The Policy-Studies
Handbook

The Policy-Studies Handbook

Stuart S. Nagel
University of Illinois

LexingtonBooks
D.C. Heath and Company
Lexington, Massachusetts
Toronto

*Dedicated to the new breed of political-science
and social-science students, who are
especially interested in developing careers that
involve teaching, research, or being a
practitioner in the evaluation of alternative
public policies*

Library of Congress Cataloging in Publication Data

Nagel, Stuart S   1934–
    The policy-studies handbook.

1. Policy sciences—Handbooks, manuals, etc. I. Title
H61.N28   361.6'1   80-7688
ISBN 0-669-03777-x

Copyright © 1980 by D.C. Heath and Company

Published simultaneously in Canada

Printed in the United States of America

International Standard Book Number: 0-669-03777-x

Library of Congress Catalog Card Number: 80-7688

Contents

List of Figures and Tables   ix

Preface and Acknowledgments   xi

Part I   *The Policy-Studies Field in General*   1

Chapter 1   **The Subject Matter and the People**   3

Subject Matter   3
People   8

Part II   *Process and Substance in Policy Studies*   25

Chapter 2   **Basic Concepts and Processes**   27

Stages in Policy Research   27
Stages in Policy Formation and Implementation   30
Policy Analysis across Nations and Disciplines   32

Chapter 3   **Specific Policy Problems**   37

Problems with a Political-Science Emphasis   37
Problems with an Economics Emphasis   41
Problems with a Sociology-Psychology Emphasis   46
Problems with a Natural-Science or Engineering
    Emphasis   49

Part III   *Institutions of the Policy-Studies Field*   55

Chapter 4   **Training Programs**   57

Present Policy-Studies Activities   58
Changes in Policy-Studies Activities   61
Recommendations for Improved Research, Com-
    munication, and Training   63
Issues Involved in Having a Balanced Policy-
    Studies Program   66

Chapter 5   **Research Centers**   77

Questionnaire Results   77

Empirical Generalizations for Understanding
        Centers   83
Normative Generalizations for Improving Centers   85

Chapter 6   **Funding Sources**   93

Questionnaire Results   93
Suggestions for Applicants   97
Suggestions for Funding Sources   100

Chapter 7   **Publication Outlets and Associations**   107

Policy-Relevant Scholarly Associations   109
Policy-Relevant Journals   114
Policy-Relevant Book Publishers   121
Interest Groups   125

Chapter 8   **Government Agencies**   131

The Respondents and the Questions   131
Political-Science Research   132
Political-Science Personnel   135

Part IV   *Methodological and Disciplinary Perspectives*   143

Chapter 9   **Methods of Policy Analysis**   145

Finding an Optimum Choice without Contingent
        Probabilities   148
Finding an Optimum Choice with Contingent
        Probabilities   151
Finding an Optimum Level on a Continuum of
        Alternatives   153
Finding an Optimum Mix in Allocating Scarce
        Resources   156
Miscellaneous Methods   159
Value Decisions and Policy Analysis   162
Summary of the Main Formulas in Optimizing
        Analysis   164

Chapter 10   **Disciplinary Contributions to Policy Studies**   175

Policy Studies across the Social Sciences   175
Policy Studies by Political-Science Fields   178

Epilogue: Policy Analysis as a Career Activity   207

Index of Names   211

Index of Subjects   216

About the Author   222

List of Figures and Tables

Figures

1–1	The Cover Letter for Policy-Studies Personnel	10
1–2	The Questionnaire for Policy-Studies Personnel	11
10–1	Mutual Relations between U.S. Government Structures and Functions	192

Tables

1–1	The Most Frequently Mentioned Specific Policy Problems	13
1–2	The Most Frequently Mentioned General Approaches to Policy Studies	14
1–3	Current Employment Positions of Policy-Studies People	17
1–4	Background Characteristics of Policy-Studies People	20
1–5	Past and Current Research Activities of Policy-Studies People	23
4–1	Present Policy-Studies Activities	58
4–2	Changes in Policy-Studies Activities	62
4–3	Research Needed	63
4–4	Improved Communication Ideas	64
4–5	Improved Training Ideas	65
5–1	Policy Problems Emphasized by Policy-Research Centers	79
5–2	Clients, Funding, and Decision Making by Policy-Research Centers	80
5–3	Staffing of Policy-Research Centers	81
6–1	Policy Problems Emphasized by Funding Sources	95
6–2	General Eligibility Criteria of Funding Sources	96
6–3	Size, Duration, and Number of Grants Awarded	97

7–1   Some Scholarly Associations Interested in Applying
        Social Science to Policy Problems   108

7–2   Activities and Funding of Policy-Relevant Scholarly
        Associations   111

7–3   Some Independent Scholarly Journals that Publish
        Application of Social Science to Policy Problems   115

7–4   Contents, Criteria, and Funding of Policy-Relevant
        Journals   117

7–5   Book Publishers Especially Interested in Political
        Science and Policy Studies   122

7–6   Target Audiences and Marketing Procedures of Policy-
        Relevant Book Publishers   124

7–7   Interest Groups that May Use Social Science in Their
        Activities   126

7–8   Activities of Policy-Relevant Interest Groups   128

8–1   Books Mentioned More than Once by Government
        Practitioners   132

8–2   Research Needs Suggested by Practitioners   134

8–3   Improved Communication Ideas Suggested by
        Practitioners   135

8–4   Improved Training Ideas Suggested by Practitioners   137

Preface and Acknowledgments

The purpose of *The Policy-Studies Handbook* is to bring together for a professional and student audience the basic professional issues and references involved in the policy-studies field. The intention is to develop a handbook roughly analogous to those prepared in chemistry or physics, which are designed to summarize basic principles for professional reference.

This book is organized into four parts and ten chapters. The four parts include (1) the policy-studies field in general; (2) process and substance in policy studies, which contains two chapters emphasizing process and substance, respectively; (3) institutions of the policy-studies field, including five chapters on training programs, research centers, funding sources, publishers/ association, and government agencies; and (4) methodological and disciplinary perspectives, which contains two chapters emphasizing methods and disciplinary contributions, respectively. The last chapter is followed by an epilogue on policy analysis as a career activity. Within each of those ten chapters, there is an analysis of the subjects with relevant bibliographies interspersed. Much of the analysis involves survey data from many sets of knowledgeable people, systematic content analyses of relevant literature, and a synthesis of ideas, experiences, and information.

The policy-studies field is only in its infancy, but it has developed rapidly enough to merit this type of handbook. One can consider the field as having begun in the early 1970s with the establishment of such journals as *Policy Sciences, Policy Analysis, Policy Studies Journal,* and a revised *Public Policy.* An important initial stimulus for creating the field was the intense concern in the late 1960s for civil rights, the war on poverty, peace, women's liberation, environmental protection, and other social problems. The implementation of that concern was facilitated by the development and spread of statistical and mathematical methods, computer software, and interdisciplinary relations. The relative attractiveness of the government as an employer and research sponsor also increased as the role of universities in employment and research funding decreased. A more recent stimulus has been the concern for obtaining more government output from reduced tax dollars.

The development of the field has manifested itself in new articles, journals, convention papers, books, book series, organizations, courses, curricula, grants, job openings, summer institutes, schools, and other indicators of academic and practitioner activity. What these manifestations have in common is a concern for applying the social sciences and other fields of knowledge to determining the nature, causes, and especially the effects of alternative government decisions or policies designed to deal with specific social problems.

These activity indicators are likely to remain high into the indefinite future because the causal forces on which they are based are strong and continuing. These forces include the attractiveness of the government as an employer and research sponsor, relative to less policy-oriented university support. They also include the increased capability of academic and nonacademic researchers to perform systematic policy analysis as a result of new methodologies, computer facilities, interdisciplinary units, and data sources. Concern for social problems has shifted to more technical, less emotional problems, such as inflation and energy. It is difficult to say that social problems and sensitivity to them will increase, but society is always likely to be trying to improve conditions in order to increase the satisfaction of its members.

The Policy Studies Organization (PSO) has been heavily involved in these developments. It was founded in 1971 by a group of political scientists who were interested in promoting the application of political and social science to important policy problems. That interest resulted in the establishment of the *Policy Studies Journal,* which began in 1972 as a small quarterly. It is now a lengthy journal that is being published with about eight issues per annual volume as a result of many special symposium issues that supplement the regular quarterly issues. The PSO has also published a series of directories dealing with government agencies, training programs, funding sources, research centers, individual researchers, publication outlets, and associations. Many of the materials that appear in this book were originally written for those directories or for the literature reviews that appear in the *Policy Studies Journal.* A number of people have commented on the helpfulness of those materials, and those comments have partly prompted bringing the materials together in this form.

Many of the sections of this book were coauthored by Stuart Nagel and Marian Neef, including the material on training programs, research centers, funding sources, and government agencies, which was originally developed as part of a series of coedited directories for the Policy Studies Organization. Much of the material on methods of policy analysis also stems from their collaboration in developing examples of how methods from operations research, management science, decision sciences, and deductive modeling could be applied to public-policy problems. The author is also indebted to Nancy Munshaw for her work on the analysis of the subscribers to the *Policy Studies Journal, Policy Analysis,* and *Public Policy,* as well as to Kathy Burkholder for her work on the analysis of policy-relevant publication outlets and associations. All three were recently graduate students at the University of Illinois. They are part of a new breed of political-science and social-science students who are especially interested in developing careers that involve teaching, research, or being a practitioner in the evaluation of alternative public policies. I dedicate this book to them.

An additional factor in the development of the policy-studies field since 1970 has been the superb cooperation of various publishers and funding sources who have helped make possible the many products of the Policy Studies Organization and other sources of policy-studies literature. Among the publishers is Lexington Books, a division of D.C. Heath and Company, particularly Mike McCarroll, vice president and general manager, and Caroline McCarley, editor in charge of the Policy Studies Organization Series. They are responsible for publishing more than thirty volumes in the PSO series. The publishers also include Sage Publications, particularly Sara Miller McCune, publisher and president. She has published about ten volumes of the Sage-PSO Yearbooks in Politics and Public Policy and four volumes of the *Policy Studies Review Annual.* Other publishers who have substantially contributed to the field include Transaction Books, particularly the editor-in-chief, Irving Louis Horowitz, and Marcel Dekker, Inc., who will publish the forthcoming *Encyclopedia of Policy Studies.* Among the funding sources, much of the cost for the above-mentioned directories, journal issues, and symposium books has been covered by the National Science Foundation, Ford Foundation, Rockefeller Foundation, Daniel and Florence Guggenheim Foundation, and numerous federal departments, such as Health, Education, and Welfare, (HEW), Transportation, Agriculture, Energy, Justice, Labor, Housing and Urban Development (HUD), and Commerce. Those government agencies are both a source of financial support and a potential beneficiary of the policy-analysis results of the studies produced. Thanks are also owed to such organizations as the American Political Science Association, the American Society for Public Administration, and other policy-relevant social-science organizations. The author is also grateful to Joyce Nagel for the work she has done on all of the many projects that are brought together in this book. In bringing together the variety of relevant materials, this book should further promote the application of quality scholarship to important policy problems.

Part I
The Policy-Studies
Field in General

1 The Subject Matter and the People

Subject Matter

The purpose of this book is to describe the new developments in the increasingly important field of policy-analysis research. By "policy-analysis research" we mean the how-to-do-it methods associated with determining the nature, causes, and effects of government decisions or policies designed to cope with specific social problems. In that sense, the research methods could focus on (1) taking policies as givens and attempting to determine what causes them, (2) taking social forces as givens and attempting to determine for what policies they are responsible, (3) taking policies as givens and attempting to determine what effects they have, or (4) taking effects or goals as givens and attempting to determine what policies will achieve or maximize those goals. One new development in policy-analysis research is an increasing concern with the fourth type of analysis. That kind of optimizing perspective is emphasized in this book, although we are also concerned with recent developments in the third type of analysis, which is generally associated with evaluation research, and also the first two types of analysis, which are especially associated with a political-science or political perspective. This material is also concerned with new institutions for implementing these relatively new developments in policy analysis.

The increased concern for evaluating alternative public policies has manifested itself in new articles, books, journals, book series, conference papers, organizations, courses, curricula, grants, job openings, legislative provisions, evaluative agencies, and other indicators of activity. The increased concern began especially in the late 1960s as part of the general public's concern for civil rights, the war on poverty, peace, women's liberation, environmental protection, and other social problems. The implementation of that concern was facilitated by the development and spread of computer software, statistical and mathematical methods, and interdisciplinary relations. The relative attractiveness of the government as an employer and research sponsor also increased as the role of universities in employment and research funding decreased. A more recent stimulant has been the concern for obtaining more government output from reduced tax dollars.

Policy analysts are mainly involved in determining the effects of alternative public policies in working for government agencies, nonuniversity

3

research centers, university research centers, teaching units, or interest groups. The work is generally not full-time policy-analysis work; rather, policy analysis tends to be part of a full-time position in public administration, research, or teaching. The government agencies are executive agencies such as HEW and HUD, legislative agencies such as the Congressional Reference Service and the General Accounting Office, or judicial agencies such as the Federal Judicial Center and the National Center for State Courts. The government agencies could also be at the federal, state, or local level.

In order to acquire the training needed for policy-analysis work, it is normally necessary to acquire a graduate degree in one of the social sciences, preferably economics, political science, social psychology, planning, or one of the newer interdisciplinary policy-studies programs. Some of the leading interdisciplinary programs include those at the Harvard Kennedy School, Princeton Woodrow Wilson School, University of Michigan Institute of Public Policy Studies, Berkeley Graduate School of Public Policy, Duke Institute of Policy Sciences and Public Affairs, and the Minnesota Hubert Humphrey Institute of Public Affairs. The methodological training of policy analysts includes courses in social-science research methods, especially methods that relate to questionnaires, interviewing, sampling, goal measurement, prediction, causal analysis, data processing, systematic observation, and report writing. The methodological training also includes courses in optimum decision making such as those offered in business administration, industrial engineering, and economics under titles like operations research or management science. The substantive training of policy analysts generally includes courses that deal with how and why alternative policies get adopted and implemented, as well as courses that cover the basic issues and references in various specific policy fields. Most policy analysts combine such general training with expertise concerning at least a few specific policy problems.

The study of government policy problems is clearly an interdisciplinary activity, at least in the sense that many disciplines have something to contribute to the study. For any social scientist or practitioner, it would be too much to acquire expertise in all the relevant perspectives. Indeed, it is too much to become an expert in all the subfields within one's own discipline. Nevertheless, there probably is a consensus that if one is interested in developing competence in policy-studies work, he or she should be familiar in a general way with the potential contributions and drawbacks of the various social sciences. Such familiarity will at least enable one to know when to call on a social scientist or a social-science treatise, just as a layperson has a general idea of the meaning of what is said by a doctor or a lawyer.

One particularly interesting set of issues worth raising in the discussion of public-policy analysis is the role of values in policy analysis. Policy analysts cannot be totally value-free since they are seeking to achieve or maximize given values, but they can take extra precautions to keep social or personal values from interfering with their statements of fact. These precautions can include drawing on multiple sources and individuals for cross-checking information, making available raw data sets for secondary analysis, and making assumptions more explicit. Policy analysts can also attempt to justify the values they are seeking to achieve by showing how they relate to higher, widely accepted values. They can especially vary the normative and factual inputs into their models to see how that variation or sensitivity analysis affects the policy recommendations. They can also be especially sensitive to democratic political constraints and constitutional legal constraints.

How can one define good policy analysis, or good analysis of the effects of alternative public policies? For one thing, good policy analysis is empirically valid in the sense that it conforms to reality. It is useful to policymakers or policy appliers in that it provides new insights that are clearly communicated. It is useful to society in aiding in the production of desired social consequences. It is also performed with a minimum of time and expense.

What institutional structures—in terms of government agencies, policy research centers, and academic units—are needed to facilitate good policy analysis? The most appropriate government agencies are those which recognize the value of using social science in program evaluation, which have staff people with program evaluation skills, and which know how (and are willing) to arrange for outside evaluations that exceed the in-house skills. The most appropriate research centers are those that combine the creativity of academia with the conscientious concern of nonuniversity centers for meeting time and specification deadlines. The most appropriate academic units are probably the interdisciplinary policy-studies programs, but also the disciplinary programs which encourage students to develop a specialty along policy-studies lines.

Why should one want to develop skills for evaluating alternative public policies? For researchers in academia, government, or research institutes, doing so may provide opportunities for such things as jobs, grants, articles, books, promotions, conferences, and teaching. Policymakers and other consumers of policy research can take more informed positions on controversial issues if they have an understanding of policy-analysis methods. Policy analysis can also be intellectually challenging and can produce feelings of social usefulness. In addition to being practical, it is also relevant to developing theories or generalizations concerning the causes and effects of public policies, which is an important part of social science. It is hoped that this book will help stimulate those benefits which policy analysis can potentially provide.

Bibliography on Policy Studies or Policy Analysis

Policy studies (or *policy analysis*) can be defined as the study of the policy problems with which governments deal, why government policy is what it is, and the impact and evaluation of government policy. Those three aspects of policy studies might be referred to as *policy substance, policy causation,* and *policy evaluation.* A policy-studies bibliography might be logically divided into those three categories. The following bibliography emphasizes political-science literature, although some relevant literature from economics and sociology is also included.

General Matters

[1] Dror, Yehezkel. *Design for Policy Sciences.* Elsevier, 1971.
[2] Dror, Yehezkel. *Ventures in Policy Sciences: Concepts and Applications.* Elsevier, 1971.
[3] Dye, Thomas. *Policy Analysis: What Governments Do, Why They Do It, and What Difference It Makes.* University of Alabama Press, 1976.
[4] Gregg, Phillip, ed. *Problems of Theory in Policy Analysis.* Lexington-Books, D.C. Heath, 1976.
[5] Katz, Arnold, and Lear, Julia. *The Policy Analysis Source Book for Special Programs.* National Planning Association, 1975.
[6] Lasswell, Harold. *A Pre-View of Policy Sciences.* Elsevier, 1971.
[7] Stuart Nagel, ed. *Policy Studies and the Social Sciences.* Lexington-Books, D.C. Heath, 1975.
[8] Nagel, Stuart, and Neef, Marian, eds. *Political Science Utilization Directory.* Policy Studies Organization, 1975.
[9] Nagel, Stuart, and Neef, Marian, eds. *Policy Studies Directory,* 2d ed. Policy Studies Organization, 1976.
[10] Ranney, Austin, ed. *Political Science and Public Policy.* Markham, 1968.
[11] Wade, Larry. *The Elements of Public Policy.* Charles Merrill, 1972.
[12] Journals like *Policy Analysis, Public Policy, Policy Studies Journal, Policy Sciences,* and *Public Interest.*

Substance

[13] Christenson, Reo M. *Challenge and Decision: Political Issues of Our Time.* Harper & Row, 1976.
[14] Gorham, William, and Glazer, Nathan, eds. *The Urban Predicament.* Urban Institute, 1976.
[15] Holden, Matthew, Jr., and Dresang, Dennis L., eds. *What Government Does.* Sage Publications, 1975.
[16] Nagel, Stuart, ed. *Policy Studies in America and Elsewhere.* Lexington Books, D.C. Heath, 1976.

[17] Owen, Harry, and Schultze, Charles, eds. *Setting National Priorities: The Next Ten Years.* Brookings, 1976.
[18] Peltason, J.W., and Burns, James M. *Functions and Policies of American Government.* Prentice-Hall, 1967.
[19] Smigel, Erwin O., ed. *Handbook on the Study of Social Problems.* Rand McNally, 1971.

Causation

[20] Anderson, James E. *Public Policy-Making.* Praeger, 1975.
[21] Dye, Thomas. *Understanding Public Policy.* Prentice-Hall, 1972.
[22] Heidenheimer, Arnold; Heclo, Hugh; and Adams, Carolyn T. *Comparative Public Policy: The Politics of Social Choice in Europe and America.* St. Martin's Press, 1975.
[23] Hofferbert, Richard. *The Study of Public Policy.* Bobbs-Merrill, 1974.
[24] Jones, Charles O. *An Introduction to the Study of Public Policy.* Wadsworth, 1970.
[25] Lindblom, Charles. *The Policy-Making Process.* Prentice-Hall, 1968.
[26] Spadaro, Robert N.; Dye, Thomas; Golembiewski, Robert; Stedman, Murray; and Zeigler, L. Harmon. *The Policy Vacuum: Toward a More Professional Political Science.* LexingtonBooks, D.C. Heath, 1975.

Evaluation

[27] Black, Guy. *The Application of Systems Analysis to Government Operations.* Praeger, 1968.
[28] Dolbeare, Kenneth M., ed. *Public Policy Evaluation.* Sage Publications, 1975.
[29] Dror, Yehezkel. *Public Policy-Making Reexamined.* Chandler, 1968.
[30] Kassouf, Sheen. *Normative Decision-Making.* Prentice-Hall, 1970.
[31] McKean, Roland N. *Efficiency in Government through Systems Analysis.* Wiley, 1966.
[32] Meltsner, Arnold. *Policy Analysis in the Bureaucracy.* University of California Press, 1976.
[33] Mishan, E.J. *Cost Benefit Analysis.* Praeger, 1976.
[34] Nagel, Staurt, with Neef, Marian. *Operations Research Methods: As Applied to Political Science and the Legal Process.* Sage, 1976.
[35] Quade, E.S. *Analysis for Public Decisions.* Elsevier, 1975.
[36] Scioli, Frank, Jr., and Cook, Thomas J. *Methodologies for Analyzing Public Policies.* LexingtonBooks, D.C. Heath, 1975.

[37] Wasby, Stephen. *The Impact of the United States Supreme Court: Some Perspectives.* Dorsey, 1970.
[38] Weiss, Carol. *Evaluation Research: Methods of Assessing Program Effectiveness.* Prentice-Hall, 1972.

People

This section summarizes the findings of a questionnaire sent to people in the field of policy studies, as indicated by their subscribing to *Policy Studies Journal, Policy Analysis,* or *Public Policy.* The section describes their policy-problem interests, general approaches, employment positions, background characteristics, and research activities. A survey of this type may be especially helpful to enable people in this relatively new and diverse field to get to know one another better and to enable others to have a better understanding of who the policy-studies people are.

The questionnaire on which this section is based also has been used to develop the *Policy Studies Personnel Directory.* The directory provides entries for each respondent, describing his or her answers to the questionnaire, including verbatim responses concerning current research activities. The directory also contains extensive indexes to facilitate communication among and with policy-studies people.[a]

The Questionnaires and the Respondents

In spring 1978, cover letters and questionnaires were mailed to the 1,431 individual subscribers to the *Policy Studies Journal,* the 626 subscribers to *Policy Analysis,* and the 221 subscribers to *Public Policy,* but not to the library or institutional subscribers of the journals. Many of those recipients subscribe to more than one of those three journals. Therefore, one would not expect to receive a total of 2,278 questionnaire returns, although the exact amount of overlap is not known. The total number of people for whom information was obtained, and thus the total number of entries in this directory, is 1,051. These three journals are probably the leading journals in the field of policy studies in terms of quantity of subscribers, scholarly orientation, and the frequency with which they are cited. The mailing list of subscribers to *Policy Sciences* was not made available by the publisher. Journals such as *Public Interest* and *Society/Transaction* are designed to appeal to a more popular

---

[a]The edited, verbatim individual responses are presented in the *Policy Studies Personnel Directory.* Copies of this 260-page directory can be obtained for $3 from the Policy Studies Organization, 361 Lincoln Hall, University of Illinois, Urbana, Illinois 61801.

market than these journals. Some of the entries in the directory also resulted from information sent by people who responded to an announcement describing the forthcoming directory in *Policy Sciences* and *Current Public Policy Research.*

Figure 1–1 shows the cover letter used, and figure 1–2 shows the accompanying questionnaire. The questionnaire seeks information concerning the affiliation, address, education, policy interests, prior publications, and current research activities for each respondent. The policy interests are divided into specific policy problems, such as environmental protection, health, and criminal justice, and into general approaches to policy studies, such as policy administration, comparative policy, and research methodology. One unusual aspect of the questionnaire is that it allows room for an open-ended essay of up to one hundred words on each respondent's current policy-research activities. Those essays are generally reproduced verbatim in the directory entries. The other questions also provide substantial flexibility by allowing the respondents to phrase their own interests rather than check off items on a structured list. That arrangement should facilitate clarifying each person's policy interests. For indexing purposes, the responses often are coded into more commonly used categories.

The nature of the questionnaire may have reduced the sample size to a smaller percentage of the recipients than it otherwise might have been. By asking open-ended questions, a greater burden is placed on the recipients of the questionnaire, but more useful information is possibly obtained from those who do respond. One might also reason that the persons most likely to respond are those with the strongest policy interests. By asking for prior publications, the questionnaire may have deterred responses from people who do not have extensive publication records, although they have strong policy interests, such as government people. Perhaps in the next edition of this directory, that item should explicitly include unpublished reports, although some respondents did mention unpublished reports. In order to include more people in the directory, many of the entries consist of information which was provided as part of the process of renewing one's subscription to *Policy Studies Journal,* rather than responding to the questionnaire in figure 1–2. Those renewal forms ask for address and policy interests, but not education and current research activities.

A majority of the respondents are subscribers to *Policy Studies Journal,* rather than *Policy Analysis* or *Public Policy.* That may simply reflect the fact that *Policy Studies Journal* has substantially more individual subscribers, since it is associated with joining an organization and its subscription fees are less than those of the other two journals. Subscribers to *Policy Studies Journal* (*PSJ*) may also have disproportionately responded because of a sense of organizational loyalty or esprit de corps since the cover letter came from the

POLICY STUDIES ORGANIZATION

to promote the application of political and social science to important policy problems

361 LINCOLN HALL
UNIVERSITY OF ILLINOIS AT URBANA-CHAMPAIGN
URBANA, ILLINOIS 61801
(217) 359-8541

TO: Members of the Policy Studies Organization and Other Policy Researchers

FROM: Stuart S. Nagel

SUBJECT: Information for the Policy Studies Personnel Directory

As you are probably aware, the Policy Studies Organization has published a series of four directories dealing with (1) policy studies activities of political science departments and interdisciplinary programs, (2) policy research needs of governmental agencies, (3) policy grants available from funding sources, and (4) activities of policy research centers. We are now interested in developing a directory describing the activities of policy research personnel like yourself.

You have been chosen for inclusion in the directory because you are either a member of the Policy Studies Organization or a subscriber to the journal Policy Analysis or Public Policy. You may receive more than one questionnaire if you fit into more than one of these three categories. I shall greatly appreciate your briefly answering the questions on the enclosed form regarding yourself to whatever extent you wish to do so within our space limitations. The answers in slightly edited form will appear in the directory along with an introductory analysis, relevant bibliographies, and an index.

In compiling this directory, we are using this somewhat open-ended format rather than a more structured questionnaire in order to make the directory more interesting to read and to make this letter more interesting to respond to. We are anticipating that those responding will be people who are especially interested in increasing the visibility of their present and past policy research, and who would like to determine who is doing related research with whom they might be able to share ideas to their mutual benefit. Users of the directory may also include government agencies, funding sources, academic recruiters, and research centers, as well as individual researchers. The indexes and cross-reference lists will facilitate such uses.

I look forward to receiving the above information from you before about April 1. When the directory is printed, one free copy will be sent to each member of the Policy Studies Organization, and each person included in the Directory. Others may obtain copies at $2.50 per copy, which is also the price per issue of the Policy Studies Journal, although four or five issues per year are available for an $8.00 membership. Thank you for your help in developing this potentially useful directory for promoting the application of social science to important policy problems.

Figure 1–1. The Cover Letter for Policy-Studies Personnel

INFORMATION FOR THE POLICY STUDIES PERSONNEL DIRECTORY

1. Your Name _____

2. Your title and affiliation _____

    _____

3. Your address _____

    _____

4. Your academic degrees (indicate years, field involved, and schools from which
    the degrees were received) _____

    _____

    _____

5. What specific policy problems are you interested in, such as environmental
    protection, health, criminal justice, foreign policy, or other specific
    problems? Indicate a maximum of five problem areas.

    (1) _____   (2) _____

    (3) _____   (4) _____

    (5) _____

6. What general approaches are you interested in, such as policy administration,
    comparative policy, research methodology, research utilization, policy
    formation, or other general approaches? Indicate a maximum of five general
    approaches.

    (1) _____   (2) _____

    (3) _____   (4) _____

    (5) _____

7. What articles or books have you published that deal with the causes and effects
    of alternative public policies? Indicate a maximum of five citations.

    (1) _____

    (2) _____

    (3) _____

    (4) _____

    (5) _____

8. In a maximum of 100 words, indicate what your current policy research activities
    are:

    _____

    _____

    _____

    _____

    _____

Please mail the above information to the Policy Studies Organization, 361 Lincoln
Hall, University of Illinois, Urbana, Illinois 61801. Thank you for your help.

Figure 1–2. The Questionnaire for Policy-Studies Personnel

Policy Studies Organization. The exact quantity of respondents from each set of subscribers cannot be determined since there is no item on the questionnaire asking respondents to which journals they subscribe. Partial information was obtained by the fact that the *PSJ* mailing list was sent out first, then that of *Policy Analysis,* and then that of *Public Policy,* with each questionnaire typed slightly differently. The characteristics of the three sets of subscribers do seem to be roughly alike in that the five tables in this introductory analysis tend to look alike regardless which set of respondents they are based on. The *PSJ* respondents, however, do represent a higher proportion of political scientists and academics, although an unknown number of them are also subscribers to *Policy Analysis* and *Public Policy.*

Specific Policy Problems

Table 1–1 shows the most frequently mentioned specific policy problems. The number of respondents in tables 1–1 and 1–2 is the full sample of 1,051, since every respondent had an opportunity to choose any of the policy problems or general approaches, regardless of whether their information came from the questionnaires or the PSO renewal forms. Table 1–1 indicates that the subscribers to the three journals (especially the *Policy Studies Journal*) are particularly interested in the environment, health, education, economic regulation, poverty, energy, criminal justice, science policy, human services, foreign policy, and taxing/spending as the top ten policy problems. Each of those problems, however, has no more than 25 percent of the total respondents among its adherents, with most of those problems down to about 10 percent. This indicates the diversity of concerns among policy-studies people. Not only are there only a few fields with a large percentage of adherents, but also there are about thirty fields among which most of the respondents are somewhat evenly spread. They range from manpower and labor down to arts and leisure, since none of those fields is represented by more than 8 or less than 1 percent of the respondents.

This list is useful in seeing what policy problems may need to be represented by symposia or articles in the policy journals. If an analysis were done of the journals, possibly one would find that those problems are represented in roughly the same proportion as these respondents. Saying such an equality is desirable, however, presupposes that the importance of a policy problem can be determined by the number of researchers interested in studying it. This may not be so, since those percentages are influenced by grant money available, job openings, disciplinary backgrounds, and other variables besides the severity of the problems in terms of a societal benefit/cost perspective.

Some problems are more identified with certain disciplines than others, as is indicated by a cross tabulation between the specific policy-problem interests

Table 1–1
The Most Frequently Mentioned Specific Policy Problems

Specific Problem	Number of Respondents (N = 1,051)	Percentage of Respondents	Most Interested Discipline
1. Environment	261	25	Planning
2. Health	230	22	Economics and sociology
3. Education	192	18	Education
4. Economic regulation	186	18	Economics
5. Poverty and welfare	143	14	Sociology
6. Energy	130	12	Economics
7. Criminal justice	124	11	Law
8. Science and technology	117	11	Natural sciences
9. Human services	116	11	Sociology
10. Foreign policy	112	11	Political science
11. Taxing and spending	108	10	Economics
12. Manpower and labor	81	8	Sociology
13. Transportation	60	6	—
14. Housing	54	5	Planning
15. Defense and military	53	5	Political science
16. Minorities	46	4	Psychology
17. Aging	45	4	Psychology
18. Land use	42	4	Planning
19. Agriculture	33	3	—
20. Civil rights	30	3	Political science and sociology
21. Civil liberties	29	3	Political science
22. Population	29	3	Sociology
23. Women	28	3	—
24. Communication	27	3	—
25. Electoral	26	3	Political science
26. Family policy	24	2	Sociology
27. Government labor	23	2	—
28. Water resources	22	2	—
29. Mental health	17	2	—
30. Consumer protection	17	2	Economics
31. Rural policy	17	2	—
32. Legislative reform	13	1	Political science
33. Court administration	12	1	—
34. Government organization	8	1	—
35. Law enforcement	7	1	—
36. Arts and leisure	7	1	—

and the disciplinary backgrounds of the respondents. *Disciplinary background* means the field in which the respondents received their highest degrees. For example, the most interested discipline with regard to environmental-protection matters is the discipline of urban and regional planning. That means a higher percentage of planners expressed an interest in environmental policy than any of the other major disciplines included among

Table 1–2
The Most Frequently Mentioned General Approaches to Policy Studies

General Approach	Number of Respondents (N = 1,051)	Percentage of Respondents
1. Policy formation	475	45
2. Administering public policy	351	34
3. Empirical research methods	256	24
4. Evaluation	241	23
5. Comparative public policy	233	22
6. Urban-policy problems	199	19
7. Policy implementation	177	17
8. Research utilization	172	16
9. Policy studies in general	97	9
10. Planning	88	8
11. Intergovernmental relations	80	8
12. Analysis of policy impact	79	7
13. Local government	65	6
14. Social values and public policy	65	6
15. State-government policy	58	6
16. Theory of public policy	56	5
17. Organization theory	45	4
18. Citizen participation	43	4
19. Modeling, optimizing, deduction	38	4
20. Decision-making theory	35	3
21. Community development	33	3
22. Service delivery	31	3
23. Systems analysis and theory	25	2
24. Bureaucratic politics	24	2
25. Regional policy	24	2
26. Political economy	23	2
27. General policy science	21	2
28. Futuristics and forecasting	21	2
29. Management	19	2
30. Ethics in policy	18	2
31. Diffusion of innovation	15	2
32. Social indicators	12	1
33. Crosscultural	10	1
34. Teaching policy studies	8	1
35. Determinants of public policies	6	1

the respondents. It does *not* mean that more planners have an interest in environmental policy than the number of respondents from each other discipline. In that regard, political scientists are probably more heavily represented among each specific problem than any other discipline, since there are so many more political scientists among these policy-studies respondents.

The percentage of political scientists interested in any specific problem, however, tends to be rather low, with the exception of such traditional political-science topics as foreign policy, defense policy, civil rights/civil liberties, electoral reform, and legislative reform. The economists and business-administration people show a special interest in health, economic regulation, energy, taxing and spending, and consumer protection. The sociologists and social-work people are especially interested in health, poverty, human services, manpower, population, and family policy. The psychology and education people stand out regarding their interest in minorities, aging, and educational policy. The law people represent the most interested discipline with regard to criminal justice, and the natural-science people with regard to science and technology. In addition to environmental protection, the planning and urban-affairs respondents have unusually high percentages with regard to housing and land use. Where a dash is shown in the last column of table 1-1, there was no discipline that had a percentage substantially above average. That last column does indicate the diversity of disciplines involved in policy studies, although it understates the fact that on any specific policy problem, many disciplines may have important contributions.

There are some close relations between certain pairs of specific policy problems, as, for example, between transportation policy and housing policy. The explanation for such relations may be that similar subject matters or disciplinary backgrounds are involved in studying those problems, with planning being especially relevant to this pair. Other closely related pairs include foreign policy and defense policy, law enforcement and court administration, energy policy and environmental policy, and legislative reform and electoral reform. Although these empirical relations are close, perhaps it would be socially desirable if foreign-policy people had more of an interest in fields like health, poverty, and agriculture, and not such an overwhelming interest in defense. Likewise, perhaps it might be socially desirable if the court administration people were not so oriented toward law enforcement (rather than civil liberties), so they could view the courts as institutions designed more to separate the innocent from the guilty than to reduce the crime rate. The extent to which different policy problems tend to cluster, however, cannot be meaningfully determined with this questionnaire. The respondents were limited to listing six problems, and they had a tendency to be diverse and thus not waste one or more of their problems by mentioning something that might duplicate what they had previously mentioned. Clustering could be more meaningfully determined if each respondent were given a list of thirty or so policy problems and asked to check off all those in which she or he was interested, or score them 3, 2, or 1 for high, medium, or low intensity of interest. In this introductory analysis, generally relations are discussed only if they have greater than +.20 or −.20 correlation coefficients.

General Approaches

Table 1–2 shows the most frequently mentioned general approaches to analyzing policy-studies problems. Here the distribution of respondents is more skewed toward a concentration in the top ten approaches, as contrasted to the top ten specific policy problems. Those leading general approaches include policy formation, administering public policy, empirical research methods, evaluation, comparative public policy, urban-policy problems, policy implementation, and research utilization. The first two approaches represent the two sides to the policy-studies coin and the PSO logo. Policy formation corresponds to a concern for the causes of alternative public policies, with a special emphasis on the role of policymakers rather than on social forces. Administering public policy corresponds to a concern for the effects of alternative public policies, with a special emphasis on the role of policy appliers rather than that of ultimate policy recipients. Those concerns are particularly relevant to political science, but a high percentage of the economists, sociologists, psychologists, and other respondents also indicated an interest in policy formation and policy administration. That may reflect the fact that non-political scientists who subscribe to these political-oriented journals have more of an interest in those political science approaches than other people in those same disciplines who do not have a policy-studies orientation. The non-political scientists, however, carry with them the specific policy problems that are of special interest to those other people in their respective disciplines. The number of respondents for some general approaches and specific problems may have been increased by mentioning them among the examples in the questionnaire.

Unlike table 1–1 and the specific policy problems, table 1–2 and the general approaches do not correspond so clearly to various disciplines. In other words, among the questionnaire respondents from the same disciplines shown in table 1–1 and later in table 1–4, there are few clear-cut relations between disciplines and general approaches, although for each discipline there does seem to be at least one general approach in which people in that discipline express an especially strong interest, relative to the other disciplines and to the other approaches. For example, political scientists seem to stand out with regard to a concern for policy formation and policy administration. Economists and business-administration people stand out on empirical research methods; sociologists and social workers, on social values; planners, on urban-policy problems; and psychology and education, on research utilization.

One might also note that even though each of those five major disciplinary orientations has about 45 percent of its respondents expressing an interest in policy formation and a similar across-the-board percentage on the other top approaches, each discipline in its own literature tends to have a different way of viewing those general approaches. On empirical research methods, for example, political scientists tend to emphasize survey research; economists, deductive modeling; sociologists, participant observation; planners, aggregate data analysis; and psychologists, pretest and posttest experimental and quasi-experimental methods. On policy formation, political scientists tend to emphasize the institutional rules or interest groups in making policy; economists often conceptualize the policymakers as operating within a benefit/cost framework; sociologists tend to think in terms of social forces, including social classes; planners and urban-affairs people emphasize demographic and environmental characteristics; and the psychology and education people frequently look to personality, socialization, and individual interaction variables. Interdisciplinary programs and the Policy Studies Organization attempt to combine these diverse orientations.

Employment Positions

Table 1–3 shows the current employment positions of the questionnaire respondents and the other people who have entries in the directory. The number of respondents varies for each variable in tables 1–3, 1–4, and 1–5,

Table 1–3
Current Employment Positions of Policy-Studies People

Employment Position	Number of Respondents	Percentage of Respondents
Type of Employer (N = 785)		
Departmental academics	458	58
Interdisciplinary academics	159	20
Government people	98	12
Nonuniversity research	70	9
Type of Academic Employer (N= 574)		
Ph.D.-granting	370	64
M.A./B.A.-granting	204	36
Rank of Academics (N = 425)		
Full professor	151	36
Associate professor	108	25
Assistant professor	138	32
Instructor/lecturer	28	7
Type of Government Employer by Branch (N = 67)		
Administrative	52	78
Legislative	15	22
Judicial	1	1
Type of Government Employer by Level (N = 67)		
Federal	33	49
State	21	31
Local	13	19

partly because of missing information (such as when a respondent gave a home address rather than an employment address) or because not all the respondents are applicable (as in the breakdown of type of academic employer, which would only apply to academic respondents). With regard to *general types of employers,* table 1–3 shows that 58 percent of the respondents are in regular academic departments, such as political-science departments; 20 percent are in interdisciplinary programs, such as Princeton's Woodrow Wilson School of Public and International Affairs or the Berkeley (California) Graduate School of Public Policy; 12 percent are in government; and 9 percent are in nonuniversity research or consulting.

Those four types of employment differ on some relevant dimensions of this analysis. On the matter of general approaches, the government people are especially interested in administering public policy. The departmental academics have more theoretical concern for the general approach of policy formation. The research-centers people, relatively speaking, emphasize empirical research methods. The interdisciplinary academics are very diverse and have no special concentration with regard to general approaches. On the matter of specific policy problems, there is not enough homogeneity within these four types of employment for them to relate clearly to one specific problem more so than the other problems and the other types of employment.

Relating employment positions to background characteristics and research activities shows several things: People in academia and research centers report more graduate degrees and research productivity than people in government. People in government, however, are more likely to have political science as their highest degree. That does not mean that political scientists are more likely to be found in government than in academia. It means only that a majority of the government respondents in this survey are political scientists, but so are a majority of respondents in almost all the major categories. It is like the finding that a majority of rich people in the United States are white, and a majority of poor people in the United States are also white, simply because most of the people in the United States are white. Likewise, most of the policy-studies people (that is, the subscribers to *Policy Studies Journal, Policy Analysis,* and *Public Policy*) are political scientists.

Among the respondents who are *employed in academia,* 64 percent are in Ph.D.-granting institutions, and 36 percent are in M.A./B.A.-granting institutions. Those respondents at Ph.D.-granting schools are more likely to be in interdisciplinary programs, have higher graduate degrees and more books, but have lower professorial ranks. The lower professorial ranks, in spite of the greater number of books, may be due to the fact that the Ph.D.-granting schools require relatively more publications than the M.A./B.A. schools for promotions, and the M.A./B.A. schools place relatively more emphasis on teaching. The respondents at M.A./B.A.-granting schools show more interest in administering public policy, which may be relevant to their public-administration programs, whereas the respondents at Ph.D.-granting schools show more theoretical interest in the implementation process. There are no clear-cut relations with specific policy problems, given the lack of homogeneity within the two types of schools regarding policy-problem interests.

On the matter of professorial rank, academic policy-studies people seem to have lower ranks than academics in general, indicating they may be among the younger, more avant-garde members of the academic profession. About one-third are full professors; one-fourth, associate professors; one-third, assistant professors; and the rest, instructors or lecturers. There is a substantial positive correlation between professorial rank and (1) age, (2) books published, and (3) being a male rather than a female. The rank-sex relation is probably due mainly to the age-sex and rank-age relations, although the rank-sex relation may partly reflect past and present discriminatory hiring and promotions.

Among the respondents *employed in government,* 78 percent are in administrative agencies, and 22 percent work with legislatures. Only one government respondent indicated he or she works in the courts. In comparing the administrative respondents with the legislative ones, some relationships are quite expected. For example, legislative respondents are more interested in legislative reform, and administrators are more interested in governmental organization. A higher percentage of legislative respondents than administrative ones expressed an interest in ethics in policy studies. A higher percentage of administrative respondents had backgrounds in political science.

On the matter of governmental level, about one-half the respondents work with the federal government; one-third, with state governments; and one-fifth, with local governments. The state and local government people are especially interested in criminal-justice matters, urban and regional planning, policy implementation, and social-work problems. The federal government people are especially interested in science and technology policy, as compared to the state and local people. This does not mean that science policy is the main concern of the federal government people; it means only that it is an interest which distinguishes them from the state and local people. That interest is manifested in the Office of Technology Assessment for which there are generally no state or local counterparts.

Background Characteristics

Table 1–4 shows the background characteristics of the policy-studies people included in this directory. Those background characteristics can be divided into educational characteristics and demographic ones. The *educational characteristics* relate to the discipline of each respondent's highest degree,

Table 1–4
Background Characteristics of Policy-Studies People

Background Characteristic	Number of Respondents	Percentage of Respondents
Disciplinary Background (N = 580)		
Political science	435	68
Economics and Business Administration	43	7
Sociology and social work	32	5
Miscellaneous social science	29	5
Psychology and education	23	4
Planning and urban affairs	20	3
Natural science and engineering	19	3
Interdisciplinary policy studies	18	3
Humanities	10	2
Law	10	2
Highest Degree Mentioned (N = 704)		
Ph.D. or other doctorate	536	76
M.A. or other master's degree	168	24
B.A. or other bachelor's degree	1	0
Years between B.A. and Ph.D. (N = 423)		
5 and under	99	23
6–10	229	54
11–15	60	14
16–20	17	4
Over 20	18	4
Region Where Currently from (N = 1,033)		
South	261	25
Northeast	239	23
Midwest	211	20
Far West	188	18
Washington, D.C.	71	7
Foreign	69	7
Sex (N = 1,029)		
Male	884	86
Female	145	14
Age (N = 570)		
Under 30	88	15
30–39	299	52
40–49	115	20
50–59	49	9
60 and over	19	3

what that highest degree is, and the years between the B.A. and the Ph.D., where the highest degree is the Ph.D. As previously indicated, a majority of the respondents have their highest degree in political science. More specifically, 68 percent have such political-science backgrounds, and the other disciplines constitute the remaining 32 percent, with no other discipline having more than 7 percent. The reason for the high percentage of political scientists in this policy-studies survey partly relates to the fact that the Policy Studies Organization and *Policy Studies Journal* began as a group within the

American Political Science Association (APSA). There is, however, a high percentage of political scientists among subscribers to *Policy Analysis, Public Policy,* and *Policy Sciences,* and those journals have no origins that relate to the APSA. Political scientists are probably especially interested in policy studies because, by definition, *policy studies* refers to applying social science to the nature, causes, and effects of government policy; and political science, by definition, is concerned with government matters. In the past, however, political scientists have emphasized general policy formation and policy administration without showing much concern for specific policy problems.

The rank order of other disciplines in table 1–4 with regard to being represented among the policy-studies respondents is economics and business administration, sociology and social work, psychology and education, planning and urban affairs, natural science, humanities, and law. The category of miscellaneous social science includes such disciplines as geography, anthropology, and history. It is interesting to note that few of the respondents have a background in interdisciplinary policy studies (only 3 percent), but many are currently in interdisciplinary programs (20 percent), indicating that more policy-studies people in the future are likely to have interdisciplinary policy-studies backgrounds. There are many relations between the discipline of one's degree and one's general and specific policy interests, as previously discussed.

The policy-studies people are well educated, at least among those who responded to the questionnaire. Almost all those who mentioned their degrees indicated having a graduate degree, with three-fourths having the Ph.D. degree. Most of them took from six to ten years to obtain their Ph.D. degrees after receiving their bachelor's degrees. Having a Ph.D. degree tends to correlate with being in academia, especially at a Ph.D.-granting school, and being at a higher professorial rank. Among government employees, having a Ph.D. tends to correlate with being in the federal government. Having a long gap between the B.A. and the Ph.D. degrees tends to correlate with being an older respondent. It also correlates with being in an administrative rather than a legislative agency, since administrators often take continuing-education courses for advanced degrees. There is a positive relation between (1) having a longer gap between receiving the B.A. and the Ph.D. degrees and (2) being a female; but the correlation is not greater than the .20 which we have been using as the threshold for discussing relations. Among academics in general, there may be a higher relation between being female and the educational gap, which is caused by older women returning to school to get advanced degrees. That relation does not appear as strongly among policy-studies people, however, possibly because policy-studies women tend to be younger and may be more likely to go directly from undergraduate to graduate work.

The *demographic characteristics* in table 1–4 relate to region, sex, and age. On region, the respondents are disproportionately from the United States, with only 7 percent being from other parts of the world. Those other places in rank order include Canada, England and the Commonwealth countries,

Western Europe, Israel and the Middle East, Latin America, and the Far East. No one responded from an Eastern European country. Within the United States, the respondents are about evenly spread across the four regions, but the number of respondents may be higher in the South and the Far West than one would expect from their populations. Perhaps the Sun Belt universities are expanding disproportionately in these times of retrenchment and are thus disproportionately hiring young political and social scientists who have a policy-studies orientation.

On the matter of age, a majority of the respondents are between thirty and thirty-nine, whereas one might expect a majority of academics to be at least in the range of forty to forty-nine. The younger age of policy-studies people as compared to most academics may reflect (1) education during a period of intense concern with policy problems in the 1960s, including poverty, civil rights, war, environment, and women's rights; (2) nontenured teaching during a period of academic cutbacks, but expansion in jobs, grants, and research opportunities relating to policy evaluation; and (3) a kind of youthful idealism with regard to being able to apply social science to important policy problems. It is difficult to compare the age breakdown of policy-studies people with that of political scientists in general (that is, APSA members) because APSA surveys tend to include a large percentage of students, whereas only 4 percent of the policy-studies respondents were students. On other demographic characteristics, there is much similarity between policy-studies people and political scientists in general, although not on subject-matter interests. Being older in the policy-studies survey correlates with such expected variables as taking longer to obtain the Ph.D., publishing more books, being at a Ph.D.-awarding school, and having a higher professorial rank.

On the matter of sex, being male correlates with being older among the respondents, although the correlation is not high. Being male thus correlates with most of the same variables that being older correlates with, like professorial rank although not education gap (as previously mentioned). The policy interests of older and male policy-studies people do not differ substantially from the policy interests of younger and female respondents, except on such an obvious matter as the fact that female respondents are more apt to be interested in women's rights than male respondents. One might think the older respondents would be more interested in aging policy than the younger respondents, but there is little relation, possibly because of the newness of aging policy and because the relatively older respondents are not old enough to be presently benefiting from alternative policies toward the aged.

Research Activities

Table 1–5 shows some quantitative data on the past and current research activities of policy-studies people. They do seem to be quite active, at least among the questionnaire respondents. Of the 1,051 directory entries, 734 are based on filled-out questionnaires rather than PSO membership forms. Of those 734 questionnaires, 533 completed the section asking for articles or books published. Of those 533 respondents, table 1–5 shows 62 percent mentioned having published at least one book, and 16 percent mentioned three to five books. The questionnaire provided for listing only a maximum of one's five most relevant books, so as to save entry space. Of the 533 usable respondents on this item, 37 percent mentioned at least one article, although no books. The questionnaire respondents may have been even more active in publishing than their responses indicate, since many of them narrowly interpreted published research on "the causes or effects of alternative public policies." Perhaps the questionnaire should have more broadly asked for research "applying social science to public-policy problems."

On the matter of current research productivity, more people inserted something into that part of the questionnaire. This may be because many of the respondents have current research activities but few prior publications, since they are relatively new academics or since they are government people who do research for in-house consumption rather than publication. Of the 734 returned questionnaires, 88 percent mentioned at least one current research project. Almost a majority of 47 percent mentioned many (that is, three or more) or a few large projects. Both number of books published and current research productivity correlate well. They also both correlate well with being older and being higher in professorial rank.

In answer to the question of who the policy-studies people are, one can say they are both a diverse and a nondiverse group. They are diverse in the sense of having a variety of policy-problem interests, including such popular topics as environment, health, education, economic regulation, poverty, energy, crime,

Table 1–5
Past and Current Research Activities of Policy-Studies People

Research Activity	Number of Respondents	Percentage of Respondents
Number of Books Published (N = 533)		
None, but one article mentioned	58	11
None, but two or more articles	148	28
One book mentioned	158	30
Two books	85	16
Three to five books	84	16
Current Research Productivity (N = 734)		
No research mentioned	87	12
One project mentioned	96	13
More than one, but not many	208	28
Many, or a few large projects	343	47

science policy, human services, and foreign policy. They are nondiverse in the sense that a high percentage are political scientists, having an interest in policy formation and administration, and employed as productive academics, at least among the policy-studies people subscribing to the main policy-studies periodicals. They are also nondiverse in that they do not differ greatly from political scientists in general, except for their policy-problem interests. It is hoped that this chapter and the *Policy Studies Personnel Directory* will help clarify what the policy-studies field involves, facilitate communication among and with policy-studies people, and promote the application of political and social science to important policy problems.

Part II
Process and Substance in Policy Studies

2 Basic Concepts and Processes

Stages in Policy Research

Basic Concepts in Policy Studies

Policy studies can be defined as research that relates to determining the causes or effects of alternative public policies. By public policies are meant government decisions with regard to ways of handling various problems that are generally considered to require collective rather than individual action. Those problems include ones emphasized by political science, economics, sociology, psychology, natural science, and other disciplines.

An alternative way of conceptualizing policy studies (rather than in terms of specific policy problems) is in terms of general perspectives that cut across all policy problems. One such general perspective is to think in terms of the stages involved in policy-studies research. The primary stage is developing basic concepts with regard to such matters as the categories of policy causes and policy effects, as well as the even more basic concept of what is public policy. Causes tend to relate to such concepts as social norms, environmental contexts, conflicting interests, policy decisionmakers, and evidentiary facts. Effects tend to relate to such concepts as behavioral versus attitudinal effects, intended versus unintended effects, short-run versus long-term effects, and effects on policy appliers versus on policy recipients. Other stages in policy research besides the conceptualization stage include the methodological development of research designs for testing the validity of various hypothesized causes and effects and the subsequent utilization of such policy research. Another general perspective is to think in terms of the stages involved in the development of policies rather than in doing research on them. Those stages include policy formation, which relates to how and why statutes get adopted in legislatures, precedents in courts, and administrative decisions among government executives and administrators. Those stages also include policy implementation, which deals with the problems of applying policies after they have been adopted, including compliance and impact. Still other general perspectives can emphasize how a variety of policy problems get treated across different nations and cultures or across different academic disciplines.

On basic concepts in policy studies, see Yehezkel Dror, *Design for Policy Sciences* (Elsevier, 1971); Thomas Dye, *Policy Analysis: What Governments Do, Why They Do It, and What Difference It Makes* (University of Alabama Press, 1976); Harold Lasswell, *A Pre-View of Policy Sciences* (Elsevier, 1971); Robert Lineberry, *American Public Policy: What Government Does and What Difference It Makes* (Harper and Row, 1977); Stuart Nagel, ed., *Policy Studies in America and Elsewhere* (LexingtonBooks, D.C. Heath, 1976); and Austin Ranney, ed., *Political Science and Public Policy* (Markham, 1968).

Methods of Policy Analysis

Methods of policy analysis can be classified in various ways. One classification might be in terms of whether quantitative or nonquantitative methods are used. Nonquantitative policy research includes (1) journalistic descriptions of incidents of policy formation or implementation, (2) philosophical analyses of normative values or ultimate social causes, (3) historical descriptions of previous attempts to deal with various policy problems, (4) anthropological or ethnographic studies dealing with the handling of policy problems in diverse cultures (although generally one culture at a time), and (5) legal analyses of the laws and judicial interpretations dealing with certain policy problems. Such nonquantitative policy research tends to be essential or at least useful background material for formulating quantitative hypotheses or for integrating quantitative findings. Nonquantitative research also is often directly useful to researchers or practitioners in developing policy theories or in making policy decisions. Some of the above types of nonquantitative analyses are often supplemented with quantitative data.

Quantitative policy research tends to be of two kinds or a combination of both. One type involves inductive statistical analysis working with data on many specified persons, places, or things. From the data one can induce relationships between inputs and outputs stated in terms of the percentages in cross-tabulation tables, the averages in analysis of variance, or the empirical equations in regression analysis. The data can be from many places at one time, from a single place at many points in time, or from both many places and many time points. An especially popular type of statistical analysis involves working with an experimental group (that has been subjected to a new policy or an alleged policy cause) and a control group (which has not) in order to determine the effects of the policy or the policy cause. The stimulus may be randomly allocated to entities within the groups or may be allocated through a process of self-selection, as, for example, where some states choose to adopt a policy and other states choose not to.

The other kind of quantitative policy research involves deductive reasoning from premises which have been arrived at through empirical statistical analysis, intuitively accepted assumptions, citation of prior authority, or other means. Causal deductive models tend to have this form: (1) X precedes Y, (2) X covaries with Y, (3) no Z, when controlled for, will substantially change the covariation, and (4) therefore X causes Y. Prescriptive deductive models tend to have this form: (1) X causes Y, (2) Y is desirable, and (3) therefore adopt X. Both forms can be made more realistic and sophisticated by adding more categories to the variables, more variables, nonlinearity, constraints, and uncertainties. Deductive modeling often can be quite helpful in determining the effects of policy changes without requiring the policy to be adopted first, as in the before-and-after experimental or quasi-experimental method.

On the methods of policy analysis, see William Coplin, ed., *Teaching Policy Studies* (Symposium Issue of *Policy Studies Journal,* 1978); Kenneth Dolbeare, ed. *Public Policy Evaluation* (Sage Publications, 1976); Stuart Nagel and Marian Neef, *Policy Analysis: In Social Science Research* (Sage, 1978); Stuart Nagel with Marian Neef, *Operations Research Methods: As Applied to Political Science and the Legal Process* (Sage, 1976); Edward Quade, *Analysis for Public Decisions* (Elsevier, 1975); Frank Scioli, Jr., and Thomas J. Cook, *Methodologies for Analyzing Public Policies* (Lexington-Books, D.C. Heath, 1975); Edith Stokey and Richard Zeckhauser, *A Primer for Policy Analysis* (Norton, 1978); and Gordon Tullock and Richard Wagner, eds., *Deductive Models in Policy Analysis* (Symposium Issue of *Policy Studies Journal,* 1977).

Utilization of Policy Research

Research utilization refers to the use of scholarly research by policymakers and policy appliers. That simple definition logically raises two sets of complicated issues. One set deals with how to get scholarly researchers to work with policy-relevant subjects in a more useful way. The other set deals with how to get policy practitioners to be more aware of the useful studies which researchers may be doing.

Recent and continuing stimuli to doing policy research in the academic world have included (1) new methodological tools and data sources for doing more meaningful policy analysis; (2) the stimuli of social movements dealing with such matters as civil rights, peace, poverty, environmental protection, and sexual equality; (3) closer interdisciplinary relations, especially those facilitated by new academic programs and organizations; (4) the increasing relative attractiveness of job opportunities and grants in policy-related fields; and (5) a feeling that there has been a near saturation regarding the application of quantitative methods to non-policy-relevant topics.

Devices to facilitate communicating the increased policy research to policy practitioners include (1) more research projects that involve academic-practitioner collaboration; (2) more research centers that can combine the creativity and broadness that are often associated with university research with the responsibility for meeting specifications and deadlines that is often associated with nonuniversity research; (3) more journals that can communicate technical findings in nontechnical language to a wider audience; (4) more requirements in legislation that proposed programs be accompanied by environmental impact statements, technological assessment, and social assessment and that ongoing programs be periodically evaluated; and (5) more staff personnel associated with legislatures, administrative agencies, and courts whose function is to distill and translate scholarly research to make it more usable to busy policymakers and to inform the research community more clearly as to what is needed.

On utilization of policy research, see Ronald Havelock, *Planning for Innovation through Dissemination and Utilization of Knowledge* (University of Michigan, Center for Research on Utilization of Scientific Knowledge, 1969); Irving Horowitz, ed., *The Use and Abuse of Social Science* (Transaction Books, 1975); National Science Foundation, *Knowledge into Action: Improving the Nation's Use of the Social Sciences* (Government Printing Office, 1969); Carol Weiss, ed., *Using Social Research in Public Policy Making* (LexingtonBooks, D.C. Heath, 1976); and Michael White, Michael Radner and David Tansik, eds., *Management and Policy Science in American Government: Problems and Prospects* (LexingtonBooks, D.C. Heath, 1975).

Stages in Policy Formation and Implementation

Policy Formation

In this context *policy formation* refers to how and why statutes get adopted in legislatures, precedents in courts, and administrative decisions among government executives and administrators. The phrase *policy formation* emphasizes the generality of those alternative ways of getting policies adopted. Each specific policy-adoption method raises more narrowly focused issues on how to reform those policy-adoption procedures in order to achieve more effective, efficient, or equitable policy making. Thus, the specific problem area of legislative reform is concerned with improving legislative decision making; that of criminal justice and judicial administration, with improving judicial decision making; and that of policy implementation and public administration, with improving administrative decision making. Not only is the study of policy formation helpful in improving the policy-making process and of theoretical interest in itself, but also it can be valuable in obtaining a better understanding of the feasibility of alternative public policies. Thus, studying policy causation can be quite relevant to arriving at prescriptions concerning optimal or desirable action where one's goals logically include political feasibility.

Scholars analyzing the policy-making process tend to emphasize its incremental nature. This sometimes leads them to advocate making policy recommendations that do not substantially deviate from prevailing policy. Advocating only a small change, however, when one could have a much larger change may be even more wasteful in an opportunity-cost sense than advocating a large change which is unlikely to be adopted, but which may serve to publicize the policy and facilitate its later adoption or a desirable compromise. Determining the probability that a policy will be adopted generally involves an insider's knowledge of the values of the specific decisionmakers or the knowledge of what has happened to related policies which have come before that specific decision-making group. However, that kind of determination may lack theoretical significance in the sense of generating ideas with regard to why some policies get adopted and others do not. Nonetheless, overly general principles are of little value in making decisions such as saying policies get adopted which have majority support, the backing of dominant forces or strong leaders, or whose time have come in terms of the social or technological context. As in much policy-studies research, what is needed is a combination of practical methods, which can provide specific answers, and insightful theories, which are broadly applicable but not clichés.

On policy formation, see James E. Anderson, *Public Policy-Making* (Praeger, 1975); Raymond Bauer and Kenneth Gergen, eds., *The Study of Policy Formation* (Free Press, 1968); Thomas Dye, *Understanding Public Policy* (Prentice-Hall, 1972); Charles Jones, *An Introduction to the Study of Public Policy* (Wadsworth, 1977); and Charles Lindblom, *The Policy-Making Process* (Prentice-Hall, 1968).

Policy Implementation

Just as meaningful policy evaluation should take political feasibility into consideration, likewise evaluation should also consider administrative feasibility or the problems of policy implementation. A Supreme Court decision declaring unconstitutional segregated schools, illegal searches, or religious activities in public schools is not very meaningful if there is little compliance on the part of lower-level government officials such as trial courts, state legislature, police officers, or school superintendents. The amount of compliance tends to be related to such matters as the clarity of the policy, the extent to which it deviates from custom, the prestige of the policymakers and policy appliers, the positive and negative sanctions available to obtain compliance, the monitoring of noncompliance, and the presence of facilitating and inhibiting environmental conditions. In general, compliance occurs when the would-be noncomplier perceives the expected benefits minus costs of compliance to be greater than the expected benefits minus costs of noncompliance.

Compliance is, however, only one aspect of an effectively implemented policy. For example, even if every school district were desegregated, the Supreme Court's desegregation policy could still be considered not a success if it failed to improve the self-perceptions of black students on which the Supreme Court partly based its decision. Likewise, the policy would probably be considered a failure if every school district were desegregated, but the costs included continuing violence, expenditures of huge social resources for transportation or policing, and increased racial antagonism in noneducational activities. Thus an effectively implemented policy is one that not only complies with but also maximizes or achieves its intended goals while minimizing adverse side effects or at least keeping them within constraints. Achieving that kind of implementation requires that above-mentioned forces favorable to compliance plus such factors as careful planning, communications, flexibility, funds, insightful personnel, and possibly good policy-analysis research.

On policy implementation, see Eugene Bardach, *The Implementation Game* (M.I.T. Press, 1977); George Frederickson and Charles Wise, eds., *Public Administration and Public Policy* (LexingtonBooks, D.C. Heath, 1977); Erwin Hargrove, *The Missing Link: The Study of the Implementation of Social Policy* (Urban Institute, 1975); Samuel Krislov, Malcolm Feeley, Keith Boyum, and Susan White, *Compliance and the Law: A Multi-Disciplinary Approach* (Sage, 1972); Jeffrey Pressman and Aaron Wildavsky, *Implementation* (University of California, 1978); and Stephen Wasby, *The Impact of the United States Supreme Court: Some Perspectives* (Dorsey, 1970).

Policy Analysis across Nations and Disciplines

Policy Analysis across Nations and Cultures

Having a cross-national perspective on policy problems can be justified for developing broader theories of the causes and effects of alternative public policies than can be developed by merely working with states or cities within the United States or another single country at one point or even many points in time. Having such a perspective also has practical significance in terms of providing insights into which policies ought to be adopted in light of given goals, constraints, and environmental circumstances. For example, an analysis of the effects of abortion policies in the United States made during the 1960s might lead one to conclude that making abortions easier to obtain has virtually no effect on decreasing deaths from illegal abortions, unwanted births, or other social indicators. In reality, however, the slope (or marginal rate of return) of relevant social indicators to the leniency of abortion policy might be quite substantial if the units of analysis had been countries where there is a wider range of scores on the leniency variable than among U.S. states. Like many policies, abortion policy may have an S-shaped relation to its goals such that the slope is relatively flat at low levels and high levels on the policy, but relatively steep in the middle. Determining the role of possibly fundamental policy causes like industrialization, capitalism-socialism, and democracy-dictatorship also cannot be meaningfully done within the limited variation of U.S. states rather than United Nations members.

The main problem in cross-national policy comparisons is the difficulty of holding constant other variables that may affect the goal indicators besides the policy variable. The traditional approach has been to use a cross-sectional analysis of many countries at one time and then divide the countries into similar subsamples, or to use some form of predictive regression analysis that attempts to statistically control for differences among the countries. Those approaches, however, are limited by the number of countries available and by the difficulty of determining what variables to control for. As an improvement on that methodology, one can use a time-series analysis. By comparing a set of ten, or N, countries before and after they adopt a policy, one generally controls for extraneous variables better than comparing ten countries that had adopted the policy with ten countries that had not. Other methodological problems in cross-national analysis involve determining the degree of reciprocal causation between policies and other variables, obtaining relevant and reliable data, and being aware of the substantive context in which the relations are operating. These are problems in any policy-studies research, but especially in one with a cross-national perspective. The extra benefits in broadness of understanding may, however, be worth the extra costs.

On policy analysis across nations and cultures, see Douglas Ashford, ed., *Approaches to Comparative Public Policy* (Sage, 1978); Alexander Groth, *Comparative Politics: A Distributive Approach* (Macmillan, 1971); Arnold Heidenheimer, Hugh Heclo, and Carolyn Adams, *Comparative Public Policy: The Politics of Social Change in Europe and America* (St. Martins Press, 1975); Richard Rose, ed., *The Dynamics of Public Policy: A Comparative Analysis* (Sage, 1975); and Harold Wilensky, *The Welfare State and Equality: Structural and Ideological Roots of Public Expenditures* (California, 1975).

Policy Analysis across Academic Disciplines

Policy problems can be classified in terms of their closest research disciplines, as has been done in the contents for this book. Any given policy problem, however, is inherently multidisciplinary in the sense that each policy problem is capable of benefiting from the perspectives of a variety of disciplines, including the social sciences, natural sciences, and humanities. Sociology, for example, has developed a substantial amount of factual knowledge and theory in broad fields like social control, socialization, and social change, which can be helpful in understanding the effects of alternative policies and the behavior of policymakers and policy appliers. Of all the social sciences, the field of economics has clearly developed the most sophisticated mathematical models for synthesizing normative and empirical premises in order to deduce means-ends policy recommendations. Institutional economists have been especially relevant in discussing the role of economic class structures, ownership systems, and technology in determining policy choices. Psychology is the social science that has probably done more to develop techniques of statistical inference, cross tabulation, survey research, and multivariate analysis. Psychology also provides an important focus on the role of the individual or small groups, particularly with regard to attitudes, perceptions, and motivations.

Anthropology, geography, and history provide a broader perspective over space and time than the other social sciences do. Without philosophy, especially normative social philosophy, policy studies might tend to lack direction with regard to what they are seeking to achieve. On the other hand, without the quantitative and computer science tools that are ultimately associated with mathematics, policy studies might tend to overemphasize evaluative gut reactions and armchair speculation. Natural science is also quite relevant substantively to certain specific policy problems like environmental protection, energy developments, and food production. The field of law has important policy-studies elements when it involves studying why the law is what it is or the effects of alternative laws. Political scientists have traditionally devoted much of their intellectual resources to analyzing how government policy gets made, with special emphasis on the role of interest groups and more recently on the role of individual decisionmakers. Political scientists are now turning more toward the analysis of specific policy-problem areas, rather than just abstract studies of the policy-making process. If one is interested in developing a competence in policy-studies work, he or she should be familiar in a general way with the potential contributions and drawbacks of the various social sciences. Such familiarity will at least enable one to know when to call on a social scientist or a social science treatise, the way a layperson has a general idea of when to call upon a doctor or a lawyer and a general understanding of what the doctor or lawyer says.

On policy analysis across academic disciplines, see James Charlesworth, ed., *Integration of the Social Sciences through Policy Analysis* (American Academy of Political and Social Science, 1972); Irving Horowitz and James Katz, *Social Science and Public Policy in the United States* (Praeger, 1975); Daniel Lerner and Harold Lasswell, eds., *The Policy Sciences* (Stanford University Press, 1951); Duncan MacRae, *The Social Function of Social Science* (Yale University Press, 1876); and Stuart Nagel, ed., *Policy Studies and the Social Sciences* (LexingtonBooks, D.C. Heath, 1975).

3 Specific Policy Problems

Problems with a Political-Science Emphasis

Foreign Policy

Foreign-policy problems have been especially important in political science, although such problems have historical, economic, demographic, psychological, technological, and ethical aspects, as well as relevance to other disciplines. Perhaps the most meaningful division of the issues is into those that deal with international conflict versus issues of international cooperation. The conflict issues relate to conflict prevention, mainly through alliances and international organization, and conflict resolution, mainly through negotiation and sometimes war. The cooperation issues relate to cooperation in trade, environmental protection, energy, communications, transportation, postal service, food, labor, health, education, and banking.

An alternative way of organizing foreign-policy issues would be in terms of the country or region whose foreign policy is being studied, which is a kind of cross-national perspective that can be applied to any policy problem. A related organization of the issues would be to think of foreign policy just from a U.S. perspective, but to divide the issues in terms of the countries and regions with which the United States interacts. That kind of geographical perspective, however, tends to miss issues that cut across U.S. relations with other countries and tends to focus unduly on current events rather than on matters of a more lasting nature.

Another meaningful way of organizing foreign-policy issues involves emphasizing the goals and means of state departments or foreign ministries in dealing with other countries. These goals include winning allies, consumers for U.S. products, sources of raw materials, and human rights for foreign nationals. The means include trade, economic aid, military aid, propaganda, subversion, the institutions of diplomacy, and international organization. Closely related to this division of goals and means are issues that relate to the structures, personnel practices, and administrative procedures used within the State Department and the government in general to make the means more efficient in furthering the goals and to make both means and goals more responsive to elected officials and the public.

On foreign policy, see Graham Allison, *Essence of Decision: Explaining the Cuban Missile Crisis* (Little, Brown, 1971); Richard Merritt, ed., *Foreign Policy Analysis* (LexingtonBooks, D.C. Heath, 1975); and James Rosenau, *The Scientific Study of Foreign Policy* (Free Press, 1971).

Defense and Arms-Control Policy

Defense policy emphasizes developing a capability for deterring foreign aggression, and arms-control policy emphasizes mutual reduction or restraint in armament development. Defense policy issues include (1) balancing air, naval, and land power; (2) balancing massive strategic power versus the ability to fight limited wars or engagements; (3) balancing the ability to engage in conventional warfare versus guerrilla and counterinsurgency activities; (4) civil defense with regard to shelter programs, antiballistic missiles, industrial relocation, and aftermath planning; (5) civilian control over the military; (6) intelligence-gathering activities; (7) problems involved in recruiting, training, and retaining military personnel; (8) coordinating military capabilities with one's allies; (9) the development and implementation of new weapons technologies; (10) policy toward the use of atomic, chemical, and bacteriological weapons systems which are oriented toward civilian destruction; (11) administrative structures to facilitate rational responses to defense problems; and (12) internal-security matters, especially in time of war.

Arms-control issues include (1) provisions for monitoring compliance with agreements, which formerly meant debating the degree of on-site inspection, but which now can be handled partly through satellite surveillance; (2) the extent to which there should be a mutual reduction in armaments or merely restraint in the development of new armaments; (3) the extent to which there has to be a settlement of political issues before or after arms-control agreements; (4) the administrative structures for negotiating arms and control agreements; (5) bilateral versus multilateral arms-control agreements; (6) balancing conventional arms control and nuclear arms control; (7) disengagement or arms-free zones; (8) agreements to limit arms sales and military aid to other countries; (9) agreements concerning the banning of certain types of nuclear weapons testing; and (10) the role of the United Nations in achieving arms control.

On defense and arms-control policy, see Alexander George and Richard Smoke, *Deterrence in American Foreign Policy: Theory and Practice* (Columbia University Press, 1974); Robert Levine, *The Arms Debate* (Harvard University Press, 1963); and William Whitson, *Foreign Policy and U.S. National Security* (Praeger, 1976).

Electoral Policy

Government policy regarding who participates in the process of choosing policymakers is especially important since it indirectly influences all policy fields. Basic issues of electoral policy deal with eligibility to vote, procedures for registration and voting, nomination procedures, and campaign funding and methods. Voting eligibility over the years has dealt with expanding the franchise to include nonpropertied persons, minority religions, blacks, women, young people, and new residents. Current trends involve increasing the franchise by making registration and voting easier, such as through mobile registration units, postcard registration, election-day registration, and extended voting hours and places. The United States has traditionally expressed more concern about the error cost of deterring eligible voters from doing so, unlike other countries where registration and voting are relatively easy.

Nomination procedures have tended in the United States from nomination by a small group of politicians to nomination by conventions and by direct primaries, which involve the potential participation of all party members or voters. Recent years have seen a concern for placing restrictions on campaign contributions and expenditures, along with increased support for government subsidies of campaign costs, mainly to lessen the indebtedness of candidates to campaign contributors. In the election of the President, there is a constant concern with proposals for changing the electoral-college system to a system that would allocate each state's electoral-college vote to the candidates in proportion to their popular vote or simply elect the President on the basis of the popular vote alone.

On electoral policy, see Richard Carlson, ed., *Issues on Electoral Reform* (National Municipal League, 1974); William Crotty, ed., *Paths to Electoral Reform* (LexingtonBooks, D.C. Heath, 1979); William Crotty, *Political Reform and the American Experiment* (Thomas Crowell, 1977); and Edward Tufte, ed., *Electoral Reform* (symposium issue of *Policy Studies Journal,* 1974).

Legislative Reform

Like electoral policy, the field of legislative reform indirectly influences all policy fields. A key related issue is the apportionment of legislative districts. Traditionally, metropolitan districts have involved more people per legislative representative than rural districts, but recent Supreme Court decisions have stimulated near equality of people per legislative representative. Redistricting can still be done in such a way as to disproportionately favor one political party over another even with equal population, although that kind of gerrymandering may be reduced as a result of future Supreme Court decisions requiring some degree of closeness between the political-party percentages in the electorate and in the legislature.

With regard to legislative procedure, the subject of legislative reform has generally referred to (1) reducing the role of filibustering and other delaying tactics, which enable a minority of legislators to prevent the majority from voting on pending bills, (2) reducing the role of seniority in choosing committee chairpersons rather than election by committee members, and (3) having more frequent and longer legislative sessions, especially at the state level. With regard to legislative personnel, legislative reform often refers to the need for (1) higher and more enforced ethical standards for legislators; (2) more staff and salary and longer terms, to attract better legislators and enable them to serve more effectively; and (3) more restrictions on pressure-group activities so legislators can be more attuned to their wider constituencies.

On legislative reform, see Donald Herzberg and Alan Rosenthal, eds., *Strengthening the States: Essays on Legislative Reform* (Doubleday, 1972); Leroy Rieselbach, ed., *Legislative Reform* (LexingtonBooks, D.C. Heath, 1978); and Susan Welch and John Peters, eds., *The Impact of Legislative Reform* (Praeger, 1977).

Civil Liberties

The field of civil-liberties policy is generally discussed in terms of three types of issues relating to free speech, equal protection, and due process. The equal-protection aspects of civil liberties are emphasized in discussing blacks, women, and other minorities, and the due-process or fair-procedure aspects are emphasized in discussing crime and criminal justice. The most important civil-liberties issues, however, is the free-speech issue which deals with how far society should go in allowing without penalty both popular and unpopular viewpoints to be advocated or communicated in any medium of communication as long as the communication does not involve untruthful defamation, obtaining money under false pretenses, invasion of privacy, the likely promotion of bodily injury, or certain types of hard-core pornography.

Free speech is generally considered the most important constitutional right because, without it, one could not adequately communicate existing defects and new ideas with regard to the other twenty or so policy problems dealt with in chapter 3. Free speech increases the probability that the most effective means toward given ends will become accepted. It also provides a check on corrupt and inefficient leadership and administrative personnel. The Supreme Court has recognized its importance by applying the First Amendment to all levels of government and by narrowing the exceptions to free speech, especially over the last fifty years, although with intermittent plateaus and some retreats. The expansion of the right to express unpopular viewpoints may be largely attributable to having an increasingly more educated population which is more adaptable to change and more aware of how often currently accepted viewpoints were formerly unpopular. Free speech in the United States traditionally has meant only a hands-off policy by the government regarding unpopular ideas, and not an affirmative policy that includes providing free access to the communication media. That affirmative aspect, however, is increasing by way of Federal Communications Commission (FCC) equal-time rules, public broadcasting, and public campaign financing.

A special form of free speech in the United States is the freedom of popular and unpopular religions to carry on their activities without government interference. In the field of religious speech, it is especially important to let all viewpoints be heard since truth and effectiveness are so much more difficult to determine in this field. Along with the restriction of no government interference with religion goes the restriction of no government aid to religion since aid can also lead to interference, favoritism, decreased private initiative, retaliatory action, and intense divisiveness, especially in a multireligious society.

On civil liberties, see Jonathan Casper, *The Politics of Civil Liberties* (Harper and Row, 1972), John Gardiner, ed., *Public Law and Public Policy* (Praeger, 1977); Jay Sigler, *American Rights Policies* (Dorsey, 1975); and Stephen Wasby, ed., *Civil Liberties: Policy and Policy-Making* (Lexington-Books, D.C. Heath, 1976).

Problems with an Economics Emphasis

Economic Regulation

The policy field of economic regulation mainly covers the problems involved in government efforts to reduce unemployment and inflation and thereby keep the economy prosperous. Doing so may mean increased government spending and/or decreased taxes when private-sector activity seems inadequate for full employment. Theoretically, it also means decreasing government spending and/or increasing taxes when private-sector activity is inflationary as a result of a relation between demand and supply that is forcing prices up. For political reasons, however, the anti-inflationary policy may not be as feasible as the proemployment policy. For economic reasons, unemployment and inflation may increase simultaneously, thereby further confusing what is the appropriate policy and possibly generating the issue of whether to institute more direct wage, price, profit, interest, and other controls.

The economic-regulation field also deals with (1) regulation of specific industries where natural monopolies tend to exist or competition has been traditionally considered undesirable, such as railroads, airlines, communications, and retail energy; (2) seeking to maintain competition through the use of antitrust laws directed particularly toward price collusion; (3) consumer-protection matters, particularly dealing with deceptive business practices; (4) union-management relations, including union recognition of elections and the need for bona fide bargaining; and (5) investor protection, particularly regarding truth in securities sales. In recent years there has been an increased concern for deregulation of the pricing of some possibly overregulated industries (like the airlines) and for increased regulation of the quality and safety of certain products (with the airlines also being an example). In recent years there has also arisen an increased tolerance toward government ownership of industries that seem inherently unprofitable to private business if extensive service is to be provided, such as municipal and intercity land passenger transportation.

On economic regulation, see Marver Bernstein, *Regulating Business by Independent Commission* (Princeton University Press, 1955); James Anderson, ed., *Economic Regulatory Policies* (LexingtonBooks, D.C. Heath, 1976); and Mark Nadel, *The Politics of Consumer Protection* (Bobbs-Merrill, 1972).

Housing and Land Use

Housing and land-use policy is especially important from both a consumer's perspective, since shelter is such a basic commodity, and an owner's perspective, since the field deals with fundamental property rights. One set of housing issues relates to providing adequate housing for low-income people. Those issues include (1) eligibility criteria and processing procedures for government-aided housing; (2) the use of clustered public housing versus scattered-site public housing; (3) a balance between government-owned housing and government rent or building subsidies in private landlord-tenant relations; (4) government programs to facilitate home ownership for the poor; (5) urban renewal and rehabilitation procedures; (6) government policy toward reducing racially segregated public and private housing; and (7) issues dealing with allowable defenses in landlord-tenant disputes over rent or housing conditions. Many of these issues also affect middle-class housing problems.

Land-use issues cover government policy toward land that is not necessarily used for housing. These issues involve such matters as (1) zoning ordinances which designate certain areas as qualifying for industrial, commercial, residential, agricultural, or other uses; (2) statutes specifying requirements for new subdivisions; (3) problems concerning the location of highways, airports, parks, and other municipal facilities; (4) the siting of power plants, natural areas, mining, and other uses which tend to be state-regulated; and (5) procedures for citizen involvement in land-use policy decisions.

On housing and land use, see Henry Aaron, *Shelter and Subsidies* (Brookings, 1972); Robert Healy, *Land Use and the States* (Resources for the Future, 1976); Robert Linowes and Don Allensworth, *The Politics of Land Use: Planning, Zoning and the Private Developer* (Praeger, 1973); and Harold Wolman, *Politics of Federal Housing* (Dodd, Mead, 1971).

Transportation and Communication

In the broader field of economic regulation, the transportation and communication industries stand out because they are subject to so much government policy and regulation. One could organize those issues in terms of forms of transportation, such as railroads, airlines, trucking, shipping, automobiles, and busing, and forms of communication, such as radio, television, telephones, and journalistic media. One could also organize the issues in terms of the geographical units involved, such as international, interstate, interurban, or local. However, it may be more meaningful to think in terms of issues that cut across these categories. One such general issue involves the procedures for allowing new firms to enter into the regulated industries of transportation and communication. On the one hand, one could argue that increased competition would benefit the consumer by stimulating lower prices and better products. On the other hand, one could argue that increased competition often would be economically wasteful where it means having duplicate telephone facilities or municipal bus services. Another issue relates to the regulation of prices to balance reasonableness from a consumer perspective with the need for maintaining the profit incentives from a managerial perspective, especially in the absence of some forms of competition that might otherwise exist. These issues also relate to (1) the regulation of product quality and safety, (2) the extent to which certain services can be abandoned or must be maintained even though unprofitable, and (3) the regulation of union-management relations where ordinary strikes cannot be so readily tolerated given the essential nature of transportation to the national economy and to land areas.

There are other transportation and communication issues besides economic regulation. For example, there are free-speech problems involved in government policy designed to provide more equal access to the mass media and to limit violence and sex in television and movies. In the field of transportation, there are also environmental-protection problems, particularly with regard to air and noise pollution. There are also land-use problems with regard to the location of airports, highways, and railroad yards, as well as poverty policy problems with regard to how to bring the cost of transportation more within the reach of low-income people. At one time an important policy issue involved the need for government subsidies to develop railroads, airlines, and communication satellites when those activities represented struggling infant industries. New transportation forms may still need substantial government support for research and development and to create a market, such as non-internal-combustion automobiles, supersonic transports, and innovative municipal rapid transit. The broadest current policy issues in transportation and communication deal with the extent to which those should be unregulated industries, regulated ones, or, in some instances, government-owned.

On transportation and communication, see Richard Adler and Douglass Cater, eds., *Television as a Cultural Force* (Aspen Institute Program on Communications and Society, Praeger Publishers, 1976); Alan Altshuler, ed., *Current Issues in Transportation Policy* (LexingtonBooks, D.C. Heath, 1979); Milton Pikarsky and Daphne Christensen, *Urban Transportation Policy and Management* (LexingtonBooks, D.C. Heath, 1976); and George Smerk, *Urban Mass Transportation: A Dozen Years of Federal Policy* (Indiana University Press, 1975).

Taxing and Spending Policy

A key issue with regard to taxation policy deals with what kind of taxes the government should levy to pay for government expenditures, with the main choices being taxes on income and wealth, which tend to be relatively progressive in terms of ability to pay, versus taxes on consumption, which tend to be relatively regressive. Within each type of taxation there are controversial issues concerning what forms of income or consumption should be taxed and at what levels. Other key taxation issues relate to (1) the extent to which government income should come from borrowing rather than taxation; (2) the extent to which the general level of taxes should be raised or lowered to restrain or stimulate the economy; (3) the use of taxes to discourage various activities as well as raise revenue; (4) how to administer the tax program in order to minimize costs and noncompliance; and (5) how to coordinate the taxing of federal, state, and local governments so as to minimize duplicative and sometimes conflicting programs.

Government spending policy could refer to how the government should spend its money to fight poverty, crime, or pollution; to support education, health, or defense; or for other government activities. Those issues, however, are more meaningful to discuss as part of each specific policy problem. Spending policy can also refer to the methodology for evaluating the wisdom of expenditures in general. That kind of benefit/cost analysis, though, is more relevant to a discussion of the methods of policy analysis. The main spending-policy issue, as such, deals with the procedures for developing government budgets in order to provide coordination across agencies, application of evaluative methodologies, more effective use of spending to stimulate or restrain the economy, and more efficient and equitable budget cutting in light of decreased revenues. Budgeting procedures can be viewed from the perspectives of the central budgeting bureau, the individual line agencies, legislative oversight, or agencies responsible for auditing.

On taxing and spending policy, see Joseph Pechman, *Federal Tax Policy* (Brookings, 1977); Lawrence Pierce, *The Politics of Fiscal Policy Formation* (Goodyear, 1971); Ira Sharkansky, *The Politics of Taxing and Spending* (Bobbs-Merrill, 1969); and Aaron Wildavsky, *The Politics of the Budgetary Process* (Little, Brown, 1974).

Poverty and Welfare

The policy field of poverty and welfare involves a number of issues. The main ones deal with matters of income maintenance and welfare, or how to provide funds to bring poor people closer to a minimum annual family income. Subissues of that general controversy relate to (1) whether welfare programs should be decentralized with different standards and procedures in each state or a more uniform approach be adopted throughout the country; (2) how welfare payments should be related to employment incentives, especially where one or two parents are capable of working; (3) what should be the eligibility criteria, benefit levels, and obligations to repay; and (4) what procedures should be provided for investigations, caseworkers, and hearings.

Other important poverty issues deal with the problems of poor people in various roles which they have in common with other people, but in which poverty increases the likelihood of one's being taken advantage of. These roles include (1) being an employee with little bargaining power for better wages, hours, working conditions, and nondiscriminatory treatment; (2) being a tenant who may be more subject to housing-code violations in private housing and lack of due process in public housing; (3) being a consumer more subject to credit collection abuses, broken warranties, and defective merchandise; (4) being a family member where charges of delinquency, neglect, and abuse may be more prevalent; (5) being a person more lacking in good health and in the funds and facilities to obtain it; and (6) being a child who is provided with relatively poor school facilities and possibly other government services. Some of these issues overlap other policy-problem fields like economic regulation, housing, race relations, education, and health, but those problems have special features when they are discussed in the context of low-income people.

On poverty and welfare, see Dorothy James, ed., *Analyzing Poverty Policy* (LexingtonBooks, D.C. Heath, 1975); Theodore Marmor, *Poverty Policy* (Aldine, 1971); Gilbert Steiner, *Social Inequality: The Politics of Welfare* (Rand McNally, 1966); and Clair Wilcox, *Toward Social Welfare: An Analysis of Programs and Proposals Attacking Poverty, Insecurity, and Inequality of Opportunity* (Irwin, 1969).

Problems with a Sociology-Psychology Emphasis

Blacks, Women, and Other Minorities

The key issue with regard to public policy toward minorities is how to minimize previous discrimination so as to enable the individuals involved to more fully utilize their skills and talents to the benefit of society and themselves. In the U.S. context, the groups against whom discriminatory barriers have been directed mainly include blacks and other racial minorities, Latinos and other national minorities, women, young people, old people, the handicapped, those with unconventional sexual orientations, and minority religious groups. Court cases and statutes have especially involved blacks, but increasingly touch other groups as well.

The types of discriminatory barriers have related mainly to denials not based on merit with regard to equal access to opportunities in political participation, education, equality in criminal procedure, employment, housing, and public accommodations. These barriers have tended to decrease in recent years as minorities have become more vigorous in pressing for changes, as the dominant groups have become more affluent and willing to make concessions, and as both minority and majority persons have become better educated to the harm done by discrimination. Now such discrimination may be more clearly seen as detracting from a society's ability to make maximum use of the skills and talents of its members, as well as having a depressing effect on the productivity of the majority. A key problem is how to remove those barriers with a minimum of the friction and alienation which may occur in both directions as a result of realistic or unrealistic rising expectations or perceptions of reverse discrimination.

On blacks, women, and other minorities, see Thomas Dye, *The Politics of Equality* (Bobbs-Merrill, 1971); Jo Freeman, *The Politics of Women's Liberation* (McKay, 1975); Marian Palley and Michael Preston, eds., *Race, Sex, and Policy Studies* (LexingtonBooks, D.C. Heath, 1979); and Harrell

Rodgers, ed., *Racism and Inequality: The Policy Alternatives* (Freeman, 1975).

Crime and Criminal Justice

This field basically involves two sets of somewhat conflicting issues. On the one hand are the issues that relate to reducing street crime, white-collar crime, and criminal behavior by public officials. On the other hand are issues that relate to safeguarding the innocent from conviction and harassment by criminal-justice decisionmakers. Methods for reducing crime tend to relate to three kinds of activities. One kind of activity involves increasing the probabilities of wrongdoing being detected, adjudicated, and negatively sanctioned. Increasing those three probabilities may require greater professionalism on the part of criminal-justice decisionmakers, although some advocate increasing those probabilities by relaxing the constraints on police surveillance, evidence needed for convictions, and the imposition of severe penalties like capital punishment. A second kind of activity involves decreasing the benefits that come from illegal behavior. Doing that may require changing the nature of peer-group recognition and hardening the targets of criminal wrongdoers. A third kind of activity involves increasing the costs that come from illegal behavior. For many people that means longer prison sentences under harsher conditions, but for other people that might mean increasing the realistic opportunities lost as a result of illegal behavior, which may be the main reason middle-class people do not take the risks involved in committing street crimes.

Methods for safeguarding the innocent from conviction and harassment (while at the same time enabling the guilty to be caught) include the right to (1) no retroactive or vague criminal statutes, or statutes declaring named persons to be guilty of wrongdoing, (2) arrest or search only where there is substantial likelihood of guilt, (3) no involuntary confessions or self-incrimination, (4) release pending speedy trial, (5) hired or provided counsel at and before trial, (6) formal notice of charges, (7) unanimous decision by a group of one's peers, (8) question adverse witnesses and call one's own witnesses, (9) no excessive punishment, and (10) no repeated prosecution for the same matter. The right to counsel is probably the most important, since without an attorney to enforce them, the other rights may be meaningless. Providing counsel to the indigent, however, is a costly problem, but one which the Supreme Court has now imposed on all government systems in the United States in criminal cases.

On crime and criminal justice, see John Gardiner and Michael Mulkey, eds., *Crime and Criminal Justice: Issues in Public Policy Analysis* (LexingtonBooks, D.C. Heath, 1975); Herbert Jacob, ed., *The Potential for Reform of Criminal Justice* (Sage, 1974); and Stuart Nagel, *Improving the Legal Process: Effects of Alternatives* (LexingtonBooks, D.C. Heath, 1975).

Education

Educational issues can be organized in terms of the level of education involved, such as preschool, elementary, college, or adult, or in terms of the government level involved, such as local, state, national, or international. Some of the issues overlap other policy problems, such as academic freedom for faculty and students relevant to civil-liberties policy, desegregation of students and faculty relevant to minorities policy, and the allocation of government funds and personnel to schools in low-income areas relevant to poverty policy. Those are especially important issues since they involve fundamental aspects of the First Amendment and of equal protection under the law.

Issues more specifically relating to educational policy include (1) the extent to which the federal government should provide aid to local schools and with what strings attached, especially regarding desegregation and non-discrimination; (2) how to provide both citizen involvement and independent professionalism in the administration of the schools; (3) how to provide balance in the curriculum among classical, vocational, life-adjustment, college-preparation, and other educational goals; (4) the need for special education programs for the handicapped, non-English-speaking, culturally deprived, and other groups; (5) what role the government should play with regard to parochial schools and religious education; (6) government subsidies to private colleges, university research, and college scholarships and loans; (7) the involvement of the courts in suspensions, dismissals, and disciplinary proceedings of students and faculty; and (8) government regulation and mediation relevant to the unionization of educational personnel, collective bargaining, and strikes.

On education, see Samuel Gove and Frederick Wirt, *Political Science and School Politics* (LexingtonBooks, D.C. Heath, 1976); Michael Kirst, ed., *State, School, and Politics: Research Directions* (LexingtonBooks, D.C. Heath, 1972); and Frederick Wirt and Michael Kirst, *The Political Web of American Schools* (Little, Brown, 1972).

Population Policy

The key issue with regard to government population policy relates to what role government should play in seeking to control population growth in view of the limited resources of the nation and world. In that regard, there are a variety of relevant government programs and policies, including (1) the subsidizing of birth-control purchases through public aid and foreign aid; (2) government programs designed to raise standards of living and thereby stimulate more middle-class values, which include having smaller families (partly because educating children is more expensive in middle-class families and children are less of an economic aid); (3) government programs designed to educate the public with regard to the availability of birth-control methods; (4) subsidies for birth-control research; (5) legalization of abortion, which in some countries is a frequent birth-control method; and (6) government programs designed to increase and conserve natural resources so as to be able to satisfy the needs of a larger population.

A second key issue concerning government population policy relates to government involvement in population movements. This involvement includes policies relating to (1) immigration of people to the United States, both legal and illegal; (2) migration from rural areas to cities, with resulting congestion problems and the need for government aid in making the transition; (3) migration patterns across nations, which sometimes lead to minorities subject to discrimination, social unrest, and foreign-policy problems; and (4) migration patterns within the United States toward the Sun Belt, which sometimes leads to competition among the states in offering more lenient industrial-regulation laws in order to attract or retain business firms and thus employment opportunities.

A third key population-policy area relates to the aging of populations (particularly the U.S. population) as a result of a lowered birthrate and better health care. Having an older population raises problems with regard to social security coverage, Medicare and special health problems, recreation and leisure activities, housing and nursing homes, and discrimination in employment opportunities against the aged, but also problems in the need for younger workers to move up in the job hierarchy.

On population policy, see Peter Bachrach and Elihu Bergman, *Power and Choice: The Formulation of American Population Policy* (LexingtonBooks, D.C. Heath, 1972); Richard Clinton, *Population and Politics: New Directions in Political Science Research* (LexingtonBooks, D.C. Heath, 1973); Michael Kraft and Mark Schneider, eds., *Population Policy Analysis: Issues in American Politics* (LexingtonBooks, D.C. Heath, 1978); and Keir Nash, *Governance and Population* (Commission on Population Growth in the American Future, Government Printing Office, 1972).

Problems with a Natural Science or Engineering Emphasis

Science and Technology Policy

A key issue in science and technology policy is how to determine the social and other effects of new technological developments before they occur, so that appropriate government policies can be instituted. For example, what are the likely broad effects of supersonic transports, electronic calculators, birth-control pills, solar energy, new antibiotics, cable television, or other technological developments? Being able to predict the effects of the automobile on suburbanization, on the depletion of oil resources, and on air pollution could conceivably have enabled the government to have more actively subsidized the development of electric and steam transportation when the automobile industry was in the process of deciding among electric, steam, and gasoline combustion engines. Congress now has the Office of Technology Assessment to aid in making such predictions. Requiring environmental-impact statements to accompany major government decisions is also an important aspect of contemporary technological assessment.

Another key science and technology issue is how governments at various levels can stimulate scientific research and development in order to accelerate socially useful knowledge and inventions. Governments attempt to achieve that goal in various ways, including (1) subsidizing university and non-university research through grants and contracts; (2) having agency staffs of in-house scientists, especially in defense, agriculture, and public-health programs; (3) supporting state universities where much research is conducted; (4) providing scholarships and loans to help create new scientists; (5) providing a patent and copyright system to make inventions and ideas profitable; (6) providing a market in which to purchase new technological developments, especially in transportation, defense, information processing, and teaching devices; and (7) facilitating government utilization of research that may have been developed independent of government policies, as mentioned in discussing the utilization of policy research.

Another science-policy issue concerns government regulation of scientific developments that can be socially detrimental if abused, such as genetic engineering, nuclear experimentation, drug development, experiments with or interviewing humans, and abuses of laboratory animals. A related science-policy issue concerns government regulation or subsidization to make useful scientific developments such as life-sustaining devices and pollution-control devices more widely available where the market forces of supply and demand are such that the developments would not become widespread without government involvement, as in the health-policy and environmental-policy fields.

On science and technology policy, see L.K. Caldwell, *Science, Technology and Public Policy* (Indiana University Press, 1967, with periodic supplements); Daniel Greenberg, *The Politics of Pure Science* (New American Library, 1976); and Joseph Haberer, ed., *Science and Technology Policy* (LexingtonBooks, D.C. Heath, 1977).

Health Policy

The key issue in government health policy is probably what role the government should play in seeking to provide minimum health care for all persons regardless of income. One choice is a laissez-faire policy of allowing the medical profession, the drug industry, and the medical insurance companies to handle the problem by charging in accordance with ability to pay, with some free services to the indigent. At the other extreme is a form of socialized medicine in which doctors mainly work for the government and provide service to patients without charge since the taxpayers, in effect, pay the medical fees. In the middle are various government programs designed either to subsidize private medical insurance or to incorporate medical insurance into a social insurance system like social security. Subissues of the insurance alternative relate to whether all people or mainly the aged and the poor should be covered; whether all medical problems or mainly medical catastrophes should be covered; whether premiums should be paid by employers, employees, or general taxpayers and at what levels; and to what extent the government should show concern for the quality of the medical services for which it is paying.

Other health-policy issues besides health delivery programs include (1) regulation of the drug industry with regard to prices and quality of products; (2) subsidizing medical education to generate more doctors, especially in some geographical areas and some specialties; (3) subsidizing hospital facilities and requiring as part of the subsidy some consideration for the medical problems of the poor; (4) control of contagious diseases, drinking water, and sanitation; (5) industrial health and safety regulation; (6) subsidizing medical research to find cures and preventatives for cancer and other diseases; and (7) special provisions for mental health problems, although all the above issues relate to both mental and physical health.

On health policy, see Theodore Marmor, *The Politics of Medicare* (Aldine, 1973); David Mechanic, *Politics, Medicine, and Social Science* (Wiley, 1974); Herman Somers and Ann Somers, *Doctors, Patients, and Health Insurance: The Organization and Financing of Medical Care* (Brookings, 1961); and Robert Alford, *Health Care Politics* (University of Chicago Press, 1975).

Environmental Protection

The policy field of environmental protection involves a number of major issues. The main issue concerns the extent to which the effects of various types of pollution are detrimental enough to warrant large-scale regulatory and grant programs. Water pollution, for example, is damaging to public health, recreation, aesthetics, commercial fishing, agriculture, and industrial water supplies. Air pollution is even more damaging to public health, because of the inability to clean the air, as well as to plant life, materials, visibility, and climate. However, massive environmental programs use resources and human effort that could be better devoted to problems of domestic and worldwide poverty. Such programs may also interfere with industrial production and the raising of living standards. Sometimes there may be too much emphasis in environmental programs on middle-class aesthetics and recreation, as contrasted to the public-health problems of pollution, especially in inner-city areas. The concern for developing new energy sources may sometimes conflict with environmental standards, although energy conservation and environmental protection tend to go together.

Other important environmental-protection issues deal with such matters as (1) devising government structures to reduce pollution, which is a public-administration matter; (2) devising government procedures to reduce pollution, which is largely an administrative-law matter; (3) devising pollution reducing incentives, which is where environmental economics can be especially helpful; and (4) whether and how to compensate victims of pollution, provide for displaced workers, and protect consumers from bearing antipollution costs. Like all policy problems, environmental policy is a multidisciplinary matter.

On environmental protection, see Frank Grad, George Rathjens, and Albert Rosenthal, *Environmental Control: Priorities, Policies and the Law* (Columbia University Press, 1971); Stuart Nagel, ed., *Environmental Politics* (Praeger, 1975); and Walter Rosenbaum, *The Politics of Environmental Concern* (Praeger, 1973).

Energy Policy

The field of energy policy is relatively new in importance since until recently the supply of energy has been taken for granted and the demand has not been so large. However, the need for government action has increased as a result of a forthcoming restricted supply of oil and gas and a greatly expanded worldwide demand resulting from motorized transportation, electrification, industrialization, and increased population. Government energy policy takes a variety of general forms, including research and development of new energy sources, stimulation of measures to conserve existing energy sources, and regulation of energy industries with regard to entry, prices, environmental protection, and safety. Other general ways of organizing energy-policy issues are either in terms of the energy sources of coal, oil, natural gas, nuclear energy, and hydroelectric power or in terms of production, physical distribution, retailing, and consumption problems.

More specific issues deal with (1) the siting of nuclear-power plants and the handling of nuclear wastes; (2) the development of coal resources without the adverse effects of air pollution and strip-mining; (3) the regulation of energy prices to stimulate energy production, but also to prevent excess profits and to provide an equitable balance between industrial and residential users; (4) the use of taxes to discourage excessive gasoline consumption; (5) the international defense implications of the proliferation of nuclear energy and the shifting balances of power as a result of the increased importance of oil locations; (6) the need to stimulate oil productivity while simultaneously guarding against oil spills and pipeline accidents; (7) the need to limit the potentially corrupting influence of oil and other energy lobbyists in obtaining government favoritism; (8) how far the government should go in seeking to stimulate the development of solar, geothermal, wind, ocean, and other new energy forms; and (9) the balance between domestic production and foreign imports.

On energy policy, see David Davis, *Energy Politics* (St. Martin's Press, 1974); David Freeman, *National Energy Policy* (Twentieth Century Fund, 1974); Robert Lawrence, ed., *Critical Issues in Energy Policy* (Lexington-Books, D.C. Heath, 1978); and Richard Mancke, *The Failure of U.S. Energy Policy* (Columbia University Press, 1974).

Agricultural Policy

In recent years agricultural policy has undergone a dramatic shift from policies mainly designed to restrict supply and increase demand (in order to provide greater farm income) to a set of policies mainly designed to increase supply and restrict demand (in view of increasing world food shortages), although some overlap exists between the two. Former policies that have been cut back include crop restrictions, government purchases, and direct farm-income payments. Current policies involve foreign sales, food stamps, and school lunch programs, not just to increase demand but also to aid the needy. Current policies also increasingly emphasize the development of greater farm auton-omy and farm productivity in view of expanded world markets. A government policy that particularly reflects the general shift is the movement from a tariff policy designed to keep out foreign agricultural competition to talk of an export control policy that would limit agricultural sales abroad so as to prevent domestic shortages.

Other less dramatic government policies in the field of agriculture and food deal with such matters as (1) consumer protection concerning the quality of food products, (2) farm-labor regulation, (3) environmental protection, particularly with regard to pesticide-runoff problems, (4) government crop insurance and farm credit, (5) rural electrification and public utilities, (6) regulation of agricultural marketing with regard to both trading practices and transportation, (7) humane livestock regulation, (8) agricultural research and research utilization, (9) resettlement problems of displaced farm labor, and (10) conservation and irrigation of farmland.

On agricultural policy, see Don Hadwiger, William Browne, and Richard Fraenkel, eds., *The New Politics of Food* (LexingtonBooks, D.C. Heath, 1978); Dale Hathaway, *Government and Agriculture* (Macmillan, 1963); Vernon Ruttan, Arley Waldo, and James Houck, eds., *Agricultural Policy in an Affluent Society* (Norton, 1969); and Ross Talbot and Don Hadwiger, *The Policy Process in American Agriculture* (Chandler, 1968).

Part III
Institutions of the
Policy-Studies Field

4 Training Programs

As its title indicates, this chapter serves two purposes: The first is to describe what is happening in university policy-studies activities within political-science departments and within interdisciplinary programs; the second purpose is to analyze a set of prescriptions for improving policy-studies activities, which have been recommended by academics and by government practitioners. By policy-studies activities in this context, we mean research, teaching, and related activities that deal with the applications of political and social science to the study of the causes and especially the effects of alternative government policies. Causes include, among other things, the role of public administrators in making policies or prospective decisions, and effects include the varied implementation of government policies.

In order to determine what is and what should be happening according to knowledgeable persons, we conducted a survey in 1976 of chairpersons of political-science departments and directors of interdisciplinary programs. We also conducted a related survey in 1975 of members of the American Political Science Association who were holding positions in federal, state, or local governments. This chapter emphasizes the results of the university survey. A previous article emphasized the results of the practitioners' survey,[1] but comparisons are made throughout this chapter between the responses of the academics and of the practitioners.

The schools surveyed include all universities or colleges that offer either the Ph.D. degree or the M.A. degree in political science as indicated on the chairperson mailing lists of the American Political Science Association. The schools surveyed also include the interdisciplinary policy-studies programs on the membership list of the National Association of Schools of Public Affairs and Administration which have a political-science component, but which are not exclusively political-science, public-administration, or business-administration programs. Of the 298 schools surveyed, 42 percent at least partly responded, and information was obtained for 10 percent of the others from a similar survey made in 1973.

The exact wording of the questionnaire and the verbatim responses of the respondents are available elsewhere and need not be repeated here.[2] Instead, this section emphasizes the highlights of the results of the survey with regard to such policy-studies activities as special degrees, research, teaching, interdisciplinary activities, funding, journal publication, and hiring and placement. It also emphasizes the recommendations for improving those activities, especially with regard to research, training, and communication among academics and government practitioners. Part of the analysis includes a comparison with an earlier survey of academics in 1973 so as to bring out trends in policy-studies activities. The quantitative presentation is supplemented with examples of quotations and a synthesizing analysis of the controversial issues raised by the respondents.

Present Policy-Studies Activities

Table 4–1 shows the percentage of the respondents saying yes, no, or something in between to each of the eight items dealing with their present policy activities. The number responding to each item varies since some respondents left some items blank as an indication of lack of knowledge, an implied no, or an oversight. Of the 103 respondents to the item asking about *special degrees* related to policy studies (other than the M.A. and Ph.D. degrees in political science), 74 percent answered yes. They were generally referring to the M.A.P.A., which variously stands for the master's degree in public administration, public affairs, or policy analysis. Special degrees also included doctorates in public administration or policy analysis and master's degrees in public systems engineering, planning, public service, criminal justice, and science policy. The greatest number of special degrees seems to be offered by the University of Michigan's Institute for Public Policy Studies which offers (in addition to the M.A. and Ph.D. in political science) the master of public policy, master of public administration, master of science in public

Table 4–1
Present Policy-Studies Activities

Item	Number Responding	Percentage Saying No	Percentage Saying "Sort of" or "in Planning"	Percentage Saying Yes
1. Special degrees	103	23	3	74
2. Organized research	102	45	3	52
3. Special teaching	103	24	7	69
4. Organized interdisciplinary	102	32	4	64
5. Special funding	98	46	3	51
6. Taking over *Policy Studies Journal*	88	68	26	6
7a. Hiring	95	54	6	40
7b. Placing	71	75	1	24
8a. Newsletter	85	79	5	17
8b. Government training	87	55	5	40
8c. Other policy-studies activity	80	79	5	16

systems engineering, and the doctorate in public policy. Many departments responded like North Texas State University by saying, "We do not have a separate field for teaching and research in policy studies, nor a separate degree. However, we have been increasing our course offerings in the area and expect this trend may continue."

Of those responding 52 percent indicated they had organized policy-studies *research* programs other than just relevant individual faculty research. These specialized programs emphasize research in such policy fields as health (for example, NYU), environmental protection (University of California at Davis), science policy (Purdue), communications (Michigan), energy (M.I.T.), transportation (Tufts), foreign policy (Johns Hopkins), urban policy (Northwestern), housing (Minnesota), policy theory (Indiana), poverty (Wisconsin), education (Columbia), criminal justice (Albany), population (North Carolina), teaching policy studies (Syracuse), and agriculture (Iowa State). Many schools mentioned having not a specialized research program, but extensive research activities, such as the response from Ohio State University which said, "We do not have a single policy studies research program in our department. However, several projects have developed to the point that they have served as a source of employment for graduate students, have provided a focus for course offerings, and have provided a basis for M.A. theses and Ph.D. dissertations. These projects focus on policy-making in the executive branch, foreign policy decision-making, the implementation of employment legislation, and the implementation of compensatory education programs." Research integrated into the teaching curricula seems especially strong at the L.B.J. School at the University of Texas, where its respondent said, "Students in their second year pursue an independent research project which generally includes analysis of a public policy issue for a public sector client, agency, or legislative committee."

Of the respondents 69 percent indicated they have a special *teaching* curriculum or field within political science called something like policy studies. At the graduate level, the University of California at Riverside said, "Public policy is, and for four or five years has been, one of the six fields a student may elect in our Ph.D. program. The public policy field, as we define it, includes both substantive areas of policy (such as government and business, government and science, intergovernmental relations, educational policy and politics, etc.) and the major policy-making institutions (courts, Congress, Presidency)." At the undergraduate level, the Massachusetts Institute of Technology said, "MIT has a number of programs in policy studies . . . in addition, we are planning an undergraduate concentration in public policy." Other schools often indicated that public policy is treated as a subfield within U.S. government (for example, Georgetown) or as an interdisciplinary outside field (for example, Duke.)

Of the respondents 64 percent indicated that their schools have an organized *interdisciplinary* policy-studies program. For example, Idaho State said, "Research generated through the Government Research Institute has involved some fifty students over the past three years in projects that are interdisciplinary and have conceptual relevance to policy studies and their analysis in the classroom. These programs have been organized and supervised by a team of faculty members representing Political Science and Sociology disciplines, with an occasional input from the Department of Economics." Minnesota also said, "Students are urged to include courses from outside the department. In addition, a weekly colloquium offers students and faculty the opportunity to hear speakers on varied aspects of public policy. Joint degrees are in effect with the Law School, Program in Hospital and Health Care Administration, and School of Social Work." The interdisciplinary policy-studies programs like those at Harvard, Michigan, Washington, and elsewhere by definition include people and perspectives from a variety of social-science disciplines and sometimes also natural science, humanities, and the professional schools like law, social work, education, and business.

Of the respondents 51 percent indicated that their departments or schools were recipients of special *funding* concerning policy-studies activities. The sources particularly included the National Science Foundation, Ford Foundation, Law Enforcement Assistance Administration (LEAA), Department of Transportation (DOT), HEW, HUD, National Institute of Mental Health, Department of Defense (DOD), Sloan, Carnegie, National Aeronautics and Space Administration (NASA), and the Office of Education. The Ford Foundation has been especially helpful to about a dozen interdisciplinary policy-studies programs such as those at Duke, Yale, Princeton, and Stanford. Money, however, seemed to be a problem, partly as indicated by the relatively low percentage of schools indicating a willingness to take over the operation of the *Policy Studies Journal* given the financial burden that might mean. The University of Massachusetts said, "Sorry, we're broke," and the University of California at Davis said, "Possibly, if suitable budgetary arrangements could be made," although Georgia State said, "We would be glad to discuss the possibility."

Although the political-science marketplace in general is rather tight because of budgetary problems, 40 percent of 95 respondents indicated they were *hiring* in the policy-studies field. Unlike in other political-science fields, the number of schools hiring exceeds the number of schools seeking to place public-policy graduates since a lower 24 percent of 71 respondents indicated they had people available to place. The market for hiring and placing in the policy-studies field seems to be especially active at the junior level for lack of funds to hire senior people, and possibly because junior people may be more likely to have relevant policy-analysis training. The University of Washington at Seattle said, "The Graduate School of Public Affairs plans to make two or three appointments for the fall of 1976." A typical response illustrating that hiring is greater than placing in the public-policy field (as contrasted to other fields) came from Cornell, which said, "One of the currently vacant positions is in American Government/Public Policy, but no other openings are likely as Cornell has generally frozen hiring. Our program is only beginning to have Ph.D.'s with a program in Public Policy, so we do not have any placement experience yet."

Table 4–1 could have been broken down into the Ph.D. departments, the M.A. departments, and the interdisciplinary programs. Doing so would indicate that the interdisciplinary policy-studies programs are the most active in the sense of having special degrees, organized research, special teaching, interdisciplinary activities, special funding, a willingness to participate in the *Policy Studies Journal,* and hiring and placement. The Ph.D. departments are the next most active, and the M.A. departments third, although there are many M.A. departments that are more active than some Ph.D. departments. Among the Ph.D. departments, the degree of activity correlates positively with the ranking of the department by the American Council of Education. This indicates that policy studies has acquired a greater respectability among the higher-ranked departments than was the case with the 1973 academic survey (which resulted in the first *Policy Studies Directory*), where that correlation was negative. It may also indicate that the higher-ranked departments are now less likely to leave policy studies exclusively to the interdisciplinary programs at those schools. The correlation analysis also shows that if a department responds favorably on one item, it is also likely to respond favorably on each other item, given that policy studies tends to relate simultaneously to many aspects of the operations of political-science departments.

Changes in Policy-Studies Activities

Table 4–2 shows the percentage of a select group of respondents that reported an increase, a decrease, or no change in each of the eight items. That subgroup consisted of those thirty-six who responded to both the 1976 questionnaire and the 1973 one, thereby holding constant those respondents across both surveys. We cannot meaningfully compare the total percentage saying yes in the 1976 questionnaire with the percentage saying yes in the 1973 questionnaire since the first one included only Ph.D. departments and not M.A. departments or interdisciplinary programs, and since the same Ph.D. departments did not respond to both questionnaires.

A department shows an increase on an item either by having said no in 1973 and "sort of" or yes in 1976 or by saying "sort of" in 1973 and yes in 1976. A department shows a decrease by having said yes in 1973 and

Table 4–2
Changes in Policy-Studies Activities

Change in Item Regarding:	Number Responding on the Change Variable	Percentage Decrease	No Change (%)	Percentage Increase	Net Increase (Percentage Increase minus Percentage Decrease) (%)
1. Special degrees	36	0	50	50	50
2. Organized research	34	3	65	33	30
3. Special teaching	35	0	69	31	31
4. Organized interdisciplinary	35	3	63	34	31
5. Special funding	32	9	66	23	14
6. Taking over *Policy Studies Journal*	26	30	50	20	−10
7a. Hiring	32	38	31	32	−6
7b. Placing	17	30	59	12	−8
8a. Newsletter	27	0	82	19	19
8b. Government training	24	4	58	37	33
8c. Other policy-studies activity	23	4	78	17	13

something less than yes in 1976. The no-change category generally involves saying yes to both questionnaires on an item, although sometimes saying no to both, or "sort of" to both. With regard to the first item involving special degrees, 50 percent of the thirty-six departments who responded to that item in both 1973 and 1976 showed an increase, 50 percent showed no change, and none showed a decrease. A net increase on each item was calculated by subtracting the percentage decrease from the percentage increase and ignoring the no-change category. Thus, the net increase on the special-degrees item was 50 percent.

Reading down the net-increase column, we can see there was a substantial net increase in departments reporting special policy-studies degrees, extension training of government personnel, organized research, special teaching, and organized interdisciplinary activities. More moderate net increases occurred in newsletters, special funding, and miscellaneous policy-studies activities. Net decreases, however, occurred in hiring and placement activities, given the increased tightness of the academic and government job markets. Hiring and placement, however, are still quite active in the policy-studies field, as indicated by the fact that 40 percent of all the respondents in table 4–1 said they were hiring and 24 percent said they were placing. A net decrease was also reported in willingness to take over the *Policy Studies Journal,* possibly because of a feeling that the costs would be too great in view of the expanded nature of the *Policy Studies Journal* and the contracted nature of departmental budgets.

Recommendations for Improved Research, Communication, and Training

The second part of the questionnaire was designed to provide recommendations and other ideas for improving the policy relevance of political-science research, communication, and training. Those three key topics were discussed in the recent *Political Science Utilization Directory* (Policy Studies Organization, 1975) by present or former government practitioners in federal, state, or local government who were members of the American Political Science Association. Table 4–3 summarizes the results with regard to *recommendations for research* conducted by political scientists that might be helpful in government decision making. The practitioners from the 1973 survey, on the other hand, placed less emphasis on research methodology and policy formation and more emphasis on substantive policy and public administration. Both groups emphasized the need for more evaluation and impact studies, as is illustrated by the practitioner respondent from LEAA who commented, "We need prescriptive rather than descriptive research. Simply to tell a political decision-maker that a policy will be endorsed by one constituency rather than another probably only repeats something he already knows." A small but substantial subgroup from both the academics and the practitioners also emphasized economic analysis, cost/benefit analysis, and related research. Respondents from the interdisciplinary programs especially stress the need for interdisciplinary research, such as the respondent from the Maxwell School of Citizenship and Public Affairs who said, "Political

Table 4–3
Research Needed

Item Mentioned	Number of Mentions	Percentage of Mentions	Percentage of Respondents[a]
Methods of decision making	27	39	53
Evaluation of policy; policy-impact studies	22	32	43
Economic analysis and new methodologies from other fields	5	7	10
Implementation studies	5	7	10
Effects of pressure-group activities	5	7	10
Syntheses of existing knowledge rather than additional case studies	3	4	6
Studies of small government units	2	4	4
Total	69	100	136

[a]Percentage of fifty-one respondents mentioning a type of research needed. This column sums to more than 100 percent because some respondents mention more than one item.

scientists should be employed in evaluative studies of the impact of existing programs, along with other social scientists."

Table 4–4 summarizes the recommendations with regard to how political scientists might better *communicate* their research to people in government and receive feedback in return. The respondents emphasize the need for exchanges of research summaries, conferences, and workshops with practitioners. The practitioners also advocated similar devices, as indicated by the respondent from the National Institutes of Health who said, "Academic political scientists should spend some time in government as advisors, consultants, interns, residents, special assistants to Cabinet members, and Congressional committees, etc. Government employees should spend a semester or two at a university every five years. There is a great need for such continual interchange." Given the agreement on both sides, all that is perhaps needed are some facilitating personnel and funds in various government line agencies and research agencies designed to encourage relevant research utilization. The academics and practitioners also agreed on the need for journal articles with less jargon. The main disagreement relates to the fact that the academics may be more optimistic regarding what academic research has to offer than the practitioners are. The interdisciplinary policy programs at the University of California at Berkeley, Harvard, and Yale participate in publishing the useful policy journals *Policy Analysis, Public Policy,* and *Policy Sciences,* respectively, although the respondent from the Princeton University Woodrow Wilson School mentioned that we need "the preparation of far better reviews of the state-of-the-art than have been issued either by government or the research community."

Table 4–4
Improved Communication Ideas

Idea Mentioned	Number of Mentions	Percentage of Mentions	Percentage of Respondents[a]
Exchange specially written summaries of research with government people	17	32	33
Conferences, workshops, and special seminars with practitioners	13	25	25
More face-to-face contact with practitioners on a planned basis	8	15	16
Establish and distribute journals which are of interest to practitioners	8	15	16
Eliminate jargon from professional journals	5	9	10
Set up extension centers somewhat like county agents in agriculture extension	2	4	4
Total	53	100	104

[a]Percent of forty-nine respondents mentioning a type of research needed. This column sums to more than 100 percent because some respondents mention more than one item.

Table 4–5 summarizes the recommendations for how political-science *training* can better prepare people for working in government or doing work outside of government that is relevant to government decision making. Here, as in research, the academics emphasized methodology, especially quantitative techniques, whereas the practitioners stressed substantive knowledge about how government actually functions and expertise in specific policy areas. Both groups strongly endorse internships in government and field experience, and they both advocate the increased emphasis on public-policy studies. The methodological emphasis of the academics is illustrated by West Virginia University, which responded by saying, "Presently, many institutions turn out people who may be well-trained in the substantive aspects of American politics and government or applied policy science, but do not have a solid grounding in the science of political science," or the response from Cornell which said, "A first requirement is that political scientists have a solid training in economics ... because the discipline is most relevant to the framing of questions of choice and because so many choices are framed in economic terms." A representative practitioner involved in planning at the statewide level said, "The best training we have found is the actual experience in doing policy analysis for elected decisionmakers. Some kind of actual training which required taking an issue, looking at it, and preparing recommendations for particular action is the most effective preparation for people in our kind of an agency." Optimism as to the meaningfulness of the new interdisciplinary training programs is expressed by the respondent for the University of California at Berkeley Graduate School of Public Policy who said, "A profession is now developing in which people are trained to examine

Table 4–5
Improved Training Ideas

Idea Mentioned	Number of Mentions	Percentage of Mentions	Percentage of Respondents[a]
More training in quantitative techniques	17	25	33
Internships in government	16	24	32
Promote application of analysis to public policy	9	14	18
Increased emphasis on decision-making techniques	7	11	14
Knowledge about how government actually functions	5	7	10
Field experience in government offices	4	6	8
Have practitioners help teach courses	3	4	6
Interdisciplinary training	2	3	4
Sabbatical leaves to work in government	2	3	4
Economics as a minor	2	3	4
Total	67	100	133

[a]Percentage of fifty-one respondents mentioning a type of research needed. This column sums to more than 100 percent because some respondents mention more than one item.

alternative approaches to public policy programs, to evaluate the effects of policies, and to facilitate the implementation of programs once adopted."

Although the Ph.D. departments may have more policy-studies activities, the respondents from the M.A. departments tended to be more articulate with regard to offering recommendations for research needed, improved communication, and improved training. On one hand, perhaps becoming more involved in trying to operate a policy-studies program makes one more cautious about making recommendations after seeing more of the complexities involved. On the other hand, some of the Ph.D. departments may be overly cautious with regard not only to making recommendations, but also to getting involved in the application of political science to important policy problems. An error of holding back when one could make a significant theoretical and practical contribution may be much more costly in terms of the opportunity costs than an error of moving forward with recommendations and programs before they are fully tested.

Issues Involved in Having a Balanced Policy-Studies Program

Reading both the responses to the questionnaire and related literature enables one to better perceive the basic issues and relevant considerations involved in having a policy-studies program within a political-science department or in an interdisciplinary unit which has political science as a leading component. These interrelated issues seem to emphasize the eleven discussed below. The consensus, as indicated, seems to be that on each issue there is a need for balancing divergent approaches in order to have what a policy-studies program should be.

1. To what extent should the program be an undergraduate rather than a graduate program, and the Ph.D. rather than the M.A. program? For political-science departments that have only undergraduate courses, this is not an issue, although they could be thinking about maintaining a balance between the policy-studies training of undergraduates who are not likely to do graduate work and those who are. The departments included in the 1976 questionnaire all offer at least the master's degree, and for them the undergraduate-graduate distinction is relevant. A program that involves undergraduate, M.A., and possibly Ph.D. policy-studies work provides diversity of faculty experiences and student interaction, an increased quantity of students to generate the critical mass that might be needed for a more effective program, and a recruitment source for the more advanced aspects of the program. Teaching policy studies to undergraduates can be especially helpful with regard to learning how to simplify the presentation of materials that otherwise might be unduly quantitative or theoretical, and such simplification can also help improve communication with government practitioners. Establishing a three-level program can be made easier by including a number of advanced undergraduate courses that can be taken for either graduate or undergraduate credit. Further discussion of the undergraduate aspects of a policy-analysis program is included in the report by David Smith, "Policy Analysis for Undergraduates," for the Ford Foundation Public Policy Committee in 1975, which he summarizes in the winter 1976 issue of the *Policy Studies Journal* (pp. 234–274).

2. To what extent should the program train people for government work as contrasted to teaching work? This issue is related to the first issue in that Ph.D. programs tend to stress teaching, and undergraduate or M.A. programs tend to emphasize government work, but not necessarily. There is an increasing demand for Ph.D.'s to do government policy-evaluation work, as indicated in the responses to the *Political Science Utilization Directory* (Policy Studies Organization, 1975). Likewise, the undergraduate and M.A. programs could have a component which encourages getting the Ph.D. teaching degree. It is desirable to have interaction between students who are oriented toward becoming policy-evaluation practitioners and those oriented toward becoming teachers and research authors, since each group has perspectives and ideas that may provide insights to the other group as well as to the faculty.

3. To what extent should the program be a political-science program as contrasted to an interdisciplinary program? Since we are talking about mainly policy-studies programs within political-science departments, it follows that these programs will basically be political-science programs although with interdisciplinary elements. Of all the social sciences, political science is the most relevant to discussing the institutional aspects of policy formation and policy implementation with regard to the roles of federal, state, and local legislators; chief executives; administrators; and judges. Political science also provides relevant knowledge and theories with regard to the roles of parties, interest groups, public opinion, and political philosophy in policy formation and implementation. Those concerns are enough to make political science a meaningful focus for a policy-studies program, although a more nearly comprehensive program would require substantial supplementing from other disciplines such as economics, sociology, law, psychology, and philosophy, as is discussed in Stuart Nagel, ed., *Policy Studies and the Social Sciences* (LexingtonBooks, D.C. Heath, 1975). The supplementing can take the form of required outside courses, a required minor, political-science courses that stress the substance and method of other disciplines, and also recommended electives.

4. What about the balance between substance and method? Both substantive and methodological knowledge are needed for policy studies. On one hand, if students are just well versed in policy-evaluation methodology, but they have had no depth in any substantive policy problem area, then their work is likely to be overly abstract and possibly impractical for lack of concrete knowledge. On the other hand, individuals who are well versed in a specific policy problem area (such as poverty, environmental protection, foreign policy, economic regulation, and so on) could not consider themselves to be policy-studies or policy-analysis persons if they do not have some generalized methodological skills for analyzing policy alternatives across policy problem areas. Relevant substantive problems of special interest to political scientists are those included on the editorial board of the *Policy Studies Journal* (*PSJ*) and those that are the subject of past and scheduled *PSJ* symposia, Stuart Nagel, ed., *Policy Studies in America and Elsewhere* (LexingtonBooks, D.C. Heath, 1975). Relevant methodologies include those dealt with in books such as those by Scioli and Cook, *Methodologies for Analyzing Public Policies* (LexingtonBooks, D.C. Heath, 1975), and Dolbeare, *Public Policy Evaluation* (Sage, 1975).

5. To what extent should policy studies be a separate field within political science rather than a pervasive approach in all fields of political science? Policy studies can be both a separate field and a pervasive approach. As a separate field, policy studies is distinguished from other political-science fields partly by its methodology, which emphasizes causal analysis in explaining policy variations over time, across places, and across subject matters, as well as a methodology of means-ends analysis for evaluating alternative public policies, especially (but not exclusively) in terms of their impacts on the political system. It is also distinguished by its substance, which stresses a concern for poverty, environmental protection, foreign policy, economic regulation, and other policy problem areas. As a pervasive approach, a policy-studies perspective can be included within every field of political science, including international policy, comparative policy, policy theory, administering policy, judicial policy, state and local policy, legislative policy, and policy dynamics. The relevance of all fields of political science to a given policy problem is illustrated by Stuart Nagel, ed., *Environmental Politics* (Praeger, 1974).

6. To what extent should the program balance classroom and field experience? It is highly desirable to give policy-studies students some experience in government work, especially policy-evaluation work, to supplement their classroom learning. The problem is how to provide that experience. One method at least for Ph.D. and M.A. students is through internships, especially in state government. The need for providing more experience to more students can also be partly satisfied by having the students work with faculty members involved in real-world consulting projects. Playing simulated roles in policy gaming situations, such as those that relate to urban planning, environmental protection, foreign policy, criminal justice, and other problem areas, can also provide many useful insights. Inviting practitioners to teach and speak within the policy-studies program can provide some vicarious experience to supplement the more abstract classroom and textbook knowledge. For further information on policy-studies internships, see the publications of the Washington-based National Center for Public Service Internship Programs, such as *Public Service Internships: Opportunities for the Graduate, Post Graduate and Mid Career Professional* (1975).

7. To what extent will the program be balanced with hard money from university budget lines as contrasted to soft money from grants and possibly contracts that relate to policy evaluation? The hard money is needed to give the program security and respectability. The soft money is needed to give the program some extra funds and to provide the kind of research projects that may be especially useful as learning experiences and for developing some Ph.D. dissertations, M.A. theses, and seminar papers. Obtaining some soft-money grants and contracts may also stimulate the university to appropriate regular budget money for the program on either a seed-money basis or a continuing basis. However, obtaining hard money to establish the program can facilitate getting research grants and training grants from foundations and government agencies. Obtaining outside grant money may be especially facilitated if the political-science policy-studies program can be linked with an academic research institute which already has a good track record for policy-evaluation research, as do some institutes of government research at public and private universities. Policy-studies grant getting is the subject of the forthcoming *Policy Studies Grants Directory* (Policy Studies Organization, 1977).

8. To what extent should the program be exclusively a teaching and training program, as contrasted to being exclusively a policy-studies research institute with no substantial teaching component? A meaningful training program would have to have a research component because part of the training logically involves training to do research regardless of whether the program is training academics who teach and do research or government practitioners who administer or produce research, or at least consume research. To acquire research skills, one needs to be involved in research projects. Thus, the policy-studies program should encourage research on the part of its faculty and its graduate students. That research will increase the visibility of the program, help its recruitment, aid its placement, and aid in getting grants and contract money. However, a pure research program would be hurt by the absence of graduate students and possibly undergraduates who would be part of the training component. Those students help generate questions, comments, and ideas which improve the research. They also provide people who can participate with research assistants and research collaborators. A pure research program might have difficulty attracting sufficiently creative personnel who welcome faculty-student stimuli and who consider being exclusively in a research institute too much like a 9-to-5 job, lacking the independence that is associated with a two course per semester teaching schedule in which one may work well into the night but on self-motivated research.

9. To what extent should the program emphasize the causes of variation in public policy rather than the evaluation of alternative public policies? Increasing emphasis is now being placed in political science on quantitatively evaluating alternative public policies. That emphasis is in response to (1) new methodological tools and data banks, (2) job opportunities and grants, (3) the stimuli of intense public concern over government policy in the late 1960s and early 1970s, (4) the reaching of a possible saturation point with regard to the application of duplicative quantitative research to relatively unimportant political matters, and (5) the momentum of policy-relevant research, teaching, and institutions in political science in the mid-1970s. That evaluative emphasis is especially relevant to the mainstream of political science if it deals with evaluating alternative public policies that relate to how chief executives, public administrators, legislators, or judges ought to operate, or if it relates to subject matters that are especially within political science, such as international relations, civil liberties, or electoral policy. That evaluative emphasis may also be quite relevant to political science regardless of the type of public policies being evaluated, as long as the concern is with the authoritative allocating of things of value rather than with natural science, humanities, or other non-political-science topics. However, one cannot meaningfully evaluate alternative public policies without taking into consideration what causes some policies to be adopted and others to be rejected by policymakers, policy appliers, or policy recipients. To ignore that kind of causal analysis is to ignore the important evaluative criterion of political feasibility. Causal analysis is also quite relevant to evaluation or optimizing work in the sense that one cannot evaluate alternative public policies unless one knows something about the causal relations between those policies and whatever goal criteria are being used. That kind of means-ends causal analysis is different from what causes a type of policy or decision to be adopted, but the same kind of methodology applies to either kind of causal analysis.

10. To what extent should the program show a concern for policy problems at the local, state, and cross-national levels as well as the national level? The major interdisciplinary policy programs tend to emphasize national policy issues. Such issues seem to have more glamour than state and local issues. They are also more in conformity with the domestic emphasis in most policy programs where international relations and comparative government are not so prevalent. Increasing the involvement with state and local issues would increase job opportunities, make for better government relations (especially for public universities), and provide more concreteness to policy-analysis teaching. Increasing the cross-national perspective provides benefits in the form of being able to offer a greater variety of experiences with alternative public policies. These experiences frequently can be valuable in supplementing the U.S. national experience or even the experience of the fifty states and numerous cities, especially with regard to experimenting with programs that are more socialistic or more contrary to traditional U.S. ideology than the United States has been willing to try.

11. How can the program provide balance in terms of liberal and conservative ideologies toward controversial public-policy issues? The program should be opened to faculty, researchers, and students regardless of ideological orientation. A conscious effort should be made to give the program a reputation of bipartisanship so that people from the program would be welcome in either a Democratic or a Republican administration. Bipartisanship seems more meaningful than nonpartisanship, whereby the program members would participate in no partisan policy analysis. When participating, however, program members would be encouraged to participate as analysts designed to determine the effects of alternative public policies, not as advocates designed to argue polemically in favor of partisan public policies.

The main conclusion to be drawn from the questionnaire responses earlier in this chapter is that policy studies is alive and well in political-science departments and interdisciplinary programs across the country and still growing rapidly, although possibly at a less rapid rate than in the early 1970s. Additional quantitative support for that conclusion is given in the recent 1975–1976 APSA Survey of Political Science Departments, which again shows that the public-policy field is the fastest-growing political-science field, as measured by course enrollment trends. Of the forty-nine Ph.D. departments with twenty-one or more faculty, 53 percent reported a gain in the public-policy field, and only 9 percent reported a loss, for a difference of 42 percentage points, which is higher than in any other field. There was a similar difference of 45 percentage points in 1974–1975 and 52 percentage points in 1973–1974, indicating some plateauing of the trend. It is difficult, however, every year to have almost 50 percent of those political-science departments report another gain in the public-policy field, as they have been doing since the APSA survey began. The related field of public administration has been maintaining a close second with regard to the percentage of departments reporting a gain rather than a loss in course enrollments.

The main conclusion to be drawn from the discussion of issues in the next section in this chapter and the recommendations included earlier is that there are a variety of policy-studies perspectives regarding the relative importance of such matters as method versus substance and policy formation versus policy evaluation. Those two issues particularly divided academics and practitioners, although they agreed on the need for more policy studies within political science, more academic-practitioner interaction, and more field experience for policy students. There were also some differences of emphasis between Ph.D. departments and M.A. departments (as, for example, on method versus substance) and between political-science departments and interdisciplinary policy-studies programs (as, for example, on policy formation versus policy evaluation and interdisciplinary emphasis). There does, however, seem to be general consensus that those perspectives are not incompatible, but rather are simultaneously needed to provide balanced policy-studies programs either within political-science departments or in interdisciplinary programs.

Thus, we can conclude that a lot is happening with regard to university policy studies, but that more probably should be happening, especially with regard to simultaneously having (1) Ph.D., M.A., and undergraduate emphasis; (2) training for government and teaching; (3) political science and interdisciplinary emphasis; (4) substantive and methodological training; (5) policy as a separate subfield and a pervasive perspective; (6) more field experience to supplement the classroom; (7) support money from diverse sources; (8) teaching and research activities; and (9) causal and evaluative emphasis in the policy-studies programs. Adoptions of these considerations should help to bring closer together and make more effective the fields of policy studies, political science, and public administration.

Bibliography on Teaching Policy Studies

[1] "Basic Institutions and Facilities in Policy Studies." Symposium issue of *Policy Studies Journal,* December 1972.
[2] Bouxsein, Peter. "Training in the Policy Sciences: A Preliminary Appraisal." Unpublished report available from the University of Michigan Institute of Public Policy Studies, 1972.
[3] Bunker, Douglas. "A Doctoral Program in the Policy Sciences." *Policy Sciences* 2:33–42 (1971).
[4] Coplin, William, ed. "Symposium on Teaching Policy Studies." *Policy Studies Journal,* March 1978.
[5] Crecine, John. "University Centers for the Study of Public Policy: Organization Viability. Unpublished report available from the University of Michigan Institute of Public Policy Studies, 1970.

[6] Dror, Yehezkel. "Research in Policy Sciences," "Teaching of Policy Sciences," and "Professionalization of Policy Sciences." In *Design for Policy Sciences* (Elsevier, 1971), chaps. 13–15.

[7] Dror, Yehezkel. "Teaching of Policy Sciences: Design for a Doctorate University Program." *Social Sciences Information* 9:101–122 (1970).

[8] Eldredge, H. Wentworth. "University Education in Future Studies," *Futures* February 1975, pp. 15–30.

[9] Ericson, Richard. "The Policy Analysis Role of the Contemporary University." *Policy Sciences* 1:429–442 (1970).

[10] Gove, Samuel, ed. *The University and the Emerging Federalism: A Conference on Improving University Contributions to State Governments* (University of Illinois Institute of Government and Public Affairs, 1972.)

[11] Jones, Charles. "The Policy Approach: An Essay on Teaching American Politics." *Midwest Journal of Political Science,* 1968.

[12] Koeppen, Sheillah, ed. *DEA News* (quarterly journal of American Political Science Association Division of Education Affairs, 1975 on).

[13] Krislov, Samuel, ed. *Teaching Political Science* (quarterly journal of Sage Publications, 1975 on).

[14] Lepawsky, Albert. "Graduate Education in Public Policy." *Policy Science* 1:443–457 (1970).

[15] Lasswell, Harold, and McDougal, Myres. "Legal Education and Public Policy: Professional Training in the Public Interest." *Yale Law Journal* 52:203–295 (1943).

[16] Lasswell, Harold. *The Future of Political Science.* Atherton Press, 1963.

[17] Lasswell, Harold. "Professional Identity" and "Professional Training." In *A Preview of Policy Sciences.* Elsevier, 1971.

[18] MacRae, Duncan, Jr. "Policy Analysis as an Applied Social Science Discipline." *Administration and Society* 6:363–388 (1975).

[19] Mann, Lawrence. "The Fuzzy Future of Planning Education." In *Urban Planning in Transition* edited by Ernest Erber. Grossman, 1970.

[20] Miller, Arthur S. "The Law School as a Center for Policy Analysis." *Denver Law Journal* 47:587–608 (1970).

[21] Nagel, S., and Neef, M., eds. *Political Science Utilization Directory.* Policy Studies Organization, 1975.

[22] NASPAA. *Graduate School Programs in Public Affairs and Public Administration.* National Association of Schools of Public Affairs and Administration, 1974.

[23] NASPAA Standards Committee. *Guidelines and Standards for Professional Master's Degree Programs in Public Affairs.* National Association of Schools of Public Affairs and Administration, 1974.

[24] Nutt, Thomas, and Susskind, Lawrence. "Prospects for Urban Planning Education." *Journal of the American Institute of Planners* 36(4):229–241 (July 1970).

[25] Robinson, James. "Participant Observation, Political Internship and Research." *Political Science Annual* 2:71–106 (1969).

[26] Seidman, Larry. "A Course in the Economics of Public Policy Analysis." *Policy Analysis* 1:197–216 (1975).

[27] Smith, David. "Policy Analysis for Undergraduates." *Policy Studies Journal* 5:234–244 (1976).

[28] Sunderland, John. "Ph.D. Programs in Policy Sciences: Who, When, Where, What, and Why?" *Policy Sciences* 1:469–482 (1970).

[29] "Universities and the Teaching of Policy Sciences," parts 1 and 2. *Policy Sciences,* December 1970 and March 1971.

[30] Weiner, Harry, ed. Symposium on "Education for the Public Service." *Journal of Urban Analysis* 3(2) (1977).

[31] Yates, Douglas, Jr. "The Mission of Public Policy Programs: A Report on Recent Experience." *Policy Sciences* 8:363–374 (1977).

Brochures for Policy-Studies Academic Programs

Eastern Locations
 1. American University: College of Public Affairs graduate programs.
 2. Carnegie-Mellon University: School of Urban and Public Affairs.
 3. Columbia University: School of International Affairs and The Regional Institute.
 4. Cornell University: Program on Science Technology and Society, Curriculum Innovation; Graduate School of Business and Public Administration.
 5. George Washington University: Science, technology, and public policy.
 6. Harvard University: Kennedy School of Government Public Policy Program.
 7. Johns Hopkins University: Center for Metropolitan Planning and Research.
 8. University of Maryland: Master of policy sciences.
 9. Massachusetts Institute of Technology: Center for Policy Alternatives.
10. New York University: Graduate school in politics.
11. State University of New York at Binghamton: Public-policy analysis and administration.
12. State University of New York at Buffalo: Center for Policy Studies.
13. Pennsylvania State University: Public Policy Option, Social Science Program.

14. Princeton University: Graduate Program of Professional Education for Public and International Affairs in the Woodrow Wilson School of Public and International Affairs.
15. University of Rhode Island: Graduate education for public service and public policy making.
16. University of Rochester: Program in public-policy analysis.
17. Suffolk University: Center for State Management.
18. Syracuse University: Policy Institute; Maxwell Graduate School of Citizenship and Public Affairs.
19. Temple University: Handbook of the policy science laboratory.
20. Yale University: Institution for Social and Policy Studies.

Midwestern Locations
1. University of Cincinnati: Graduate program in public affairs.
2. Cleveland State University: Master of public administration program.
3. Indiana University: Workshop in political theory and policy analysis.
4. University of Michigan: Center for Research on Conflict Resolution; Institute of Public Policy Studies.
5. Michigan State University: Public-affairs management.
6. University of Minnesota: School of Public Affairs, graduate study in public policy—Analysis, formulation, administration.
7. Northern Illinois University: Master of arts in public affairs.
8. Northwestern University: Center for Urban Affairs.
9. Ohio State University: Mershon Center—Programs for research and education in leadership and public policy.
10. Sangamon State University: Facts about Sangamon State.
11. Washington University: Center for the Study of Public Affairs.
12. Wayne State University: Center for Urban Studies.
13. University of Wisconsin: Center for the Study of Public Policy and Administration.

Southern Locations
1. Duke University: Institute of Policy Sciences and Public Affairs; Law and public-policy program.
2. Florida Technological University: Public-policy program.
3. Georgia State University: Graduate division, School of Urban Life.
4. University of Georgia: M.A. and Ph.D. of public administration.
5. Instituto de Estudios Superiores de Administracion, Venezuela: Institute for Higher Studies in Administration.
6. Jackson State University: Graduate study in public policy and administration.
7. Memphis State University: Public administration.
8. University of Missouri, St. Louis: Extension activities report.

9. University of New Orleans: Proposed master of public administration degree.
10. University of North Carolina: Institute of Government; Institute for Research in Social Science.
11. University of South Carolina: Master of public administration program.
12. University of Texas at Austin: Statement of the purposes and programs of the Lyndon B. Johnson School of Public Affairs.
13. Tulane University: Program prospectus for master's in public administration and public-policy degree.
14. Virginia Polytechnic Institute and State University: Center for Study of Public Choice.

Western Locations
1. University of California at Berkeley: Graduate school of public policy.
2. University of California at Davis: The Institute of Governmental Affairs; public-service major.
3. University of California at Irvine: Program in social ecology.
4. California State University at Long Beach: Center for Public Policy and Administration.
5. Claremont Graduate School: Master of arts in public-policy studies.
6. Colorado State University: Environmental politics.
7. University of New Mexico: Program for Advanced Study in Public Science Policy and Administration.
8. Portland State University: Area of specialization is policy analysis.
9. Rand Graduate Institute for Policy Studies.
10. Saitama University, Japan: Institute for Policy Science.
11. Stanford University: Urban-management program of the Graduate School of Business.
12. University of Sydney: Public policy.
13. University of Washington: Graduate School of Public Affairs.

Notes

1. S. Nagel and M. Neef, "The Use of Political Science: The Practitioner's Perspective," *Policy Sciences* 8:376–380 (1975); and S. Nagel and M. Neef, eds., *Political Science Utilization Directory* (Policy Studies Organization, 1975).

2. S. Nagel and M. Neef, eds., *Policy Studies Directory* (Policy Studies Organization, 1976). Copies of this 152-page directory can be obtained for $3 to cover administrative and mailing costs from the Policy Studies Organization, 361 Lincoln Hall, University of Illinois, Urbana, Illinois 61801.

5 Research Centers

This chapter summarizes the findings of a questionnaire sent to directors of university and nonuniversity centers and institutes that conduct policy-studies research. Their research mainly attempts to determine the feasibility and effects of alternative public policies. The questionnaire is designed to obtain information relevant to understanding and improving such policy-research centers. The questionnaire results deal with policy problems, clients, funding, decision making, and staffing. Those results have been supplemented with a propositional inventory from other articles and books dealing with policy-research centers, particularly their internal relations, external relations, and substantive areas emphasized.[a]

Questionnaire Results

The Survey

A questionnaire letter was sent to numerous university and nonuniversity policy-research centers mainly in autumn 1977. The responses consist of personal letters, reports, or both. The list of sources for sending questionnaires was obtained by consulting the directories listed in the bibliography on policy-research centers at the end of this section. The most useful listings of policy research centers were contained in William Beuthel, ed., *Governmental Research Bureaus, Centers, and Institutes Affiliated with Universities in the United States* (Institute of Governmental Research and Service, University of Colorado, 1977); Archie Palmer, ed., *Research Centers Directory* (Gale Publishing, Co., 1975); and Robert Haro, *A Directory of Governmental, Public and Urban Affairs Research Centers in the United States* (Institute of Governmental Affairs, University of California at Davis, 1969). From within those lists, only policy-research centers are solicited which are at universities awarding a graduate degree in political science or policy studies or which are prominent nonuniversity policy-research centers. Responses that were usable as entries for the *Policy Research Centers Directory* were received from 107

---

[a]The edited verbatim responses to the survey questionnaire are presented on a center-by-center basis in the *Policy Research Centers Directory*. Copies of this 172-page directory can be obtained for $3 from the Policy Studies Organization, 361 Lincoln Hall, University of Illinois, Urbana, Illinois 61801.

policy-research centers. Of those, 58 are university research centers, and 49 are nonuniversity research centers. The quantity of responses usable for the frequency distributions of this section is somewhat different because the directory entries and the frequency distributions were done separately and because a response might be usable for only one of those two purposes. Few major centers were likely to be total nonrespondents since those that did not answer the questionnaire were likely to send brochures or reports from which an entry could be prepared.

The questionnaire is divided into nine parts dealing with (1) policy problems emphasized, (2) types of clients, (3) disciplines represented, (4) funding sources, (5) decision-making procedures, (6) hiring activities, (7) desired research, (8) suggestions for policy-research centers, and (9) suggestions for funding sources. The main purpose of this section is to summarize each of those nine items across policy-research centers in order to provide an overview of what is involved. The main usefulness of the directory is in the specific information it provides on each research center. The index to the directory is also helpful in finding centers dealing with a given subject.

The Structured Responses

Table 5-1 shows the results of the analysis of the first questionnaire item concerning policy problems emphasized. The categories are arranged in the order of frequency mentioned among all 124 centers used in the frequency distribution. Environmental protection is the most frequently mentioned category since it is mentioned by 27 percent of 124 centers, 28 percent of the 78 university centers, and 26 percent of the 46 nonuniversity centers. The percentages in the first column in effect represent a weighted average of the percentages in the second and third columns, weighted by 78 and 46, respectively. Other frequently mentioned categories include criminal justice, urban affairs, health, and education. The categories that are especially popular depend largely on the availability of research funds, which in turn depends on the popularity of certain social problems and their amenability to research. Some categories that are low on the list, such as agriculture and foreign policy (but sce international), may reflect the fact that research on them tends to be conducted by government agencies rather than by university or nonuniversity policy-research centers, or it tends to be done by more specialized research centers than those included on the above-mentioned general lists from which the entries were drawn. Differences between university and nonuniversity centers occur, for example, in criminal-justice research, which is more present among university centers, possibly because the LEAA is barred from making grants or contracts to profit-making research centers. The university centers are also more involved with urban affairs, possibly reflecting the presence of

Table 5-1
Policy Problems Emphasized by Policy-Research Centers[a]

Policy Problem	For All 124 Centers (%) (number)		For 78 University Centers (%) (number)		For 46 Nonuniversity Centers (%) (number)	
Environmental protection	27	34	28	22	26	12
Criminal justice	24	30	28	22	17	8
Urban affairs	23	29	36	28	2	1
Health	22	27	22	17	22	10
Education	20	25	15	12	28	13
Housing	16	20	18	14	13	6
Welfare	15	18	15	12	13	6
Transportation	10	13	12	9	9	4
International	7	9	3	2	15	7
Organizational behavior	7	9	9	7	4	2
Technology	6	8	5	4	9	4
Intergovernment	3	4	4	3	2	1
Labor	4	5	3	2	7	3
Methodology	3	4	1	1	7	3
State government	5	6	5	4	4	2
Agriculture	2	2	0	0	4	2
Foreign policy	2	2	1	1	2	1

[a]For most variables in the questionnaire (including policy problems), respondents sometimes answer with more than one category.

institutes of state and local government research at many state universities. On a related matter, question 7 asked, "What kind of research would you like to be more involved with than you currently are?" The answers include most of the categories shown in table 5-1. Categories that were high among desired research, but not so high among current research, included state-local government relations, energy, and economic regulation.

Table 5-2 summarizes the results of the questionnaire items dealing with clients, funding, and decision making. The client most frequently mentioned is the federal government, which was mentioned by 61 percent of 105 centers who answered that question. Other major clients, in order of importance, are local governments, state governments, corporations, and foundations. The university centers differ substantially from the nonuniversity centers on the client dimension, with the university centers relying more on state and local government and the nonuniversity centers relying more on federal and corporate clients. Those differences are also reflected in the funding methods, where only the university centers can generally rely on annual appropriations from government agencies and the nonuniversity centers frequently develop proposals to corporations.

On the matter of decision-making structure, 62 percent of the centers rely mainly on senior staff for deciding what projects will be undertaken and other

Table 5–2
Clients, Funding, and Decision Making by Policy-Research Centers

Variables and Categories	All Centers (%) (number)		University Centers (%) (number)		Nonuniversity Centers (%) (number)	
Major Clients (N = 105, 64, 41)[a]						
Federal	61	64	48	31	80	33
Local	51	54	56	36	44	18
State	36	38	69	44	34	14
Corporations	23	24	9	6	44	18
Foundations	3	3	2	1	5	2
Major Funding Methods (N = 100, 65, 35)						
Proposals to government agencies	69	69	68	44	71	25
Appropriated yearly by government agencies	24	24	34	22	6	2
Proposals to corporations	11	11	8	5	17	6
Endowment income	3	3	3	2	3	1
Decision-Making Structure (N = 61, 43, 18)						
Senior staff	62	38	53	23	83	15
Collegial decisions	38	23	47	20	17	3

[a]Percentages are of the number responding to the variables among all centers, university centers, and nonuniversity centers. Those three numbers are shown next to each variable.

governing matters, whereas 38 percent rely mainly on collegial decisions. This is one of the few items in the frequency distributions that was coded with mutually exclusive categories. The nonuniversity centers are substantially more likely to rely on senior staff (83 percent), as contrasted to a bare majority of the university centers (53 percent). Another decision-making issue concerns whether the research center has independent authority or is part of a larger unit. This issue particularly affects the university centers, most of which are part of a larger unit such as a department, school, or college within a university.

Table 5–3 deals with the staffing of policy-research centers. On the matters of disciplines represented, economics and business is the most important discipline, especially among university centers. Next comes political science, although among nonuniversity centers sociology ranks higher than economics or political science in terms of disciplines mentioned, but not necessarily quantity of staff members. Law is mentioned about one-third of the time by the responding university centers, but only one-fifth of the time by the nonuniversity centers, whereas natural science is more frequently mentioned among the nonuniversity centers. On staff size, the categories are arranged in order of frequency, with categories 11 through 20 being the most common and 31 through 50 the next most common. The university centers are more heavily

Table 5–3
Staffing of Policy-Research Centers

Variables and Categories	All Centers (%) (number)		University Centers (%) (number)		Nonuniversity Centers (%) (number)	
Disciplines Represented (N = 105, 68, 37)[a]						
Economics and business	61	64	70	48	43	16
Political science	56	59	65	44	41	15
Sociology	53	56	47	32	65	24
Psychology	34	36	35	24	32	12
Other social sciences	29	30	28	19	30	11
Law	28	29	31	21	22	8
Natural science	17	18	13	9	24	9
Engineers	9	9	7	5	11	4
Planners	5	5	4	3	5	2
Humanities	3	3	0	0	8	3
Number of Staff (N = 63, 46, 17)						
11–20	29	18	35	16	12	2
31–50	23	15	24	11	24	4
1–10	21	13	26	12	6	1
21–30	10	6	9	4	12	2
Over 100	10	6	2	1	30	5
51–100	8	5	4	2	18	3
Predominant Hiring Procedures (N = 65, 48, 17)						
Permanent staff	80	52	81	39	76	13
Temporary staff for specific projects	20	13	19	9	24	4
Current Staff Needs (N = 38, 28, 10)						
Not hiring presently	55	21	64	18	30	3
Openings available	45	17	36	10	70	7

[a]Percentages are of the number responding to the variables among all centers, university centers, and nonuniversity centers. Those three numbers are shown next to each variable.

represented among the three smaller staff sizes, and the nonuniversity centers are more heavily represented among the larger staff sizes, including over 100.

On the matter of hiring procedures, about 80 percent of the centers rely predominantly on permanent researchers, whereas about 20 percent rely predominantly on people who are hired for specific projects with a core of permanent staff. That is about equally true of the university and the nonuniversity centers. On current staff needs, 45 percent of those responding to that item reported openings available, although centers with openings might be more likely to respond to the item which had a lower response rate than other items. The percentage of responding nonuniversity centers with openings available is substantially higher than among the university centers. More specifically, the following university centers reported openings available: Arizona State Center for Public Affairs, National Opinion Research Center, Duke Institute of Policy Sciences, Georgetown Public Services Laboratory, Howard Institute for Urban Affairs, Kansas Institute for Social and Environmental Studies, Michigan Center for Research on Economic Development, St. Louis Center for Urban Programs, Tennessee Bureau of Public Administration, Vanderbilt Institute for Public Policy Studies, V.P.I. Center for Urban and Regional Studies, and the Yale Institution for Social and Policy Studies. The following nonuniversity centers reported openings: Battelle Human Affairs Research Centers; Booz, Allen, and Hamilton; National Research Council; Syracuse Research Corporation; and the Urban Institute.

The Open-Ended Responses

Question 9 asked the questionnaire recipients, "What suggestions do you have for government people or private sources who do or would like to commission various policy research projects?" The responses to that open-ended question are more difficult to quantify than the responses to the other questions. The most frequently mentioned answers were as follows: (1) a policy-research directory could be quite helpful; (2) hold conferences and disseminate needs more widely; (3) have more competitive bidding, but with some advance screening to discourage researchers from preparing elaborate proposals where they have little chance of success; (4) concentrate more on research products that have broader and longer-term implications; (5) conduct better literature searches to avoid funding what has already been done; and (6) encourage creative experts to make suggestions and to submit proposals rather than rely solely on in-house-drafted requests for proposals (RFPs) and passively waiting for proposals. For further suggestions to funding agencies, see Stuart Nagel and Marian Neef, eds., "Suggestions for Funding Sources," *Policy Grants Directory* (Policy Studies Organization, 1977). Those suggestions were compiled from questionnaires directed to funding sources and from various publications, rather than from questionnaires directed to funding recipients, as here.

Question 8 asked, "What suggestions do you have for other people who work in or with policy research centers, or who would like to do so?" The most frequently mentioned answers were these: (1) beware of affiliations that may offer financial security, but are likely to unduly inhibit independence; (2) develop methodological skills and employ methodological rigor in research; (3) be more interdisciplinary and acquire more familiarity with other ongoing research; (4) communicate more clearly with the audiences to which your research is directed; (5) focus more on important policy problems, rather than trying to use a problem to illustrate methodological of theoretical matters; and (6) be conscientious in meeting deadlines, supplying reports, and covering the relevant subject matter, but be creative in offering new ideas. For further suggestions to researchers and research centers, see the literature content analysis below on "Normative Generalizations for Improving Centers."

The following propositions have been gleaned from the literature on policy-research centers which is cited in the references at the end of this section. These empirical and normative generalizations relate to (1) internal relations, especially staffing, decision-making, and work procedures; (2) external relations, especially relations with clients, funding sources, government, the general public, and other centers; (3) substantive emphasis, especially policy problems researched and other research focuses; and (4) general matters. Sometimes it is unclear where a generalization should be classified in terms of the above four categories, or even whether it is an empirical or normative generalization. These classifications, however, are meant not to be confining, but just to provide some organization. The important matter is the generalizations themselves. See the sources cited for further detail concerning the generalizations. (The numbers in brackets next to each generalization correspond to those numbered items in the bibliography on policy-research centers.)

Empirical Generalizations for Understanding Centers

Internal Relations

Multiple evaluations about a problem are useful [2].

There has been a growth of project research institutes run by faculty [19, 20].

More consulting is being done by faculty for industry [19, 28].

Administrators of research centers are becoming concerned about all the federal regulations with which they must comply [19].

The strongest influence in shaping institute programs is the institute director [9].

External Relations

The implementation of recommendations has gotten too little attention from social scientists [2, 10].

Recommendations are too often aimed at top-level decisionmakers [2, 10].

Central agencies are often not aware that an action recommended might require considerable changes in the local agencies [10].

Higher-level decisionmakers often are not aware of local political pressures [10, 29].

There is frequently a simple lack of communication between the social scientist and the policymaker about results of studies [10].

More institutes are giving information exchanges on community-development matters [5].

Loosen ties between universities and contract research centers [19, 20].

Universities are playing an increasingly prominent role in filling national needs [19, 26].

First-rate centers have to take on three new functions—promotion, coordination, and administration—of research operations [27, 35].

Substantive Emphasis

Research centers are sometimes more concerned with creating good will with administrators than with being useful [10].

Sometimes research centers follow too closely the prescriptions of their clients [10].

More research centers are emerging as educational institutes for training policy professionals and policy scientists [5].

There is increasingly targeted research [19, 20, 28].

There is increasing expenditure for research and development activities [11, 19].

In general, there is an increased interest in applied research [11, 19, 20].

Increasing technology requires more specialized centers [19, 26].

The social-indicators movement is a step toward bringing social-science information to bear on public policy [8].

Most problems of today call for interdisciplinary approaches [26, 28, 29, 30].

Individuals must have knowledge of one another's disciplines [27].

General

There is a general slowdown in U.S. research funding since the mid-1960s [19, 20, 28].

Universities face much greater competition for research funds now [19, 28].

The original distinction between contracts and grants has largely disappeared [19].

Research institutes are growing rapidly [2, 5, 9, 10, 19, 20].

Growth in academic professionalism lately is centered on both creating and transmitting knowledge [9].

There is an increasing demand for well-trained policy analysts [2, 5, 10, 19, 20, 40].

For-profit research centers with heavy involvement in social-science research represent a "new breed" of centers [31].

Normative Generalizations for Improving Centers

Internal Relations

Centers should try to achieve as interdisciplinary staff as possible [8, 10, 11, 19, 27].

Collaborative research, rather than individual efforts, is more likely to arrive at approaches to the problems of today [8, 10, 11, 19].

Research centers should devote more time to staff study, such as through the use of case-study seminars [10].

Try to maintain greater familiarity with other ongoing research in the field [10].

Do not continue to design each study afresh as if no work had gone on in the same or related areas already [2].

Organizations should employ more highly trained and experienced individuals on a contractual-grant basis to monitor projects in particular areas [2].

Centers should undertake an annual audit or analysis of evaluation-research studies and prepare a critique of them [2].

Centers should use a small internal committee to scrutinize carefully proposals and final reports [2].

Make decisions on priorities inside rather than outside the research decision [9].

Do not filter perceptions just through your own cultural experiences [12].

It is very important to develop research staff who have "staying power" [30].

Policy centers with large number of economists on the staff are most listened to [26, 31].

External Relations

A research center should view itself as one part of a larger network: nationwide, intergovernmentally, internationally [8, 10, 11, 31].

The research center should devote resources to dissemination of its findings, not just to the accumulation of them [8, 10].

Maximizing the center's visibility is a key way of improving the quality of its research [2, 31].

Encourage university-industry knowledge transfer through devices such as increased consulting activities [20].

Substantive Emphasis

In general, ally yourself more with social innovation and social change. Be more daring. Take more risks [8, 11, 19, 40].

Greater methodological rigor is needed in projecting trends for the future [5, 10].

Avoid academic "fadism" [11].

Research institutes should cooperate in trying to develop a broader national evaluation policy [2].

Try to better anticipate the policies and programs that will be considered at a federal level in the future [2].

Where programs are of extreme national importance, there should be simultaneous research conducted by many different research or evaluation centers [2].

Do not focus just on variables that can be measured most readily [12].

Try not to be unrealistically optimistic about the usefulness of evaluations for solving national problems [12].

General

Nonprofit institutes are better able than for-profit institutes to conduct research through to its ultimate application [11].

Try to maintain independence from funding sources, in terms of research findings [11, 35].

Avoid disputes that are primarily ideological in nature [10, 11, 12].

Set priorities relatively early [2, 5].

Be less opportunistic [9].

Devote much more attention to the relevance of program proposals [9].

Large-scale efforts usually have better payoffs than narrow or small-scale efforts [23, 35].

Try to get a more stable funding base [31].

From the questionnaire responses and the propositional inventory, one can conclude that policy-research centers are involved in a variety of policy problems, especially those relating to the environment, crime, urban affairs, health, and education. They are mainly supported by government funds, especially funds from the federal government. They tend to operate in a more hierarchical manner than the collegial decision making which is associated with academic departments. The disciplines of economics, political science, and sociology are well represented among the centers, with psychology, law, and other disciplines being less heavily represented. The centers tend to involve a research staff of about ten to twenty people, with a fluctuating temporary staff for special projects. Many of the responding centers indicated they were currently hiring additional staff. That reinforces the idea that policy-research centers are prospering even though much of the academic world is not doing so well financially. Although no time dimension was included in this analysis, trends in the policy-studies field do indicate that the future looks good for policy-research centers and others interested in seeing more application of social science to important policy problems.

Bibliography on Policy-Research Centers

Books

[1] Allison, David, ed. *The R&D Game: Technical Men, Technical Managers, and Research Productivity.* M.I.T. Press, 1969.

[2] Bernstein, Ilene, and Freeman, Howard. *Academic and Entrepreneurial Research: The Consequences of Diversity in Federal Evaluation Studies.* Russell Sage Foundation, 1975.

[3] Biderman, Albert, and Sharp, Laura. *The Competitive Evaluation Research Industry.* Bureau of Social Science Research, 1972.

[4] Denver Research Institute. *Contract Research and Development Adjuncts of Federal Agencies.* Denver Research Institute, 1969.

[5] Dickson, Paul. *Think Tanks.* Ballantine, 1972.

[6] Glatt, Evelyn, and Shelley, Maynard, eds. *The Research Society.* Gordon and Breach, 1968.

[7] Guttman, Daniel, and Willner, Barry. *The Shadow Government: The Government's Multi-Billion Dollar Giveaway of Its Decision Making Powers to Private Management Consultants, "Experts," and Think Tanks.* Pantheon, 1976.

[8] Horowitz, Irving, and Katz, James. *Social Science and Public Policy in the United States.* Praeger, 1975.

[9] Ikenberry, Stanley, and Friedman, Renee. *Beyond Academic Departments: The Story of Institutes and Centers.* Jossey-Bass, 1972.

[10] Lazarsfeld, Paul. *An Introduction to Applied Sociology.* Elsevier, 1975.

[11] National Academy of Sciences and Social Science Research Council. *The Behavioral and Social Sciences: Outlook and Needs.* Prentice-Hall, 1969.

[12] National Academy of Sciences. *Policy and Program Research in a University Setting.* National Academy of Sciences, 1971.

[13] Orlans, Harold. *Contracting for Knowledge.* Jossey-Bass, 1973.

[14] Orlans, Harold. *The Nonprofit Research Institute: Its Origins, Operations, Problems and Prospects.* McGraw-Hill, 1972.

[15] *Report of the Executive Director of the United Nations Institute for Training and Research.* United Nations, 1977.

[16] Ritchie, R. *An Institute for Public Policy Research.* Ottawa: Queens Printer, 1970.

[17] Rossi, Peter, and Williams, Walter. *Evaluating Social Programs: Theory, Practice and Politics.* Seminar Press, 1972.

[18] *Scientific Activities of Independent Nonprofit Institutions.* National Science Foundation, 1971.

[19] Smith, Bruce L.R., and Karlesky, Joseph. *Background Papers: The State of Academic Science.* Change Magazine Press, 1978.

[20] Smith, Bruce L.R., and Karlesky, Joseph. *The Universities in the Nation's Research Effort.* Change Magazine Press, 1977.

[21] Williams, Walter. *Social Policy Research and Analysis.* Elsevier, 1971.

[22] Wisconsin Bureau of Government. *University Bureau Research in Government: An Inventory of Current Projects.* University of Wisconsin, Bureau of Government, 1961.

Articles and Papers

[23] Abt, Clark C. "Notes for a Strategy for Big and Small Social Research." Abt Associates, 1975.

[24] Biderman, Albert. "The Nonprofit Social Policy Research Institute." Unpublished paper presented at the International Political Science Association meeting, 1975.

[25] Caplan, Nathan. "Social Research and National Policy: What Gets Used, by Whom, for What, and with What Effects?" *International Social Science Journal* 28 (1976).

[26] Coulter, Phillip. "Relevant Knowledge in Policy Research Centers." In *Policy Research Centers Directory.* Edited by S. Nagel and M. Neef. Policy Studies Organization, 1978.

[27] Crecine, John P. "University Centers for the Study of Public Policy: Organizational Viability." *Policy Sciences* 2:7–32 (1971).

[28] Friedman, Renee. "Centers and Institutes: The State of the Art." In *Policy Research Centers Directory.* Edited by S. Nagel and M. Neef. Policy Studies Organization, 1978.

[29] Goldberg, Peter. "Political Scientists in Policy Research Centers." In *Policy Research Centers Directory.* Edited by S. Nagel and M. Neef. Policy Studies Organization, 1978.

[30] Gorham, William. "Why Policy Research Institutes?" Urban Institute, 1975.

[31] Lehman, Edward, and Waters, Anita. "Relations between Control and Impact in Policy Research Centers." In *Policy Research Centers Directory.* Edited by S. Nagel and M. Neef. Policy Studies Organization, 1978.

[32] Merritt, Richard. "The Organization and Promotion of Political Research in the United States." In *Comparing Nations.* Edited by R. Merritt and S. Rokkan. Yale University Press, 1966.

[33] Merritt, Richard. "Social and Organizational Developments in Empirical Research." Unpublished paper presented at the American Political Science Association Meeting, 1963.

[34] Murray, Michael. "The Structure and Function of Policy Research Centers: An Exploratory Comment." In *Policy Research Centers Directory.* Edited by S. Nagel and M. Neef. Policy Studies Organization, 1978.

[35] Shapiro, Gilbert. "Social Science Research and the American University." *American Behavioral Scientist,* October 1964, pp. 29–35.

[36] Smith, Bruce L.R. "The Non-Governmental Policy Analysis Organization." *Public Administration Review,* May/June 1977.

[37] Speckhard, Roy. "An Essay in Public Policy Research Institutes within Large Multi-Campus Public Universities: Generalizations from a Sample of One." Unpublished paper presented at the American Political Science Association meeting, 1975.

[38] "Social Research with the Computer." Symposium issue of *American Behavior Scientist,* May 1965.

[39] "Urban Studies Research Centers." *Urban Affairs Quarterly,* 1972, pp. 317–374.

[40] Wolf, Charles, Jr. "Policy Sciences and Policy Research Organizations." *Policy Sciences* 2 (1971):1–6.

Directories

[41] Beuthel, William E., ed. *Governmental Research Bureaus, Centers, and Institutes Affiliated with Universities in the United States.* Bureau of Governmental Research and Service, University of Colorado, 1977.

[42] Gale Publishing Company. *Directory of University Research Bureaus and Institutes.* Gale Publishing Company, 1975.

[43] Gale Publishing Company. *New Research Centers.* Gale Publishing Company. Quarterly updating service.

[44] Gale Publishing Company. *Research Centers Directory.* Edited by Archie Palmer. Gale Publishing Company, 1975.

[45] Governmental Research Association. *Directory of Organizations and Individuals Professionally Engaged in Governmental Research and Related Activities 1976–1977.* Governmental Research Association, Inc., 1976.

[46] Haro, Robert. *A Directory of Governmental, Public and Urban Affairs Research Centers in the United States.* University of California at Davis Institute of Governmental Affairs, 1969.

[47] National League of Cities. *The Nation's Cities: 1974–75 Annual Directory.* National League of Cities, 1974.

[48] National Research Council. "Research Institutes, Centers, Laboratories and Museums Listed by University Coordinators." National Research Council, 1971.

[49] Urban Institute. *University Urban Research Centers.* 1971.

[50] "Urban Studies Research Centers." *Urban Affairs Quarterly,* March, 1972, pp. 317–374.

[51] Winston, Eric. *Directory of Urban Affairs Information and Research Centers.* Scarecrow Press, 1970.

6 Funding Sources

This chapter summarizes the findings of a questionnaire sent to directors of public and private agencies that fund policy-studies research. Such research mainly involves attempting to determine the feasibility and effects of alternative public policies. The questionnaire was designed to obtain information relevant to bringing together funding sources and applicants. The questionnaire results deal with the policy problems emphasized by each funding agency, their eligibility criteria, their procedures, and other relevant matters. Those results have been supplemented with a propositional inventory from other articles and books dealing with obtaining and awarding research grants and contracts.[a]

Questionnaire Results

The Survey

A questionnaire letter was sent to numerous government and private funding sources in 1977. The responses from that questionnaire provided the entries to the *Policy Grants Directory*. The responses consisted of personal letters, reports, or both. The list of sources for sending questionnaire letters was obtained from consulting the references dealing with funding sources cited in the bibliography on funding sources at the end of this section and from the experiences of the Policy Studies Organization in seeking funding for the symposium issues of the *Policy Studies Journal* and the symposium books which it publishes with D.C. Heath, Sage, and Praeger. No funding source that currently funds policy research was a total nonrespondent since they all at least provided annual reports, brochures, and related materials which could be analyzed in compiling the directory entries. There were eighty-three usable respondents to the survey. Respondents that were not usable and non-respondents included funding sources that no longer exist or that do not currently fund public-policy research. Of the eighty-three funding sources that constitute the entries in the directory, three to seven are government agencies, and four to six are private foundations or sources.

---

[a] The edited verbatim responses to the survey questionnaire are presented on an agency-by-agency basis in the *Policy Grants Directory*. Copies of this directory can be obtained for $3 from the Policy Studies Organization, 361 Lincoln Hall, University of Illinois, Urbana, Illinois 61801.

Many funding sources issue contracts, purchase orders, or requests for proposals, but in this analysis we are mainly concerned with grants in which the researcher has the primary responsibility for initiating the research idea to which the funding source reacts, rather than the reverse. The questionnaire is divided into seven parts dealing with (1) the names of relevant programs, (2) kinds of policy research funded, (3) appropriate people to contact, (4) eligibility criteria, (5) size and quantity of grants, (6) procedural matters, and (7) other information. The main usefulness of the directory lies in the specific information it provides on each funding source, particularly information that has longer-term value. The index to the directory may be especially helpful in finding a set of funding sources dealing with a given subject.

The Responses

Table 6–1 shows the *policy problems emphasized* by the funding sources. The leading policy areas are those dealing with education, environmental protection, technology, economic regulation, international relations, health, criminal justice, and equal opportunity. More general categories that receive fewer mentions include comparative, evaluation, teacher training, methodology, and theory. As expected, individual government agencies tend to be more focused on a single, more specific policy problem [although the National Science Foundation (NSF) is an exception], and individual private sources tend to deal with a greater variety and generality of problems (although the Carnegie Corporation's concern for education is an exception to that generality). The government agencies also tend to stress more current policy issues reflecting more recent political trends, whereas the private funding sources tend to reflect the less flexible intentions of their founders or to be less responsive to current developments and pressures. Government agencies also seem to emphasize the more quantitative modeling and optimizing research as contrasted to the more philosophical, journalistic, historical, or other traditional approaches. That emphasis is pointed out in the NSF entry which says of the program in political science, "Almost none of the currently funded projects has a significant institutional or historical focus, while about a sixth of the declinations appear to do so. . . . Of the grants funded in the most recent fiscal year, nearly one-third were concerned with formal modeling."

Table 6–2 deals with *eligibility criteria* for funding policy research other than types of subject matter and types of methods used. The leading criteria mentioned of that nature include the track record of the researcher and staff, whether specific recommendations are aimed at, and whether the findings will have broad applicability. Criteria that were not explicitly mentioned so frequently but may reflect implicit criteria include amount of money asked for, imagination displayed, and manageability of the project. As a representative government agency, the HUD guidelines state, "Each proposal will be

Table 6–1
Policy Problems Emphasized by Funding Sources

Policy Area of Funding Interest	Number of Mentions	Percentage of Mentions (% of 248)	Percentage of Respondents (% of 83)
Education	21	9	25
Environment and pollution	19	8	23
Technology policy	18	8	22
Economic policy	17	7	20
International relations	17	7	20
Health	14	7	17
Criminal justice	12	6	14
Equal opportunity	11	5	13
Science policy	9	3	11
Comparative	9	3	11
Communications	9	3	11
Energy	9	3	11
Evaluation	9	3	11
Foreign policy	7	3	8
Urban policy	7	3	8
Women	7	3	8
Agriculture	6	2	7
Employment	6	2	7
Land management	6	2	7
Teacher training	6	2	7
Arts and humanities	5	2	6
Methodologies	5	2	6
Population	5	2	6
Congress	4	2	5
Air and space	3	1	4
Government executives	3	1	4
Rural development	3	1	4
Theory	1	—	1
Total	248	100	297

evaluated by the following minimum criteria: (a) overall technical merit of the proposed effort, (b) potential contribution of the proposed effort to HUD's program objectives, (c) special capabilities offered by the proposer, (d) qualifications of the key personnel, (e) availability of resources in light of other research needs, and (f) uniqueness of the proposal when compared with others in the same area." As a representative private source, the Rockefeller Foundation reports say, "There are no specific eligibility criteria, but demonstrated research ability, knowledge of the issues, and previous experience in these or closely related fields are likely to be minimally necessary for individuals to be competitive." Unlike the situation in submitting articles for journal publication, the referees of grant proposals almost always know who is submitting the proposal and take his or her past record into consideration along with the specific project under consideration.

Table 6-2
General Eligibility Criteria of Funding Sources

Criteria Mentioned	Number of Mentions	Percentage of Mentions (% of 82)	Percentage of Respondents (% of 83)
Track record of the researcher and staff	31	38	37
Whether specific recommendations are aimed at	22	27	27
Whether findings will have broad applicability	12	15	14
Unique approach to the problem offered	7	9	8
Good methodology and scientific merit	6	7	7
Manageability of the project	2	2	2
Imagination displayed	1	1	1
Amount of money asked for	1	1	1
Total	82	100	97

Table 6-3 provides summary information on the *size, duration, and number of grants awarded.* The most common size category was less than $5,000, although many sources responded by saying that grants vary widely from a few thousand to a few hundred thousand dollars. The duration of grants tends to be about one year. The number of grants awarded per year tends to be between seventy-five and one hundred for the typical funding source. There is, however, great variation among the funding sources on size, duration, and number of grants, ranging from government agencies that specialize in giving grants, such as the National Science Foundation, to government agencies for which grant giving is only a small part of their activities, such as the Department of the Treasury. Private funding sources vary from giants like the Ford Foundation to many smaller foundations that tend to be more specialized. There is also substantial variation within a given agency, such as the NSF Research Applied to National Needs, as contrasted to the relatively small NSF Political Science Office. Size, duration, and quantity do not necessarily correlate since some funding sources which give few grants tend to give them in large sizes over a substantial duration, such as the Daniel and Florence Guggenheim Foundation.

On *procedural matters,* most sources tend to use structured application formats rather than more open-ended letters, although forms are more common among government sources than among private sources. Most sources have annual, semiannual, or quarterly deadlines for submitting proposals, although some process proposals continuously. A substantial majority of funding sources indicated they prefer a concept paper or preliminary proposal before a formal application is submitted. The average lead time for processing proposals tend to be four to six months. The reviewing of proposals is usually done in-house with some outside consulting and occasionally the use of special reviewing committees consisting of academic peers or other experts in the field. Proposals tend to consist of a cover sheet,

Table 6–3
Size, Duration, and Number of Grants Awarded

Size, Duration, and Number	Percentage of Mentions	Percentage of Mentions (% of Number)	Percentage of Respondents (% of 83)
Size			
Less than $5,000	12	19	14
About $10,000	8	12	10
About $20,000	6	10	7
$20,000–$50,000	6	10	7
$50,000–$150,000	5	8	6
$150,000–$500,000	2	3	2
Over $200,000	1	1	1
Salary only	8	13	10
Very wide (from $10,000 or less to $500,000)	15	24	18
Total	63	100	75
Duration			
Wide duration (1 month to 2 years)	4	31	5
1 year	4	31	5
6 months to 2 years	3	23	4
3 months to 15 months	2	15	2
Total	13	100	16
Number per Year			
1 to 6	7	18	8
1 to 15	8	21	10
20	4	11	5
40 to 50	4	11	5
75 to 100	11	30	13
150	1	3	1
500	1	3	1
1,000	1	3	1
Total	37	100	44

abstract, table of contents, research design, budget, and vitas. Given the importance of the National Science Foundation, its proposal form tends to be quite usable across many funding sources. The best times at which to apply are often the beginning of the fiscal year, when money is more plentiful, or sometimes at the end of the fiscal year, when there is a rush to spend unspent funds that will otherwise lapse.

Suggestions for Applicants

Discussing funding-source procedures logically leads to making suggestions on how to maximize the probability of receiving a grant. Listed below are thirty-two such suggestions compiled from the responses and from the references cited in the bibliography of funding sources at the end of this section under "Items Useful to Applicants." The numbers in brackets next to each suggestion correspond to those numbered items in the bibliography of funding sources.

Have a positive attitude.

Do not assume the proposal will be cut. Do not anticipate rejection, but think positively [13, 14].

If you do get rejected, think ahead to the next grant [19, 20].

Be aggressive.

Keep you contacts in and outside of your field as wide as possible [20].

If you do not get the grant, follow up to ask why [21].

Be informed.

Know as much as possible about the agencies to whom you are applying, and target the proposal to the right place [13, 14, 18, 19, 20, 21, 25, 30].

Make informal initial inquiries before submitting formal proposals [13, 18].

Look over the previous grant-award announcements from the agency to see what they have actually funded and to determine current priorities [13, 15, 19, 20, 21, 25, 27, 30].

Know the agency's review procedure for evaluation purposes [20, 21, 25, 26].

Know the methodological biases of the review committee [19, 26].

Be concise.

Be specific about the objectives and methods [13, 14, 18, 19, 20, 21, 25].

Pay attention to specific procedures, and follow them concisely [19, 20, 21, 25].

Pay special attention to the abstract since most committee members read only the abstract [26].

Use plenty of headings to signal to readers the important parts of the proposal [25].

Probably the most common error is to paint the picture in too grandiose terms or too general terms [25].

Do not submit extremely lengthy bibliographies [25].

It is a red flag to reviewers if the writer says this is a completely new idea. Find some research at least touching on the problem, and briefly compare it [25].

List concrete achievable objectives, but no more than a sentence or two apiece, in approximately the order of their importance [25].

Be professional.

Check grammar, punctuation, and so on carefully [14, 18, 19, 20, 25, 27].

Write your proposal as one professional writing to another [19, 23, 25, 26].

Pay special attention to qualifications of the investigator [14, 19, 26, 27].

Avoid citing people who may give you especially bad reviews [19].

Watch out for jargon that reviewers cannot understand [18, 25, 26, 27].

Junior investigators should start small. A rule of thumb is to ask for less than $10,000 for your first grant. A small award gives you good experience and a reputation for larger funding purposes [27].

Establish a good track record [27].

Research involving advanced quantitative techniques is more likely to be funded [18, 26].

Encourage your university, research center, or place of affiliation to establish a good library of materials relevant to obtaining grants.

Be thorough and systematic.

Set up a plan of operation for yourself and follow it through [14, 17, 18, 19, 25].

Do not think just of the large, commonly used agencies. Survey less well-known sources also.

Do not think just of getting the grant. Also do a good follow-through job.

Good review of the literature, thorough but concise, is important [26].

Check to see that the proposal is integrated across its section [25].

Do not forget to explain the significance to the field of the project [25].

Suggestions for Funding Sources

Discussing suggestions for applicants logically leads to making suggestions on the other side with regard to how funding sources can get more for their money. Listed below are thirty-four suggestions compiled from the responses and the references cited under "Items Useful to Funding Sources." The numbers next to each suggestion correspond to those numbered references.

Obtain more input from the scientific community.

Ad hoc advisory groups should be used by program directors in planning future programs and budgets. Each advisory group should meet with the appropriate program director at least once a year [37, 38, 42].

The staff managing research in the social and behavioral sciences does not effectively represent these sciences at the higher administrative levels of many foundations [37, 38, 42, 45].

More outside panels of the applicant's peers should be used [38].

In acquiring new staff members, inform relevant disciplines of new positions. Many new Ph.D. graduates might be relevant staff members since they have good recent substantive knowledge [38].

Improve communication systems.

There is often a lag time between the announcement of a new program by an agency and its recognition by all the relevant members of the scientific community. Sometimes the program has been discontinued before people even find out about it. Therefore, work out better ways to disseminate information about new programs, and try to make announcements as much in advance of the funding as possible [38].

Foundations should support a kind of "Annual Report to the Nation" which would help identify solutions of problems [37, 40].

Do not needlessly provoke public controversy [35].

Better techniques should be used to diffuse information to the general public, social researchers, and community organizations [34, 35, 42].

Close the information gap between the public and foundation grants available. *The Foundation Directory* is a good step in that direction [45].

Have better evaluation procedures.

Private foundations do not adequately evaluate the programs they fund and operate themselves. They should have better monitoring [35].

More research would be utilized by government if greater attention were given to methodological quality of the research funded [42].

Foundations should use systematic checklists in evaluating proposals and in monitoring research sponsored [36].

Fund more applied and interdisciplinary research.

Support should be given to researchers' efforts to develop a system of social indicators [31, 37].

Support should be given toward devising a national data system for social scientific purposes [31, 37].

More agency funds should be earmarked for law schools which want to engage in more social-science research [37].

Those agencies which are now less involved in social-science research should develop and expand support of basic and applied research in social sciences, when it is relevant to their missions [37].

More applied research support should be given [37].

More impetus should be given to interdisciplinary research for problem solving [37].

Foundations should fund more work in program evaluation. It could become an area of primary interest to them [35, 42, 45].

Have more long-range planning in the funding of applied research as is done with agencies funding basic research in certain areas [38].

Restructure some programs of funding to correspond more closely to the structure of the applied fields that will carry out the research. Some activities can be better accommodated in interdisciplinary programs [38].

General and miscellaneous suggestions.

There should be an annual increase in funds for behavioral and social science by the federal government between 12 and 18 percent [37].

More support should be given universities to develop and staff data archives [37].

Foundations should give financial aid to graduate students in social sciences in the same proportions as to other sciences [37].

Agencies should provide assured support for graduate students for four to five years without reapplication [37].

Support of graduate students should include funds for the direct cost of research by predoctoral students [37].

Private foundations could act more in the role of innovators [35, 45].

Private foundations should undertake more ventures with government sponsors [35].

High priority should be given to reforming government structures and procedures [35, 42].

Have substantial funding for complete inventories of theoretical propositions [31].

Start a program of research support directly to faculty capable of doing research [31].

More funding should go to a small number of distinguished researchers [31].

More collaboration should be encouraged between academics and practitioners.

Fund more symposia.

From the questionnaire responses and the propositional inventory, one can make some general observations. First, many funding sources are interested in a variety of policy problems awaiting good research proposals. Second, there are many experienced researchers who have written articles in books in which they are willing to share their experiences to help others obtain grants. Third, researchers have studied the operations of the funding sources, and they have some good suggestions for more efficient and effective policy-research funding. What now seems to be especially needed is for more grant applicants and funding agencies to get together with regard to applying social science to important policy problems.

Bibliography on Funding Sources

Data on Funding Sources

[1] American Political Science Association. *Research Support for Political Scientists.* 1977.

[2] Aroeste, Jean L., ed. *Annual Register of Grant Support.* Marquis Who's Who, Inc., annual.

[3] *Catalog of Federal Domestic Assistance.* Government Printing Office, annual.

[4] *Commerce Business Daily.* Contains daily listing of requests for proposals.

[5] Federal Grants Information Center. *Federal Grants Reporter.*

[6] *The Foundation Directory.* The Foundation Library Center, various editions to the present.

[7] *Foundation News* and the *Foundation Grants Index,* 888 Seventh Avenue, New York, New York 10019.

[8] The Funding Sources Clearinghouse, Inc. *Grants Daily Monitor.* 1976.

[9] Grant Development Institute. *Grant Development Digest.* Annual.

[10] *Grantsman Quarterly Journal,* P.O. Box 200, Pine City, Minnesota 55063.

[11] Sclar, Deanna, ed. *Annual Register of Grant Support.* Academic Media.

[12] Walton, Ann D., and Andrews, F. Emerson, eds. *The Foundation Directory.* The Foundation Library Center, 1960.

Items Useful to Applicants

[13] ABA Special Committee on Youth Education for Citizenship. *The $$ Game: A Guidebook on the Funding of Law Related Educational Programs.* ABA, 1975.

[14] Allen, Herb; Buckdruker, Elliot; Fuller, David; Silverstein, JoAnn; Strickland, Ida; and Silk, Tom. *The Bread Game: The Realities of Foundation Fundraising.* Glide Publications, 1973.

[15] Carroll, James D., and Knerr, Charles R. "Changes in Federal Support for Political Science." Paper presented at American Political Science Association annual meeting, 1975.

[16] Church, David M. *Seeking Foundation Funds.* National Public Relations Council of Health and Welfare Services, 1966.

[17] Dermer, Joseph, ed. *How to Get Your Fair Share of Foundation Grants.* Public Service Materials Center, 1973.

[18] Dermer, Joseph. *How to Raise Funds from Foundations.* Public Services Materials Center, 1972.

[19] Eckman Center. "Notes and Brochures from Grantsmanship Seminar," 8399 Topanga Canyon Blvd., Canoga Park, California.

[20] Golden, Hal. *The Grant Seekers: The Foundation Fund Raising Manual.* Oceana, 1976.

[21] Golden, Joseph. *The Money Givers.* Random House, 1971.

[22] *The Grantsman Quarterly Journal.* Various items.
[23] Hall, Mary. *Developing Skills in Proposal Writing.* Office of Federal Relations, Oregon University, 1976.
[24] Hill, William. *A Comprehensive Guide to Successful Grantsmanship.* Grant Development Institute, 1972.
[25] Krathwohl, David R. *How to Prepare a Research Proposal.* Syracuse University, 1966.
[26] Mercer, Jane R. "Research Proposal Writing from the Viewpoint of Peer Review Committees." Unpublished paper presented at American Sociological Association annual meeting, 1975.
[27] "Money & How to Get It: A Guide to Foundations, Grantsmanship, and Fellowships." *Behavior Today,* 1972.
[28] Schmandt, Jurgen. *Financing and Control of Academic Research.* L.B.J. School of Public Affairs, 1977.
[29] Useem, Michael. "Federal Government Influence on Social Research." Unpublished paper presented at American Sociological Association annual meeting, 1972.
[30] White, Virginia P. *Grants: How To Find Out about Them and What to Do Next.* Plenum, 1975.

Items Useful to Funding Sources

[31] Eulau, Heinz, and March, James G., eds. *Political Science.* Prentice-Hall, 1969.
[32] *Foundation News.* Various items.
[33] Greenberg, Daniel. *The Politics of Pure Science: An Inquiry into the Relationship between Science and Government in the United States.* New American Library, 1971.
[34] Haberer, Joseph, ed. *Science and Technology Policy: Perspectives and Developments.* LexingtonBooks, D.C. Heath, 1977.
[35] Heimann, Fritz. *The Future of Foundations.* The American Assembly, Prentice-Hall, 1973.
[36] Mahoney, Margaret E. "Evaluation Can Help Make the Managers' Life Easier." *Foundation News,* November 1976, pp. 29–34.
[37] National Academy of Sciences. *The Behavioral and Social Sciences: Outlook and Needs.* 1969.
[38] National Research Council. *Social and Behavioral Science Programs in the National Science Foundation.* 1976.
[39] Robinson, D.Z. "Government Contracting for Academic Research: Accountability in the American Experience." In *The Dilemma of Accountability in Modern Government.* Edited by B. Smith and D.C. Hague. St. Martin's Press, 1971, pp. 103–117.

[40] Rosenthal, Albert, ed. *Public Science Policy and Administration.* University of New Mexico Press, 1973.

[41] Schmandt, J. "Financing and Control of Academic Research." *International Encyclopedia of Education.* Jossey-Bass, 1977.

[42] Weiss, Carol, ed. *Using Social Research in Public Policy Making.* LexingtonBooks, D.C. Heath, 1977.

[43] Williams, C.W.; Schwartz, P.; and Tarpey, J. *Choosing Technological Opportunities for Innovation in the Public Sector.* Stanford Research Institute, March 1975.

[44] York, Carl M. "Steps toward a National Policy for Academic Science." *Science* 14 (May 1971): 643–648.

[45] Zurcher, Arnold J. *The Management of American Foundations: Administration, Policies and Social Role.* New York University Press, 1972.

7

Publication Outlets and Associations

This chapter is designed to describe policy-relevant scholarly associations, journals, book publishers, and interest groups. The information is based mainly on open-ended questionnaire responses, mailed to various entities that fit into those four categories. One purpose is to enable policy-studies and political-science people to have a better understanding of the periodical and book publishing outlets available to them and the scholarly and political organizations in which they might become active, or at least more aware. Another purpose is to enable editors, publishers, and organization directors to become more familiar with one another's activities so as to facilitate learning from one another's experiences and possible future coordination.

Further details concerning the scholarly associations, journals, book publishers, and interest groups can be obtained from the forthcoming *Policy Publishers and Associations Directory* of the Policy Studies Organization, located at the University of Illinois. The directory was originally to be entitled the *Policy Network Directory*. The change was made in recognition of the fact that the policy-studies network also includes government agencies, training programs, funding sources, research institutes, and policy-studies people, which are each the subject of a different directory of the Policy Studies Organization.

The associations come first in this analysis because they are probably the most basic in the sense that they tend to represent the scholarly disciplines with which policy-studies people usually identify. They are also the source of many of the key journals in the policy-studies field. The book publishers come third in the sense of producing products which are often the result of journal articles being pulled together. On the top of this subnetwork are the interest groups who directly or indirectly make use of the knowledge developed in journals and books in order to convert that knowledge into public policies by way of their policy-formation activities.

The basic information was compiled by sending mailed questionnaires to scholarly-association directors, journal editors, book publishers, and interest-group directors. The return rate on the mailed questionnaires was reasonably high. Of 46 associations to whom questionnaires were mailed, 28 responded; of 138 journals, 90 responded; of 82 book publishers, 50 responded; and of 42 interest groups, 29 responded. Additional information could be found for the

Table 7–1
Some Scholarly Associations Interested in
Applying Social Science to Policy Problems

National Social-Science Organizations
American Anthropological Association (*American Anthropologist*)
American Economic Association (*American Economic Review*)
Association of American Geographers (*Annals of the AAG*)
American Historical Association (*American Historical Review*)
American Political Science Association (*American Political Science Review*)
American Psychological Association (*American Psychological Review*)
American Sociological Association (*American Sociological Review*)
American Statistical Association (*American Statistical Review*)

Regional Social-Science Organizations
All the social sciences have regional associations which tend to be about as interested in applying their social-science discipline to policy problems as the national association is. In political science, for instance, there are regional associations covering the Northeast, Midwest, West, Southwest, and Southeast.

Subdiscipline Organizations Emphasizing Policy Problems
Policy Studies Organization—Political science (*Policy Studies Journal*)
Public Choice Society—Economics (*Public Choice*)
Society for the Psychological Study of Social Issues—Psychology (*Journal of Social Issues*)
Society for the Study of Social Problems—Sociology (*Social Problems*)

Organizations that Are More Applied-Science-Oriented
American Institute for Decision Sciences (*Decision Sciences*)
American Planning Association (*APA Journal*)
American Society for Public Administration (*Public Administration Review*)
The Institute of Management Sciences (*Management Science*)
Operations Research Society of America (*Operations Research*)
National Association of Schools of Public Affairs and Administration

Interdisciplinary Organizations Emphasizing Policy Problems
Association for Policy Analysis and Management
Council for Applied Social Research (*CASR Newsletter*)
Evaluation Network (*Evaluation Network Newsletter*)
Evaluation Research Society (*Evaluation Research Society Newsletter*)
World Futures Association (*World Futures*)

Some Organizations that Focus on Specific Policy Problems
Academy of Criminal Justice Sciences (*ACJS Newsletter*)
American Educational Research Association
Committee on Health Politics (*Journal of Health Politics, Policy, and Law*)
International Studies Association (*International Studies Quarterly*)

Miscellaneous Relevant Organizations
American Association for the Advancement of Science (*Science*)
Law and Society Association (*Law and Society Review*)   .

nonresponding questionnaire recipients from various directories that publish basic information such as addresses and names of officers. It was felt, however, that the most useful and interesting information would be the open-ended responses to questions about policy-relevant activities that cannot be obtained through other directories. The respondents also represent the entities within each of the four sets who are probably most interested in policy studies.

Policy-Relevant Scholarly Associations

Table 7–1 shows the major scholarly associations interested in applying social science to policy topics. They are all membership organizations, rather than research institutes, funding sources, training programs, or other policy-relevant institutions. They also have in common an interest in seeing social science applied to important policy problems. They do not include all such organizations that might be listed in general or under any specific category, but rather they are representative examples. Organizations listed under a specific discipline or interest generally have members from other disciplines and have other interests as well, but they are listed under the category that relates to their *primary* membership or concern. The organizations are listed alphabetically within each category, rather than in order of importance. Next to each association is listed its main journal publication. The organizations include national, regional, subdiscipline, applied-science, interdisciplinary, and problem-focused organizations.

The main questionnaire items sent to directors of scholarly associations such as those listed in table 7–1 were as follows:

1. What are the name and address of your association?
2. What journals, directories, or other publications does your association publish?
3. What are your membership rates, and how many members do you have?
4. How long has your association been in existence, and when does it hold general meetings?
5. What sources of funding do you have besides dues?
6. What general approaches to policy problems does your association tend to emphasize, if any, in terms of methodology, theoretical orientation, and/or disciplinary perspective?
7. What specific policy problems does your association tend to emphasize, if any, such as crime, poverty, health, environment, foreign affairs, or other policy problems?
8. Would you be interested in participating in some kind of consortium of policy journals and associations designed to facilitate the exchange of advertisements, subscriptions, and mailing lists as well as information on membership recruitment, grants, publishing, and other relevant association procedures?
9. Would you be interested in having your association participate in some collective activities with regard to communicating social-science information to legislative, executive, and judicial policymakers?
10. Would you be interested in having your association participate in the establishment or expansion of centers designed to bring academics and practitioners together to develop ideas concerning important policy problems?

11. What miscellaneous suggestions do you have that might be worth including in our directory to be read by directors and presidents of policy-relevant associations?

The questionnaire was designed particularly to obtain open-ended information useful to potential members and other association directors, rather than to obtain quantitative but generally less interesting data. The entries are particularly useful in seeing the types of activities, funding sources, and policy concerns of the associations. Table 7–2 summarizes the activities mentioned. The main activity is publishing a journal, as indicated by the fact that three-fourths of the responding associations do so. Next in importance is the publishing of books, directories, and newsletters. Most of the associations also hold conventions or other interaction activities. Less frequent activities include training programs, local chapters, employment services, research committees, insurance, interdisciplinary activities, prizes, affirmative action, accreditation, and discounts. Funding sources mainly include dues from members. Many associations also mention income from nonjournal sales, royalties, foundation grants, private donations, subscriptions that are separate from dues, government agencies, universities, and interest on savings. Many associations may also receive income from those sources, but often they did not explicitly say so, given the open-ended nature of the questionnaire as contrasted to a structured list of potential income sources to check off. University support for associations, for example, often tends to be taken for granted, since the support is often in the form of various accommodations (that do not involve an explicit budget allocation) where an association is located at a university.

In addition to activities and funding, there were a number of other items in the questionnaire. It is interesting to note, for example, that most of the larger scholarly associations are not associated with a university. Instead, they maintain their headquarters or office in Washington, New York, or Chicago. The smaller associations, however, often operate out of the academic office of the president or the editor of whatever journal they publish. Discounts on dues and subscriptions usually are provided for students at about half the going rate for regular members, and libraries and institutions usually are charged about twice the regular rate since they can afford to pay more and involve more readers. The Society for Policy Modeling has an interesting 50 percent discount for people in developing countries. The size distribution tends to be bimodal in that about 40 percent of the associations have less than 1,000 members, about 40 percent have more than 10,000 members, and 20 percent have between 1,000 and 10,000. The largest association is the American Psychological Association, with over 48,000 members. The age distribution involves about one-third of the associations being over fifty years old, one-third between ten and fifty, and one-third recently established within the last ten years. The oldest association is the American Historical Association,

Table 7-2
Activities and Funding of Policy-Relevant Scholarly Associations

Variables and Categories	Number of Associations	Percentage of Associations
Activities (N = 30)		
Publishing a journal	23	77
Publishing books, directories, etc.	15	50
Publishing newsletters and bulletins	13	43
Meetings and seminars other than conventions	6	20
Educational programs	6	20
Local or regional chapters	5	17
Employment services	4	13
Special research area committees	4	13
Group insurance	2	7
Joint activities with other associations	2	7
Prizes and awards	2	7
Affirmative action, accreditation, etc.	2	7
Publication discounts	2	7
Visiting scholars	1	3
Other	1	3
Funding besides Dues (N = 25)		
Nonjournal sales and royalties	13	50
Grants	11	43
Private donations	9	36
Subscriptions	7	29
Advertisements	4	14
Government	4	14
Universities	2	7
Savings	2	7
Other	7	29

founded in 1884. Most of the associations are interested in a broad range of policy problems, although that is largely due to the fact that the set of associations surveyed generally excluded associations interested in more specialized policy problems or uninterested in any policy problems. The response was quite favorable to the idea of more coordination across associations to facilitate exchanging information, communicating social science to policymakers, and developing ways for bringing together academics and practitioners. A wide variety of academic disciplines are represented, with political science being the most prevalent, but most of the associations considered themselves interdisciplinary. With regard to coordination and interdisciplinary activities, Edward Lehman, the executive director of the American Anthropological Association noted that "If we are to convincingly set forth the contribution social science can make, we must develop a common effort that reflects the interrelationships of the social sciences and their unity of purpose."

A key problem that many scholarly associations have is membership recruitment and fund raising, especially during current times of economic retrenchment. Some of the devices used by the Policy Studies Organization (PSO) that other associations might find helpful include the following:

1. Invite people to join PSO when they are invited to submit manuscript proposals to a *Policy Studies Journal* issue.
2. Ask members to recommend potential members.
3. Ask members to send subscription forms to their acquisition librarians.
4. Ask social-science departments to post notices on their bulletin boards.
5. Exchange advertisements with related journals.
6. Bulk mailings to library lists are provided by the American Library Association.
7. Make renewal notices part of the annual election with two follow-ups.
8. Bulk-mail to subscribers to related journals.
9. Bulk-mail to directors of relevant academic programs and research centers.
10. Exhibits at relevant conventions.
11. Free distribution of directories and special issues.
12. Grants received from government agencies, foundations, and universities to support special issues.
13. Raise dues.
14. Bulk-mail to former members, inviting them to rejoin in light of new services.
15. Royalties from expanded book-length versions of journal symposia.
16. Expenses saved by using inexpensive typesetting and printing systems.
17. In general, trying to provide a useful quarterly journal and other publications to present and prospective PSO members.

Perhaps policy-relevant associations might be able to work more closely together on various joint activities. This might be especially true of the associations in table 7–1 under subdiscipline organizations emphasizing policy problems, organizations that are more applied-science-oriented, and interdisciplinary organizations emphasizing policy problems. The more disciplinary organizations (such as the first two) may not be as oriented toward interdisciplinary action, and the organizations that focus on specific policy problems may not be sufficiently broad in this context. Some meaningful joint activities might include the following:

1. Exchange advertisements to be reproduced in the journals of the associations on an annual basis.
2. Exchange journal subscriptions.
3. Exchange mailing lists to facilitate contacting one another's members and subscribers.
4. Refer manuscripts to one another.

5. Cooperate with regard to the coordination of congressional testimony on policy problems, particularly through the congressional liaison which has been established by the National Association of Schools of Public Affairs and Administration and the Society for the Psychological Study of Social Issues.
6. Provide for panels at one another's conventions and conferences.
7. Provide copies of one another's convention programs for listing relevant papers in one another's journals.
8. Notify one another to send appropriate letters designed to influence government and other decisions concerning the encouragement of policy-relevant research and teaching.
9. Encourage the establishment or expansion of centers designed to bring together academics and practitioners to develop ideas concerning important policy problems, such as the Smithsonian Woodrow Wilson Center and the American Academy for Contemporary Problems.
10. Call a planning meeting of leaders of the policy-relevant associations to discuss additional joint activities.
11. Have a joint research conference with panels, workshops, roundtables, plenary sessions, and poster sessions of members of the associations and others, with the program organized in terms of general approaches and specific policy problems and all sessions multidisciplinary.
12. Possibly form some kind of interdisciplinary umbrella organization, consortium, or confederation of the policy-relevant associations to coordinate further their related activities to the mutual benefit of their members and policy-relevant research and teaching.
13. Cooperate in the use of a typesetter, printer, or subscription-fulfillment service, or share information on the relative merits of different ways of getting that work done.

Most of these activities can also be participated in by the leaders and subscribers of the policy-relevant journals that are not associated with the organizations.

Bibliography on Scholarly Associations

[1] Colvard, Richard, ed. "SSSP as a Social Movement," *Social Problems* 24 (Special Issue, 1976): 1–141.
[2] Handy, Rollo, and Kurtz, Paul. *A Current Appraisal of the Behavioral Sciences.* Behavioral Research Council, 1963–1964.
[3] Gale Research Company, *Encyclopedia of Associations.* Gale, 1978.
[4] Hagstrom, Warren. *The Scientific Community.* Basic Books, 1965.

[5] Hoselitz, Bert, ed. *A Reader's Guide to the Social Sciences*. Free Press, 1970.

[6] NASPPA. *Programs in Public Affairs and Administration*. National Association of Schools of Public Affairs, 1978.

[7] National Academy of Sciences and Social Science Research Council. *The Behavioral and Social Sciences: Outlook and Needs*. Prentice-Hall, 1969.

[8] Somit, Albert, and Tanenhaus, Joseph. *American Political Science: A Profile of a Discipline*. Atherton, 1964.

[9] Somit, Albert, and Tanenhaus, Joseph. *The Development of American Political Science: From Burgess to Behavioralism*. Allyn & Bacon, 1968.

[10] UNESCO. *International Organizations in the Social Sciences*. UNESCO, 1961.

[11] UNESCO. *Main Trends of Research in the Social and Human Sciences. Part 1: Social Sciences*. UNESCO, 1970.

Policy-Relevant Journals

Table 7–3 shows the major independent scholarly journals that publish applications of social science to policy problems. They are periodicals published no more often than about every two months for an audience mainly of social-science scholars or practitioners, rather than a popular newsstand audience. They also have in common that they at least occasionally publish applications of social science to important policy problems. The table does not include all such journals that might be listed in general or under any specific category, but rather it includes representative examples. The journals are listed alphabetically within each category rather than in order of importance. The table includes only journals that are not affiliated with a scholarly membership organization, although many of them may be affiliated with universities rather than commercial publishers. Even those that are associated with commercial publishers tend to have editors who are affiliated with universities. See table 7–1 for the policy-relevant journals that are publications of scholarly associations.

Policy-relevant journals could be classified in various ways, including the distinction between those that are associated with scholarly organizations and those that are independent. The ones that are associated with scholarly organizations can then be classified in the same way as the organizations in table 7–1. The ones that are independent have been classified in table 7–3 along various dimensions. One dimension contrasts policy analysis with evaluation research, with policy analysis tending to place more emphasis on political economy rather than social psychology and emphasizing a pre-

Table 7–3
Some Independent Scholarly Journals that Publish
Applications of Social Science to Policy Problems

General Policy-Analysis Journals
Policy Sciences (Elsevier)
Policy Analysis (U.C.-Berkeley Press)
Public Policy (Wiley)

Evaluation Research Journals
Evaluation and Change (Program Evaluation Resource Center)
Evaluation Quarterly (Sage)
Evaluation and Program Planning (Pergamon)

Semipopular Journals
Society/Transaction (Transaction, Inc.)
Social Policy (Independent)
Policy Review (Heritage Foundation)
Public Interest (Independent)

Journals that Focus on Specific Policy Problems, Approaches, or Disciplines
Foreign Policy (National Affairs)
Urban Affairs Quarterly (Sage)
Law and Policy Quarterly (Sage)
Journal of Policy Modeling (North-Holland)
Journal of Legal Studies (University of Chicago Press)
Journal of Urban Analysis (Gordon Breach)
Policy and Politics (Sage)
Philosophy and Public Affairs (Princeton University Press)
Social Indicators Research (Reidel)
Socio-Economic Planning Sciences (Pergamon)

adoption rather than a postadoption perspective. The second dimension separates the scholarly journals that partly seek magazine-rack distribution (semipopular journals) from the others that rely on the mail only. A third dimension separates the general journals from those that are focused on specific policy problems, approaches, or disciplines.

The main questionnaire items sent to policy-relevant journals such as those included in tables 7–1 and 7–3 were as follows:

1. What are the name and address of your journal?
2. What organization, publisher, and/or printer is your journal associated with?
3. What are your subscription rates, and how many subscribers do you have?
4. How long has your journal been in existence, and how often is it published?
5. Approximately how many articles do you publish per issue, and how long on average do they tend to be?
6. In selecting articles, what subjects and criteria do you prefer?
7. What procedures do you use in selecting articles that potential authors should be aware of, such as to whom manuscripts should be addressed,

how many copies should be sent, and what citation format should be used?
8. What sources of funding do you have besides subscriptions?
9. What general approaches to policy problems does your journal tend to emphasize, if any, in terms of methodology, theoretical orientation, and/or disciplinary perspective?
10. What specific policy problems does your journal tend to emphasize, if any, such as crime, poverty, health, environment, foreign affairs, or other policy problems?
11. Roughly what percentage of the articles which appear in your journal would you classify as being relevant to analyzing the causes or effects of alternative public policies, and would you like to see that percentage increased?
12. Would you be interested in participating in some kind of consortium of policy journals and associations designed to facilitate the exchange of advertisements, subscriptions, and mailing lists, as well as information on editing, printing, marketing, and other relevant procedures?
13. What miscellaneous suggestions do you have that might be worth including in our directory to be read by journal editors or article writers?

The responses are particularly useful for determining the contents, selection criteria, and funding sources, as summarized in table 7–4. The number of journals included in table 7–4 is substantially smaller than the number of journals which have entries in the directory because the tabular data are based on only the questionnaire responses, whereas the entries often are based on brochures and materials other than letters which were sent back in response to the questionnaire. In order of frequency of mention, the journals include articles, book reviews, research notes, review essays, comments, conference announcements, bibliographies, lists of convention papers, and lists of syllabi. Selection criteria mentioned include theory, data, relevance, practicality, originality, methodological soundness, addition to knowledge, and other less frequently mentioned criteria. For example, Everett K. Wilson, the editor of *Social Forces,* routinely informs authors who have been asked to revise and resubmit their articles that he wants simplicity and economy. By simplicity, he means avoiding "multiple syllabification producing a pompous ass of a word like utilize when we mean use, or implement when we mean do." As to economy, he says, "lean and lucid writing cuts costs by saving editorial time and pages, and within the same limited number of pages, it enables more of your colleagues to get into print." Funding sources tend to be about the same as those for scholarly associations, with university support being more important to journals and private donations being less important.

In addition to the tabular information on contents, criteria, and funding, there are a number of other items of interest in the questionnaire. Subscription rates tend to involve the same categories as dues rates for scholarly

Table 7–4
Contents, Criteria, and Funding of Policy-Relevant Journals

Variables and Categories	Number of Journals	Percentage of Journals
Contents of Journals ($N = 30$)		
Articles	30	100
Book reviews	20	67
Research notes	17	57
Review essays	11	37
Comments	10	33
Conference announcements	6	20
Bibliographies	3	10
Lists of convention papers	1	3
Lists of syllabi	1	3
Other	2	7
Selection Criteria ($N = 62$)		
Theoretical significance	27	44
Empirical data	26	42
Contemporary relevance	24	39
Practical value	20	32
Original scholarly contribution	17	27
Sound methodology	16	26
Adds knowledge	12	19
High quality	8	13
Authoritative facts	7	11
Clear and coherent	7	11
Readability	7	11
Experimental	4	6
Shortness	3	5
Documentation	1	2
Original sources	1	2
Funding besides Subscriptions ($N = 31$)		
University	11	36
Grants	6	19
Sales and royalties	5	16
Advertisements	5	16
Dues	3	10
Government	2	6
Affiliated organization	2	6
Private donations	1	3
Savings	1	3
Other	5	17
None	5	16

associations. Subscriptions, though, generally allow for discounts for multiple years and for being a member of an association. Other common adjustments consider income, being elderly, and being in the same family as a member or subscriber. The quantity of subscribers tends to be between 2,000 and 5,000, with one-third of the journals reporting that figure; one-fourth, under 1,000; one-fourth, between 1,000 and 2,000; and one-fifth, over 5,000. The journal in the directory that is most subscribed to is the *American Bar Association Journal,* with 240,000 subscribers. As with associations, there is a bimodal distribution on age of the journals, with almost half being less than ten years, one-third being older than thirty years, and about one-sixth being between ten and thirty years. The oldest journal in the directory is *World Affairs,* going back 150 years, followed by the *American Journal of Sociology,* which was established in 1895. Two-thirds of the journals are quarterlies, with about one-sixth publishing more often and one-sixth less often. The average number of articles is between five and nine, where two-thirds of the journals fell. The average length of articles is about ten to twenty typescript pages, or 2,500 to 5,000 words. Many policy problems are represented, such as criminal justice, economic regulation, education, energy, environment, foreign policy, health, science, and poverty, although the journals differ from one another more in terms of disciplinary orientation than in terms of specific policy problems. The editors tend to indicate that either all their articles are policy-relevant or very few are, possibly depending on how they define policy-relevant, rather than on the contents of their journals. Most of them expressed an interest in being more policy-relevant and in participating in some kind of consortium of policy journals to facilitate exchanging advertisements, lists, and other information.

A key problem of many would-be authors of both journal articles and books is how to work more effectively with journal editors and book publishers in order to get material published. To aid such authors, one could do a propositional inventory of the books and articles that have been written to help would-be authors. That kind of content analysis reveals the following propositions. The numbers next to each proposition refer to the journal-publishing bibliography in this section, the book-publishing bibliography in the next section, or to the questionnaires.

Presubmission Suggestions

Research support should be investigated [4].

Read the magazine for a statement of editorial policies and goals and for examples of accepted pieces [4].

Look for a publisher early in the book-writing process and work with them [4].

Consult with others who have written and published similar work [4].

Have your work reviewed by others before submission [4].

Develop a network of contacts by participating in a variety of professional

activities including reviewing, writing nonarticle material, and participating in professional associations [4].

Suggestions for Meeting Journal Selection Criteria

Reasons for rejection in order of importance and frequency are (1)
unimportant or insignificant contribution, (2) methodological short-
comings or flaws, (3) theoretical problems, (4) editorial discretion (for
example, journal goals, multiple submissions), and (5) problems in
presentation (not likely to be the sole factor) [2, 7].

Quality appears to be the determining factor in selection and rejection of
journal articles [2, 7, 11].

Opinions vary on whether there is a great deal of disagreement among
editors and reviewers on the quality of manuscripts [2, 7, 11].

Positive agreement among reviewers to accept a manuscript is less
common than agreement to reject [1, 2].

With increasing costs and pressure for space, length of articles becomes a
factor [2].

Suggestions for Meeting Additional Book-Selection Criteria

Book publishers' criteria for selection may tend to be more oriented
toward the particular item because they face uncertainty [10, book
publishing].

Chances for publication are lowest of an author who has had no prior
contact with a publishing house, middling if one has had prior contact, and
best if the manuscript has been solicited [10, book publishing].

Other selection criteria include tradition of the house, editorial taste,
status of the author, timing considerations, and financial aspects [10, book
publishing].

The author of a more specialized monograph reviewed by a series editor
has a better chance of publication than a book at a scholarly house, where
the potential author has had no prior contact with that publisher [10, book
publishing].

Disciplinary Orientation and Audience

Research today is interdisciplinary, and writers may be required to report
information in more than one field [8].

There is an increasing emphasis on "bridging the gap" between academics and practitioners; thus clear, understandable writing and attention to application are emphasized by some journals.

Some journals are also actively seeking articles by practitioners as well as academics.

Problems in Publication

Fields with less developed paradigms, such as sociology and political science, may tend to have articles judged more by particular than universal criteria because consensus is less, may have longer articles and more books because less defined material requires more space to explicate, and may take longer to process to publication because manuscripts are longer, criteria are unclear, and space is limited, requiring more reviewer time [1].

There is considerable underpublication of applied social research, resulting in loss of knowledge. This might be rectified if research organizations, sponsors, and clients encouraged publication; publishers conducted outreach and market research for potential works and audiences; and archivists and librarians encouraged market and accessibility, through an abstracting and retrieval system [1, book publishing].

As university presses find themselves under increasing financial pressure, facing rapid turnover in subject matter and competition from commercial publishers, academics can help by refereeing, supporting presses, seeking quality rather than quantity in publication, and considering alternatives for book publication such as journals and microfiche [12, book publishing].

There is an unfortunate conflict between the value placed on a book review by tenure and promotion committees and the priority given it by the reviewers and the value and priority placed on it by the journal reader [7].

Bibliography on Scholarly Journals

[1] Beyer, Janice. "Editorial Policies and Practices among Leading Journals in Four Scientific Fields." *Sociological Quarterly* 19 (1978):68–88.
[2] Bonjean, Charles, and Hullum, Jan. "Reasons for Journal Rejection: An Analysis of 600 Manuscripts." *Policy Sciences* 11 (1978):480–483.
[3] Chase, Janet. "Normative Criteria for Scientific Publication." *American Sociologist* 5 (1970):262–265.

[4] Hopkins, Anne; Lawson, Anne; Kallgren, Joyce; Marshall, Dale Rogers; and Ross, Ruth. "Guide to Publication in Political Science." APSA Committee on the Status of Women and the Women's Caucus, 1974.

[5] Marien, Michael. "A World Institute Guide to Futures Periodicals." *Fields within Fields,* Summer 1974.

[6] Merritt, Richard, and Pyszka, Gloria. "The Periodical Literature." In *The Student Political Scientists Handbook.* Schenkman, 1969, pp. 125–153.

[7] Michalos, Alex. "Social Indicators Research: A Case Study of the Development of a Journal." Paper presented at the World Congress of Sociology, 1978. (Available from the Department of Philosophy, University of Guelph, Guelph, Canada.)

[8] Mitchell, John. *Writing for Professional and Technical Journals.* Wiley, 1968.

[9] Mullins, Carolyn. *A Guide to Writing and Publishing in the Social and Behavioral Sciences.* Wiley, 1977.

[10] National Inquiry into Scholarly Communication. "Conclusions and Recommendations." *Chronicle on Higher Education,* May 7, 1979.

[11] Smigel, Erwin, and Ross, Laurence. "Factors in the Editorial Decision." *American Sociologist* 5 (1970):19–21.

[12] VanLeunen, Mary-Claire. *A Handbook for Scholars.* Knopf, 1976.

Policy-Relevant Book Publishers

Table 7–5 shows the book publishers that are especially interested in political science and policy studies. They have all advertised in the *American Political Science Review* or in the convention program of the American Political Science Association during 1977 or 1978. They are arranged alphabetically by commercial and university publishers. Those publishers that have a policy-studies series include Elsevier, Duxbury, LexingtonBooks (D.C. Heath), Marcel Dekker, Pergamon, Praeger, and Sage.

The main questionnaire items sent to book publishers such as those listed in table 7–5 were as follows:

1. What are the name and address of your publishing firm?
2. Are you associated with any other publishing firm?
3. What book series do you publish that you consider policy-relevant in the above sense, and what are some example books?
4. To what audiences do you prefer to appeal in terms of disciplinary orientation, subject-matter interests, popular appeal, classroom potential, professional use, or other criteria?

Table 7–5
Book Publishers Especially Interested in
Political Science and Policy Studies

Commercial Book Publishers

Academic Press	Kenniket Press
Addison-Wesley	LexingtonBooks (D.C. Heath)
Allen & Unwin	Liberty Press
Allyn & Bacon	Little, Brown
Anderson	Macmillan
Ballinger	Marcel Dekker
Basic Books	Mayfield
Bobbs-Merrill	McGraw-Hill
R.R. Bowker	Charles E. Merrill
Chandler Publishing	New Viewpoints
Clio Press	Palisades Publishers
Congressional Quarterly	Pantheon
Thomas Y. Crowell	F.E. Peacock
Dorsey Press	Penguin
Duxbury Press	Pergamon
Elsevier	Plenum
Foundation Press	Praeger Special Studies
Free Press	Prentice-Hall
General Learning Press	Public Affairs Press
Goodyear	Rand McNally
Greenwood	Random House
Halsted Press	Sage Publications
Harcourt Brace	St. Martin's Press
Harper & Row	Science and Technology Press
D.C. Heath	Simon & Schuster
Holt, Rinehart, and Winston	Viking Press
Houghton Mifflin	Wiley
Jovanovich	Winthrop

University Presses

University of Alabama Press	M.I.T. Press
University of California Press	University Press of New England
Cambridge University Press	New York University Press
University of Chicago Press	SUNY-Albany Press
Cornell University Press	Oxford University Press
Duke University Press	University of Pennsylvania Press
University of Georgia Press	University of Pittsburgh Press
Harvard University Press	Princeton University Press
Hoover Institution Press	University of South Carolina Press
University of Illinois Press	Stanford University Press
Indiana University Press	Syracuse University Press
Johns Hopkins University Press	University of Texas Press
University Press of Kentucky	University of Toronto Press
University of Michigan Press	University Press of Virginia

5. What formats do you prefer in terms of average, maximum, and minimum length; paperbound versus hardbound publication; and symposia of original papers, readers of reprinted articles, or authored rather than edited works?

6. Approximately how many books a year do you publish, with about how many would you consider policy-relevant, and would you like to increase the quantity of policy-relevant books that you publish?
7. What kind of marketing do you emphasize with regard to traveling agents, direct mail, free examination copies, advertisements in periodicals, exhibits at conventions, and other means?
8. What criteria do you use in pricing your books, and what do your price ranges tend to be?
9. Roughly how much editing do you do on submitted manuscripts?
10. What miscellaneous suggestions do you have that might be worth including in our directory to be read by policy researchers, teachers, and practitioners interested in authoring, editing, contributing to, adopting, buying, or using your books?

The responses particularly lend themselves to tabular presentation with regard to target audiences and marketing methods, as shown in table 7–6. Two-thirds of the publishers mention being oriented toward an academic audience, with over half mentioning undergraduate students, and almost half mentioning professionals. Less important in terms of frequency of mention are graduate students, libraries, and the public. Marketing methods tend to emphasize direct mail, advertisements, exhibits, and agents, all of which are used by more than half the publishers. Less frequently mentioned are examination copies, catalogs, book reviews, and discounts.

Among the nontabular items, most publishers are interested in manuscripts between 200 and 300 typescript pages, to be published in hardbound form, but with paperbound as a possibility if the hardbound books sell well enough to indicate a classroom market. The strong preference is for authored works, less for edited symposia, and substantially less for readers of reprinted works, contrary to the popularity of a few years ago of readers. Many publishers expressed an interest in increasing their policy-relevant books. Dan Davis of the Greenwood Press, for example, reports that he is "aggressively seeking to increase the number of policy-relevant books that we publish." As is well known, book prices are rapidly increasing, with the paperbound books selling for $5 to $10 and the hardbound books selling for $10 to $20. The quantity of editing varies greatly across and within publishers. Mike McCarroll of LexingtonBooks says editing "ranges from very little (very rare) to complete rewrites (also fortunately rare)." One publisher said "many academicians are lousy writers," and thus "we will occasionally edit very heavily." That can be desirable or undesirable, depending on whether the author and readers like the editing. A useful monthly review of policy-relevant books is provided by Michael Marien's *Future Survey,* published by the World Future Society.

Table 7–6
Target Audiences and Marketing Procedures of Policy-Relevant Book Publishers

Variables and Categories	Number of Publishers	Percentage of Publishers
Target Audiences ($N = 35$)		
Academics	23	66
Undergraduate students	20	56
Professions	15	43
Graduate students	8	23
Libraries	7	20
Public	4	11
General	4	11
Political scientists	3	9
Policymakers	2	6
Teachers	2	6
Economists	1	3
Social scientists	1	3
Marketing Methods ($N = 36$)		
Direct mail	27	75
Advertisements	26	72
Exhibits	25	69
Agents	20	56
Many free copies	16	44
A few free examination copies	7	19
Catalogs	6	17
Media review	6	17
Trade discount	3	8
Conferences	1	3
Standing orders	1	3
Other	3	8

Writing books and articles can be a rewarding experience. The benefits potentially include, in random order, (1) receiving recognition that brings job offers, promotions, and salary increases; (2) acquiring knowledge that can be used in teaching or other job activities; (3) attracting graduate and under-graduate students to one's courses; (4) making a contribution to scholarly or popular knowledge; (5) making a contribution to improving public policies and decisions; (6) facilitating grants, future article acceptances, and invitations to present papers; and (7) generating stimulating interaction among other people interested in the subjects on which one is writing. Book publishing, like article publishing, can be facilitated by doing things that (1) help generate more and better ideas, such as keeping up with the literature in one's field, having stimulating contacts, and teaching in the fields in which one wants to publish; (2) provide for more time, especially for writing, such as having a lighter and/or more compact teaching load, being in an organized routine, avoiding distractions and disruptions, and obtaining time off in the summer and every few years for a research leave; and (3) enable one to delegate more work to research assistants, students, secretaries, data processors, coauthors, and others.

Bibliography on Book Publishing

[1] Abt, Clark. "Publishing Needs of the Applied Social Research Community within the Socio-economic Structure of Social Science Publishing." Paper presented at World Congress of Sociology, 1978. (Available from Abt Associates, 55 Wheeler St., Cambridge, Massachusetts.)

[2] Applebaum, Judith, and Evans, Nancy. *How to Get Happily Published.* Harper & Row, 1978.

[3] Barzun, Jacques, and Graff, Henry. *The Modern Researcher.* Harcourt, Brace, 1957.

[4] Coser, Lewis. "Publishers as Gatekeepers of Ideas." *Annals of the American Academy of Political and Social Science* 421 (1975):14–22.

[5] Grannis, Chandler. *What Happens in Book Publishing.* Columbia University Press, 1967.

[6] Hill, Mary, and Cochran, Wendell. *Into Print: A Practical Guide to Writing, Illustrating, and Publishing.* William Kaufmann, 1977.

[7] Huenefeld, John. *The Huenefeld Guide to Book Publishing.* The Huenefeld Company, 1978.

[8] Association of American University Presses. *One Book/Five Ways: The Publishing Procedures of Five University Presses.* William Kaufmann, 1977.

[9] "Perspectives on Publishing." Annals of the American Academy of Political and Social Science 421 (1975).

[10] Powell, Walter. "Publishers' Decision-Making: What Criteria Do They Use in Deciding Which Books to Publish?" *Social Research* 45 (1978):227–252.

[11] Change Publications. *Professional Development: A Guide to Resources.* Change, 1976.

[12] Putnam, John. "The Future of Scholarly Publishing in Political Science." Paper presented at symposium "The Future of Political Science Book Publishing in the 1970's," American Political Science Association, 1972. (Available from Association of American University Presses, One Park Avenue, New York, New York 10016.)

Interest Groups

Table 7–7 shows various interest groups that may make use of social science in their activities. The list provides only a sampling of the major categories and

Table 7–7
Interest Groups that May Use Social Science in Their Activities

Business
American Bar Association (ABA)
American Medical Association (AMA)
Chamber of Commerce of the United States
Committee for Economic Development (CED)
National Association of Manufacturers (NAM)
National Federation of Independent Business
National Security Industrial Association

Labor
American Federation of Labor and Congress of Industrial Organization (AFL-CIO)
American Federation of Teachers and National Education Association
Association of State and Local Government Employees
International Brotherhood of Teamsters
United Auto Workers (UAW)
United Mine Workers (UMW)
United Steel Workers

Agriculture
American Farm Bureau Federation
Farmers Union
National Farmers Organization
National Grange

Minorities or Disadvantaged Groups
National Association for the Advancement of Colored People (NAACP)
National Council of Senior Citizens
National Organization of Women (NOW)
National Urban League
People United to Save Humanity (PUSH)
Southern Christian Leadership Conference (SCLC)

Right and Left Ideological
Americans for Constitutional Action (ACA)
Americans for Democratic Action (ADA)

General Government Improvement
Common Cause
League of Women Voters

Religious
American Jewish Congress
National Catholic Welfare Association
National Council of Churches
United States Catholic Conference

Veterans
American Legion
Amvets
Disabled American Veterans
Veterans of Foreign Wars

Consumers, Environment, and Civil Liberties
American Civil Liberties Union
Consumers Union
Environmental Defense Fund
Natural Resources Defense Council

the major groups under each category. An *interest group* can be defined as an association of individuals or organizations that attempts to influence public policy by (1) educating the public to a viewpoint favorable to the group, (2) working on behalf of political candidates, but not slating them as a political party would, and/or (3) seeking to influence the decisions of public policymakers. The methods used are not as important as the fact that the group has as one of its major purposes influencing public policy. In that sense, the most important or influential interest groups tend to be associated (in random order) with business, labor, agriculture, minorities, religions, veterans, or other economic or demographic interests. Other interest groups tend to represent more philosophical interests such as civil liberties, environmental protection, or general government improvement. Some of the groups in table 7–7 could be listed under more than one category.

The main questionnaire items sent to interest groups such as those listed in table 7–7 were as follows:

1. What are the name and address of your association?
2. What publications does your association publish?
3. How is membership in your association determined, and how many members do you have?
4. What activities does your association participate in that seek to influence or educate legislative, administrative, or judicial policymakers?
5. What activities does your association participate in that seek to influence the general public, the electorate in certain constituencies, or other segments of the public?
6. What social scientists (if any) do you have on your staff or as consultants who prepare materials for the educational, lobbying, or campaigning activities mentioned in questions 4 and 5?
7. How do you think social scientists could be more useful to your activities, and what types of issues relevant to social science is your association especially interested in?
8. Would your association be interested in participating in a conference or other activities that would bring people together to discuss the use of social science to influence or educate policymakers and members of the general public?
9. What miscellaneous suggestions do you have that might be worth including in our directory to be read by people in policy-oriented associations and by social scientists interested in the activities of such associations?

The responses particularly lend themselves to tabular presentations with regard to the activities of the interest groups, as shown in table 7–8. Of those responding, almost all mention some lobbying activity to influence legislation.

Table 7–8
Activities of Policy-Relevant Interest Groups

Variables and Categories	Number of Groups	Percentage of Groups
Actions toward Government (*N* = 25)		
Lobbying	24	96
Legal action	8	32
Electioneering	3	12
Actions toward the Public (*N* = 23)		
Education	22	96
Publications	14	61
Research	7	30
	2	9
Actions toward Members (*N* = 27)		
Education	27	100
Publications	23	85
Programs	14	52
Conferences	13	48

About one-third mention litigation activities, but only one-eighth mention election campaigning. Nearly all seek to educate the public toward their point of view. More than half have a publications program, and one-third have a research program. A good deal of their educating and publishing is also designed for their own members and not necessarily for policymakers or the public. The largest of the interest groups is the AFL-CIO with 14 million members. Many of the interest groups publish journals which are widely subscribed to, such as the *American Bar Association Journal* with 240,000 subscribers.

The most interesting responses are possibly those that relate to the question concerning the use of social scientists in the activities of the interest groups. Only about a dozen groups responded to that question. Three-fourths of those say they do use social scientists, and most of them indicate they would like the help of more social scientists. Joel Henning, the assistant executive director of the American Bar Association, wrote, "Recent efforts to develop programs in such areas as the environment, privacy, and aging suggest greater rather than less opportunity for ABA employment of individuals with social science backgrounds and skills." Mary Kurkjian, a policy analyst for the Consumers Union, wrote, "There is a need for sophisticated analysis of public policy issues which have an impact on consumers (e.g., oil pricing and insurance rate structures); social scientists could be more useful by conducting such analysis from the consumer perspective." David Cohen, the president of Common Cause, also expressed a positive reaction toward the use of social science: "Common Cause would be interested in closer contact with social scientists especially those interested in public policy formulation and implementation, because many of our issues deal with political reform." None of the interest-group respondents expressed a negative reaction toward the use of social science, although most implied (by not answering that question) they do not make much use of social scientists on their staffs or as consultants. This may be an important, insufficiently developed channel for the use of policy-relevant social science. Those responding also indicated an interest in participating in a conference or other activities that would bring people together from interest groups and the policy-studies field.

Bibliography on Interest Groups

[1] Dexter, Lewis. *How Organizations Are Represented in Washington.* Bobbs-Merrill, 1969.

[2] Holtzman, Abraham. *Interest Groups and Lobbying.* Macmillan, 1966.

[3] Mahood, H.R. *Pressure Groups in American Politics.* Scribner, 1967.

[4] Milbrath, Lester. *The Washington Lobbyists.* Rand McNally, 1963.

[5] Monsen, Joseph, and Cannon, Mark. *The Makers of Public Policy: American Power Groups and Their Ideologies.* McGraw-Hill, 1965.

[6] Salisbury, Robert, ed. *Interest Group Politics in America.* Harper & Row, 1970.

[7] Sinclair, John. *Interest Groups in America.* General Learning Press, 1976.

[8] Truman, David B. *The Governmental Process.* Knopf, 1953.

[9] Woottan, Graham. Interest Groups. Prentice-Hall, 1970.

[10] Zeigler, Harmon. *Interest Groups in American Society.* Prentice-Hall, 1972.

[11] Zeigler, Harmon, and Bauer, Michael. *Lobbying: Interaction and Influence in American State Legislatures.* Wadsworth, 1969.

[12] Zisk, Betty, ed. *American Political Interest Groups: Reading in Theory and Research.* Wadsworth, 1969.

Among the ideas expressed by the respondents to the survey, a few important general themes stand out. The first is the receptiveness toward policy-relevant research on the part of scholarly associations, journals, book publishers, and interest groups. Some suggestions were offered for how policy researchers might take advantage of that receptiveness, especially with regard to journals and book publishers. A second theme is the receptiveness of the directory participants toward some kind of interaction activity across scholarly associations and journals and across academics and interest groups. Perhaps this section and the directory on which it is based might facilitate that kind of interaction. Policy studies is an inherently interdisciplinary subject. The study of any policy problem is likely to benefit from ideas developed among a variety of scholarly associations and journals. Those associations, journals, publishers, and interest groups are important entities in the public-policy research network along with government agencies, university programs, funding sources, research centers, and individual researchers. It is hoped the future will see more coordination and sharing of information across those network entities.

8   Government Agencies

This chapter summarizes the findings of a questionnaire directed to APSA members who indicated they held government positions when they completed a form for the APSA *Biographical Directory* in 1973. The questionnaire was designed to determine how political science has been and can be used in federal, state, and local government agencies and in administrative, legislative, and judicial positions.[a]

The Respondents and the Questions

In January 1975, the questionnaire was mailed to the 425 APSA members who held government positions as of 1973. These persons were chosen as a good group of people to ask about the relevance of political science to government work since they are likely to be knowledgeable about both political science and government work and are likely to be responsive to such a survey.

This group constitutes only 5.5 percent of the entries in the APSA *Biographical Directory*. The percentage of all professional people in federal, state, and local governments who are APSA members is probably below 1 percent. These figures might suggest a lack of relevance to government work of formal political-science training and APSA affiliation.

Of the 425 letters mailed, 71 were returned as undeliverable and unforwardable, suggesting a high rate of mobility among political scientists who work in government. The remaining 354 letters produced 143 responses, of which 108 were usable.

The seven sections of the questionnaire sought to identify helpful political-science references, research needs, means of improving communication between practitioners and academics, present hiring of political scientists, future hiring prospects, potentials for improving training to better prepare people for government work, and the interest of the respondents in contributing an article to a research utilization symposium. What follows is a summary of the findings.

---

[a] The edited verbatim responses are presented on an agency-by-agency basis in the *Political Science Utilization Directory*. Copies of the 128-page directory can be obtained for $3 to cover administrative and mailing costs from the Policy Studies Organization, 361 Lincoln Hall, University of Illinois, Urbana, Illinois 61801.

Political-Science Research

Table 8–1 lists the books mentioned more than once by respondents as being helpful to their work. The most frequently mentioned book was Aaron Wildavsky's *The Politics of the Budgetary Process*. The most frequently mentioned author was James Q. Wilson. Other authors who received four or more mentions were Herbert Simon, Edward Banfield, Peter Blau, and Anthony Downs. Books and authors related predominantly to the field of public administration, with emphasis on theoretical or causal perspectives and behavioral methodology rather than a more traditional approach. The second most mentioned field was state and local government.

Although many respondents did mention books or authors, others indicated they knew of no political-science materials that would be helpful in their work. One Social Security Administration respondent, for example, commented: "Political science books and articles are not on the top of the list of readings for government people either on the Hill or at the bottom of the Hill. Most studies of politics that I have read are essentially retrospective—analytic of what has happened. I have seen little from any of the social science disciplines that identifies predictors that can be manipulated, that have political efficacy, and that can be used to solve problems in formulating or administering policies."

Table 8–1
Books Mentioned More than Once by Government Practitioners

The Book Mentioned	Number of Mentions	Percentage of Mentions	Percentage of Respondents[a]
Aaron Wildavsky, *The Politics of the Budgetary Process*	7	18	12
Edward Banfield, *The Unheavenly City*	4	10	7
James Q. Wilson, *Varieties of Police Behavior*	4	10	7
Graham Allison, *Essence of Decision*	3	8	5
Karl Deutsch, *The Nerves of Government*	3	8	5
Yehezkel Dror, *Public Policy Making Re-examined*	3	8	5
Theodore Lowi, *The End of Liberalism*	3	8	5
Anthony Downs, *Inside Bureaucracy*	2	5	3
Anthony Downs, *Inside Bureaucracy*	2	5	3
Tom Dye, *Understanding Public Policy*	2	5	3
James March and Herbert Simon, *Organizations*	2	5	3
Don Price, *The Scientific Estate*	2	5	3
Richard Neustadt, *Presidential Power*	2	5	3
Alice Rivlin, *Systematic Thinking for Social Action*	2	5	3
Total	39	100	64

[a]Percentage of respondents mentioning a book. This column sums to less than 100 percent since some respondents mention only books other than those listed.

Question 1 of the survey also yielded information on journals as well as books and authors. The most favorably mentioned journal was the *Policy Studies Journal,* no doubt reflecting acknowledgment of the source of the questionnaire. Other journals receiving four or more favorable mentions included the *Public Administration Review, Foreign Affairs,* the *American Political Science Review (APSR),* and *Foreign Policy.* But the *American Political Science Review* received almost twice as many unfavorable as favorable mentions.

The respondents sometimes complained that articles in the professional journals tended to be trivial, irrelevant, filled with jargon, infeasible, and stale. For example, a city planner from Detroit said, "Most articles in the *APSR* and other journals do not deal even remotely with the real world and those that do, come up with solutions that are totally unworkable. The suggestion that the income distribution in the U.S. should be restructured does not really help a city that is looking at an immediate budget deficit of $50,000,000 and may have to lay off a third of its work force." Offsetting comments included those from the Advisory Commission on Intergovernmental Relations: "We do draw upon a number of books authored by political scientists. Some of these provide useful general analytic frameworks, and others offer detailed descriptions of specific programs or problem areas."

Table 8–2 summarizes information about judgments concerning research needs. As with the other tables, items are included only if they are mentioned more than once. The leading need asserted is for more prescriptive research on policy choices and the range of alternatives and effects. Table 8–2 is mainly organized in terms of research subjects. For studying those subjects, the respondents tended to emphasize a need for quantitative behavioral methodologies drawing on economics, psychology, and sociology rather than law, history, philosophy, and journalism. A respondent from the Law Enforcement Assistance Administration commented, "We need prescriptive rather than descriptive research. Simply to tell a political decision-maker that a policy will be endorsed by one constituency rather than another probably only repeats something he already knows." A respondent from the Energy Research and Development Administration commented, "The most useful kind of work falls into three general areas: criticism of public policy based on sound cost-benefit analysis; development of creative policy alternatives based on the same kind of analysis; and feasibility studies including analyses of the political problems of implementing policies." The same respondent also finds helpful "publications which describe and analyze the politics of the decision-making process" partly to avoid "painful on-the-job experience."

Table 8–3 summarizes suggestions or ideas for improving professional communication. The most frequently mentioned ideas included having a clearinghouse for research and having exchange fellowships or internships

Table 8–2
Research Needs Suggested by Practitioners

Item Mentioned	Number of Mentions	Percentage of Mentions	Percentage of Respondents[a]
Research that is prescriptive in nature; more work on policy choices and the range of alternatives and effects	45	27	48
Research on state and local government concerns, and more research on urban-policy problems	20	12	21
Organizational forms of government	15	9	16
Legislative oversight, legislative leadership, and effects of decisions	13	8	14
International politics and power	12	7	13
Problems of the legal system and organization	12	7	13
New methodologies and analytic techniques	8	5	8
Cost/benefit analyses	7	4	7
Comparative	6	4	6
Civil rights and problems of minority groups	6	4	6
Effects of pressure-group activities	6	4	6
Government responsiveness to citizens' needs	5	3	5
Budgeting	3	2	3
Theory	3	2	3
Middle East policy	2	1	2
Descriptive research	2	1	2
Political parties	2	1	2
The executive	2	1	2
Total	169	100	177

[a]Percentage of respondents mentioning a type of research needed. This column sums to more than 100 percent because some respondents mention more than one item.

between government and academia. For example, a respondent from the National Institutes of Health said, "Academic political scientists should spend some time in government as advisors, consultants, interns, residents, special assistants to Cabinet members, and Congressional committees, etc. Government employees should spend a semester or two at a university every five years. There is a great need for such continual interchange." More specifically, a staff member in the House of Representatives stated that "the Congressional Fellowship Program has been one of the most positive and productive attempts to overcome the gulf between the Capitol and the campus." Almost one-fourth of the respondents (who suggested ideas for improving communication between political scientists and government practitioners) mentioned the questionnaire as being a good step. Many respondents suggested that communication could be improved by trying to write in a simpler manner, or, as a Department of Transportation respondent suggested, "If you want to talk to bureaucrats, use language that your father (or perhaps your grandfather) would understand."

Table 8–3
Improved Communication Ideas Suggested by Practitioners

Idea Mentioned	Number of Mentions	Percentage of Mentions	Percentage of Respondents[a]
Have a clearinghouse for research. Scholars could send in their research, and a brief summary could periodically be sent to practitioners, who could then reply or write brief reviews to be circulated to academics.	40	19	43
Have exchange fellowships or internships between government and academia.	32	16	34
More face-to-face contact with bureaucrats on a planned basis.	29	14	31
Have a publication which would translate research into language the government person can understand.	23	11	25
This questionnaire is a good first step.	22	11	24
Have more panels at political-science conventions which include government people.	19	9	20
Increased interest in policy research by academia will help.	17	8	18
Political scientists should participate in professional organizations to which government people belong and attend meetings, rather than expect government people just to join academics.	15	4	16
Better distribution of journals which are of interest to bureaucrats, such as *Policy Studies Journal* would help.	9	4	10
Total	206	100	221

[a]Percentage of respondents mentioning an improved communication idea. This column sums to more than 100 percent because some respondents mention more than one idea.

Political-Science Personnel

The next three items in the questionnaire deal with political-science personnel. Of the respondents 24 percent said their agencies currently had one political scientist, the respondent; 40 percent said their agencies had a few political scientists, but less than five; and 37 percent said more than five. The federal agencies with an especially large number of reported political scientists included the Census Bureau, Civil Service Commission, Congressional Research Service, U.S. Information Agency, National Park Service, State Department, Department of Defense, and the Agency for International Development. At the state and local levels, the largest number of political scientists was reported for such agencies as the Illinois Legislative Council, Kansas Legislative Research Department, Little Rock City Manager's Office, Philadelphia Central Personnel Agency, Minnesota State Planning Agency, and New York City Police Department.

About one-third of the respondents said political scientists constituted less than 10 percent of their agency's professional employees; about one-fourth claimed between 10 and 25 percent; one-fifth said between 25 and 50 percent. One-fourth reported over 50 percent, but they were referring to small agencies with only a few persons. The academic degree most frequently reported by presently employed political scientists was at the master's level, with only three agencies reporting that their political scientists were mainly at the Ph.D. level. These three agencies were units in the Civil Service Commission, the Department of Transportation, and the Supreme Court. The tasks performed by political scientists included research (mentioned by 40 percent), management (24 percent), and program evaluation (20 percent).

Although political scientists are often hired in government agencies, usually they are not hired just because they are political scientists. A staff member of a Senate committee commented, "No office deliberately sets out to hire a political scientist in the same way some set out to hire an economist. But because of some self-selection process that seems to be at work, many of the applicants for Hill positions turn out to have some training in political science." Likewise, a respondent from Health, Education, and Welfare said, "I do not know of anyone in HEW hired because of political science [substantive] qualifications. People are hired, one might say, in spite of such qualifications. The [methodological] research Ph.D. is easily adapted to evaluation and policy analysis work, so opportunity does exist."

Question 5 asked about future hiring. Of the respondents 72 percent said future hiring of political scientists would be about the same as present hiring; 19 percent said less than the present; and 9 percent said more in the future, although there were many "don't knows" to this question. Agencies expecting increased hiring in the future included the State Department, Kansas Advisory Council on Intergovernmental Relations, Minnesota State Planning Agency, Anaheim Police Department, New York City Police Department, and the Erie County, N.Y., Legislature. Those who indicated how additional political scientists would be used emphasized a shift toward more policy analysis and program evaluation and away from research and management. Those who indicated reasons for a downward trend in the hiring of political scientists mentioned that persons from other disciplines are now more needed, especially economists and sociologists. Those who anticipate an upward trend mentioned that public-policy backgrounds now make political-science graduates more attractive. They also indicated a possible shift toward more hiring at the Ph.D. level, possibly because of the more demanding policy-analysis work involved and the increased availability of Ph.D.'s given the surplus in the academic market.

Some respondents were relatively optimistic about the future hiring of political scientists, such as a House of Representatives staff member who said, "I believe that for political scientists, the opportunities will be brightest for those having a policy-oriented background, such as research work in a particular policy field." Some other respondents had a more pessimistic tone, such as a Maryland city manager who said, "Political science majors have little to offer outside of an academic setting. Those [also] trained in some specialty as computers, personnel administration, economics, foreign affairs, etc. offer more if placed in an appropriate position."

Table 8–4 summarizes the responses from the sixth question: How should political-science training better prepare people for government work? The most frequently mentioned responses related to teaching how government actually functions, providing internships, offering decision-making analysis, more training in policy problems, and more quantitative methodology. As an example, a respondent from the Law Enforcement Assistance Administration commented,

Table 8–4
Improved Training Ideas Suggested by Practitioners

Idea Mentioned	Number of Mentions	Percentage of Mentions	Percentage of Respondents[a]
Knowledge about how government actually functions	37	22	40
Internships in government similar to those in business which engineering and business programs offer	23	14	25
Courses to take greater account of conditions of uncertainty and risk elements in decision making	15	9	16
More expertise and specialization in specific policy areas, rather than just the general background as offered today	15	9	16
More training in statistics and methodology	13	9	14
More public-policy courses	12	7	13
Economics as a minor	10	6	11
Interdisciplinary training	8	5	9
Better analytical abilities	8	5	9
More integration of public administration in programs	6	4	6
Better writing and speaking skills	6	4	6
Exposure to practitioners by having practitioners lecture	5	3	5
Upgrade M.P.A. programs to the level of most M.B.A. programs	4	2	4
More sociology	2	1	2
Training in legal analysis	2	1	2
Something like moot court or business-school case analyses	2	1	2
Political philosophy	2	1	2
Total	170	102	18

[a]Percentage of respondents mentioning an improved training idea. This column sums to more than 100 percent because some respondents mention more than one idea.

The omnipresent Survey Research Center voting data analysis which pervades our graduate schools does not constitute a transferable paradigm for program evaluation; furthermore, our schools' obsession with internal validity has produced students with absolutely no sense of or interest in the external validity (relevance of the data they use). Saul Alinsky's story that a sociologist would need a $50,000 grant to find a whorehouse is probably even more applicable to our brethren. If our graduate schools could start teaching students what decision contexts (and the data which will be available or procurable in them) will be like, someone might listen to their products.

A more positive viewpoint toward some aspects of current political-science training was expressed by a member of the Bureau of the Census who said, "My methodological training in my Ph.D. program has benefited me more than any of the political science [substantive] courses I have ever taken or taught," and by a member of an agency involved in planning at the statewide level who said, "The best training we have found is the actual experience in doing policy analysis for elected decisionmakers. Some kind of actual training which required taking an issue, looking at it, and preparing recommendations for particular action is the most effective preparation for people in our kind of an agency." An especially positive note was struck by a member of the National Park Service who said, "No matter where a person is located in government, his political science training should help him in his understanding of the political factors in the decision-making process."

It might be interesting to note that there are some substantial relations between the characteristics of respondents and the nature of their responses. For example, those respondents who are younger and have spent fewer years in government provide more references to political-science literature; they are more oriented toward the federal government than toward state and local governments; they are more likely to stress quantitative behavioral research rather than more traditional research; and they are more likely to indicate a desire to contribute an article to a research utilization symposium. Similar response directions were shown by respondents who had Ph.D. degrees, teaching backgrounds, or relatively extensive publication records, as indicated by their APSA biographical entries.

Persons interested in political-science utilization can expect some help from political scientists in all levels of government, as indicated by the fact that 52 percent of the respondents said they would be willing to contribute an article to a research utilization symposium. This runs counter to the notion that political scientists in government are unwilling or unable to write articles for lack of time or incentive. It may, however, indicate that they have not been called on to join with academic political scientists in developing a more policy-relevant political science. The results of that invitation to contribute an article mentioned in question 7 will be reflected in the spring 1975 issue of the *Policy Studies Journal,* mainly devoted to a symposium on research utilization under the editorship of Carol Weiss of the Columbia Bureau of Applied Social Research. She welcomes related manuscript proposals and manuscripts on the use of social research in public-policy making.

The lists shown in tables 8–1 through 8–4 may be helpful in suggesting ideas to political-science departments, organizations, foundations, publications, and individuals as to how political science can make a more significant contribution to government decision making. There does seem to be a consensus among the respondents that political science is not making as much of a contribution as other social sciences are. More important, the respondents generally imply that political science has the potential of making a substantially greater contribution to both research communication and training for government placement. To make that potential more of a reality requires a greater or different effort on the part of political-science departments and political scientists. That effort can manifest itself in such ways as special degrees related to policy studies, policy-studies research programs, special teaching curricula within political science, interdisciplinary programs, relevant conferences and convention panels, more policy-studies articles and publications (in a more readable format), and special programs or centers where political scientists and practitioners can work together in specific policy fields.[b] Efforts like those should help build closer relations among political-science academics and practitioners and thereby promote the increased application of political science to important policy problems.

Bibliography on Policy-Research Utilization

Political-Science Utilization

[1] Charlesworth, James, ed. *A Design for Political Science: Scope, Objectives and Methods.* American Academy of Social and Political Science, 1966.

[2] Dror, Yehezkel. *Design for Policy Sciences.* Elsevier, 1971.

[3] Dror, Yehezkel. *Public Policymaking Reexamined.* Chandler, 1968.

[4] Dror, Yehezkel. *Ventures in Policy Sciences: Concepts and Applications.* Elsevier, 1971.

[5] Dye, Thomas. *Understanding Public Policy.* Prentice-Hall, 1972.

[6] Easton, David. "The New Revolution in Political Science." In *Approaches to the Study of Political Science.* Edited by Michael Haas and Henry Kariel. Chandler, 1970.

[7] Eulau, Heinz, and March, James, eds. *Political Science.* Prentice-Hall, 1969.

---

[b] For a department-by-department inventory of those efforts, see the *Policy Studies Directory* (Policy Studies Organization, 1976).

[8] Graham, George, and Carey, George, eds. *The Post-Behavioral Era.* McKay, 1972.

[9] Greenstein, Fred, and Polsby, Nelson, eds. *Policies and Policy-Making.* Vol. 6 of *Handbook of Political Science.* Addison-Wesley, 1975.

[10] Hyneman, Charles. *The Study of Politics.* University of Illinois Press, 1959.

[11] Jones, Charles. "Policy Analyses: Academic Utility for Practical Rhetoric." Paper presented at the 1975 Midwest Political Science Association meeting.

[12] Lasswell, Harold. *A Pre-View of Policy Sciences.* Elsevier, 1971.

[13] Lasswell, Harold. *The Future of Political Science.* Atherton, 1963.

[14] Mann, Thomas. "Employment of Political Scientists in the 1970's: Problems and Prospects." Paper presented at the 1973 Midwest Political Science Association meeting.

[15] Mitchell, Joyce, and Mitchell, William. *Political Analysis and Public Policy: An Introduction to Political Science.* Rand McNally, 1969.

[16] Nagel, Stuart, ed. *Policy Studies in America and Elsewhere.* LexingtonBooks, D.C. Heath, 1975.

[17] Ranney, Austin, ed. *Political Science and Public Policy.* Markham, 1968.

[18] Sharkansky, Ira, ed. *Policy Analysis in Political Science.* Markham, 1970.

[19] Somit, Albert, and Tanenhaus, Joseph. *The Development of Political Science.* Allyn & Bacon, 1967.

[20] VanDyke, Vernon. *Political Science: A Philosophical Analysis.* Stanford University Press, 1960.

[21] Also see the journals *Policy Studies Journal, Public Policy, Policy Analysis,* and *Policy Sciences.*

Social-Science Utilization

[22] Glaser, E.M., and Ross, H.L. *Increasing the Utilization of Applied Research Results.* National Institute of Mental Health, Human Interaction Research Institute, 1971.

[23] Harris, Fred. *Social Science and National Policy.* Transaction Books, 1973.

[24] Havelock, Ronald. *Knowledge Utilization and Dissemination: A Bibliography.* Center for Research on Utilization of Scientific Knowledge, University of Michigan, 1968.

[25] Havelock, Ronald. *Planning for Innovation through Dissemination and Utilization of Knowledge.* Center for Research on Utilization of Scientific Knowledge, University of Michigan, 1969.

[26] Horowitz, Irving, ed. *The Use and Abuse of Social Science.* Transaction Books, 1975.

[27] Institute for Communication Research. *Case Studies in Bringing Behavioral Science into Use: Studies in the Utilization of Behavioral Science.* Stanford University Press, 1961.

[28] Knezo, Genevieve. *Government Science Policy: Some Current Issues on Federal Support and Use of the Behavioral and Social Sciences.* Congressional Research Service, 1974.

[29] Lazersfeld, Paul. *An Introduction to Applied Sociology.* Elsevier, 1975.

[30] Lazarsfeld, Paul. *The Uses of Sociology.* Basic Books, 1967.

[31] Lerner, Daniel, and Lasswell, Harold. *The Policy Sciences.* Stanford University Press, 1951.

[32] Loavenbruck, Grant. *Research Utilization Inventory: A Survey of Current Research in Social and Health Organizations in New York City.* Community Council of Greater New York, 1974.

[33] Lynd, Robert. *Knowledge for What?* Princeton University Press, 1948.

[34] Lyons, Gene. *The Uneasy Partnership: Social Science and the Federal Government in the Twentieth Century.* Russell Sage Foundation, 1969.

[35] Nagel, Stuart, ed. *Policy Studies and the Social Sciences.* Lexington-Books, D.C. Heath, 1975.

[36] National Institute of Mental Health. *Planning for Creative Change in Mental Health Services: A Distillation of Principles on Research Utilization.* Government Printing Office, 1971.

[37] National Research Council. *The Behavioral Sciences and the Federal Government.* National Academy of Sciences, 1968.

[38] National Science Foundation. *Knowledge into Action: Improving the Nation's Use of the Social Sciences.* Government Printing Office, 1969.

[39] U.S. Congress House Committee on Government Operations. *The Use of Social Research in Federal Domestic Programs.* Government Printing Office, 1967.

[40] Weiss, Carol, ed. *Using Social Research in Public Policy Making.* LexingtonBooks, D.C. Heath, 1976.

[41] White, Michael; Radner, Michael; and Tansik, David, eds. *Management and Policy Science in American Government: Problems and Prospects.* LexingtonBooks, D.C. Heath, 1975.

[42] Also see the journals *Social Problems, Social Issues, Public Interest,* and *Society* (formerly *Trans-Action*).

**Part IV
Methodological and
Disciplinary
Perspectives**

9 Methods of Policy Analysis

The methodology of finding an optimum alternative legal policy in general can be reduced in its most simplified form to a one-sentence rule: Choose the alternative that maximizes net benefits, where net benefits are total benefits minus total costs. That rule can be symbolized as follows: When faced with choosing between X_1, X_2, and so on, choose the X, or legal policy alternative, that gives the greatest Y, where Y symbolizes net benefits.[1]

The Y (or NB, for net benefits) can be decomposed into various benefits (B_1, B_2, and so on) and various costs (C_1, C_2, and so on). A *benefit* is an effect of an X alternative that is considered desirable, whereas a *cost* is an effect of an X alternative that is considered undesirable. Sometimes benefits and costs are referred to generically simply as effects and symbolized Y_1, Y_2, and so on. The overall Y of a given X represents the sum of the separate Y scores if they are measured with a common unit and thus can be added. Otherwise, either the relation between each X and each Y must be analyzed separately, or the Y must be multiplied rather than added, with exponents indicating their relative value weights.

Given those definitions of benefits and costs, it logically follows that we want to choose legal policy alternatives that will maximize benefits and minimize costs. It is, however, usually impossible to do both simultaneously since doing nothing is likely to be the alternative that will minimize our costs (that is, bring them down to zero), but it is also the alternative that is least likely to produce any benefits. Likewise, spending great sums of money or effort may bring substantial or maximum benefits, but only at great cost. Thus, since we cannot have maximum benefits and minimum costs at the same time, a more feasible goal is to try to pick the alternative that will provide the biggest difference between total benefits $B_1 + B_2 + \cdots + B_n$ and total costs $C_1 + C_2 + \cdots + C_n$ of the alternatives available. This is analogous to a business firm seeking to maximize its profits, or the difference between total income and total expenses.

That general rule about maximizing net benefits would be more useful if we were to indicate how it varies in different general situations. The main typology of situations for methodological purposes is a simple dichotomy between legal policy problems in which the alternatives have no logical order and legal policy problems in which the alternatives do have logical order. Legal policy problems in which the alternatives have no logical order include yes-no problems, such as whether illegally seized evidence should be admissible in court[2] or whether a given defendant should be released or held in jail prior to trial.[3] Likewise there is no logical order among the alternatives where more than two nonnumerical categories are involved, such as whether to provide counsel to the poor in criminal cases through a voluntary-counsel system, an assigned-counsel system, or a public-defender system.[4] The number of categories lacking inherent order for a given legal policy problem can be huge, as is the situation in trying to choose among all the possible ways in which ninety of the downstate Illinois counties could be made into eighteen districts.[5]

Legal policy problems in which the policy or decisional alternatives do have inherent order include the problem of the optimum number of jurors to have among the alternatives of six, seven, eight, nine, ten, eleven, or twelve,[6] or the optimum percentage of defendants to hold in jail prior to trial, with the alternatives being 1, 2, 3 percent, and so on, including all the decimal possibilities between the integer percentages.[7] There is especially inherent order where the alternatives involve money or effort expenditures, such as how many dollars to allocate (out of every $100 available) to law reform versus case handling in the OEO Legal Services Program[8] or how many dollars to allocate (out of every $100 available) to Illinois, Wisconsin, and other states in order to have a maximum impact on keeping down the national crime occurrence.[9]

Although our overall goal is to pick the alternative that maximizes net benefits, often we use other terminology to mean the same thing. For example, one can talk about legislatively setting bail bonds that will maximize the difference between the probability of a pretrial defendant appearing in court (PA) minus the probability of his being held in jail (PH). In that context, PA is like total benefits, and PH is like total costs. One can also talk about releasing a percentage of pretrial defendants that will minimize the sum of our holding costs plus our releasing costs. In that context, holding costs can be considered a negative benefit. More specifically, holding costs are the releasing benefits (that is, the dollars saved by not holding a defendant) which we lose by holding a defendant, and in that sense holding costs are negative releasing benefits. Thus when we say we want to minimize the sum of our holding costs plus our releasing costs, in effect we want to maximize our releasing benefits (that is, minimize our negative releasing benefits) minus our releasing costs. In other words, costs can be considered negative benefits, and benefits can be considered negative costs. Thus, if we have considered all the relevant effects, we may be maximizing our net benefits even though we only talk about maximizing benefits or minimizing costs.[10]

Bibliography on Finding an Optimum Alternative
Policy in General

These sources discuss or use a wide variety of optimizing methods. The methods are collectively referred to by such phrases as *operations research, management science, systems analysis,* and *policy analysis.*

Basic Methods

[1] Baumol, William. *Economic Theory and Operations Analysis.* Prentice-Hall, 1965.
[2] Kassouf, Sheen. *Normative Decision Making.* Prentice-Hall, 1970.
[3] MacRae, Duncan, Jr., and Wilde, James. *Policy Analysis for the Citizen.* Duxbury, 1978.
[4] Nagel, S., and Neef, M. *Operations Research Methods: As Applied to Political Science and the Legal Process.* Sage, 1976.
[5] Quade, Edward. *Systems Analysis: An Outline for the State-of-the-Art Survey Publications.* International Institute for Applied Systems Analysis, 1976.
[6] Richmond, Samuel. *Operations Research for Management Decisions.* Ronald Press, 1968.
[7] Theil, Henri; Book, John; and Kloek, Teun. *Operations Research and Quantitative Economics: An Elementary Introduction.* McGraw-Hill, 1965.
[8] Thierauf, Robert, and Grosse, Richard. *Decision Making through Operations Research.* Wiley, 1970.
[9] White, Michael; Clayton, Ross; Myrtle, Robert; Siegel; and Rose, Aaron. *Managing Public Systems: Analytic Techniques for Public Administration.* Duxbury, 1980.
[10] Zeckhauser, Richard, and Stokey, Edith. *A Primer for Policy Analysis.* W.W. Norton, 1977.

Policy Applications

[11] Blumstein, Alfred; Kamrass, Murray; and Weiss, Armand; eds. *Systems Analysis for Social Problems.* Washington Operations Research Council, 1970.
[12] Buchanan, James, and Tullock, Gordon, eds. *Theory of Public Choice.* University of Michigan, 1972.
[13] de Neufville, Richard, and Marks, David, eds. *System Planning and Design: Case Studies in Modeling, Optimization, and Evaluation.* Prentice-Hall, 1974.

[14] Drake, Alvin; Keeney, Ralph; and Morse, Philip. *Analysis of Public Systems.* M.I.T. Press, 1972.

[15] Fromm, Gary; Hamilton, William; and Hamilton, Diane. *Federally Supported Mathematical Models: Survey and Analysis.* Data Resources and Abt Associates, 1974.

[16] Gass, Saul, and Sisson, Roger. *A Guide to Models in Governmental Planning and Operations.* Environmental Protection Agency, 1974.

[17] Greenberger, Martin; Crenson, Matthew; and Crissey, Brian. *Models in the Policy Process.* Sage, 1976.

[18] Helly, Walter. *Urban Systems Models.* Academic Press, 1975.

[19] Margolis, Julius, ed. *Analysis of Public Output.* National Bureau of Economic Research, 1970.

[20] Nagel, S., and Neef, M. *Legal Policy Analysis: Finding an Optimum Level or Mix.* LexingtonBooks, D.C. Heath, 1977.

[21] Zeckhauser, Richard; Harberger, Arnold; Haveman, Robert; Lynn, Lawrence; Niskanen, William; and Williams, Alan, eds. *Benefit Cost and Policy Analysis: An Aldine Annual on Forecasting, Decision-Making and Evaluation.* Aldine, 1974. Also see the 1973 volume edited by Robert Haveman, the 1972 volume edited by William Niskanen, and the 1971 volume edited by Arnold Harberger.)

Finding an Optimum Choice without Contingent Probabilities

Procedure

A good example of choosing without probabilities is the problem of how to provide legal counsel to the poor in criminal cases. The main alternatives are a list of volunteer attorneys (X_1), assigned counsel generally on a rotation basis from among practicing attorneys in the county (X_2), or a public defender who is a salaried lawyer hired by the government to represent poor defendants (X_3). All other things being equal, the best alternative is the one that is most inexpensive (Y_1), visible and accessible (Y_2), politically feasible (Y_3), and the most likely to result in specialized competence and aggressive representation (Y_4). A benefit can be defined as being relatively high on one of these goals, and a cost can be defined relatively low.

If we start with the goal of inexpensiveness, volunteer counsel and assigned counsel score well. However, the public-defender system is substantially more expensive. On visibility and accessibility all three alternatives are about equal in the sense that arraigning magistrates are expected to inform poor defendants of whatever system the county uses for making counsel available to them. On political feasibility or acceptability there is not likely to be any great opposition among influential lawyers to the volunteer or public-defender alternatives. They are, however, likely to object to the assigned-counsel alternative since it forces lawyers to devote time and resources to cases which they may find frustrating and even distasteful. Volunteer counsel is unlikely to yield competent, aggressive lawyers unless substantial fees are paid to the screened volunteers, which is a system that exists at the federal level only. Likewise, assigned counsel tends to result in the appointment of lawyers who may be competent in their specialty, but that specialty is not so likely to be criminal law. The public-defender system develops competent criminal defense attorneys through the specialized continuous experience, although their aggressiveness may be limited by lack of funding and personnel.

The above analysis indicates three relative benefits or advantages for volunteer counsel and one relative cost or disadvantage; two benefits for assigned counsel and two costs; and three benefits for the public-defender system and one cost. To resolve the tie between volunteer counsel and the public defender requires giving relative weights to the four goals. If we give more weight to the goals of visibility-accessibility and competence-aggressiveness as a more liberal policymaker might be inclined to do, then the public defender comes out ahead. If we give more weight to the goals of inexpensiveness and political feasibility, as a more conservative policymaker might be inclined to do, then the volunteer system comes out ahead, assuming that it is capable of providing sufficient counsel to satisfy the constitutional requirements.

This optimizing perspective of listing alternatives, goals, relations, weights and choices may also be applicable to obtaining insights into the best alternatives for solving other legal policy problems. The perspective can be made more sophisticated by using X's that are not mutually exclusive, thereby introducing combinations of the alternatives, such as an X_4 which involves a list of volunteer attorneys for poor defendants who do not like the public defender, as is done in the city of Chicago. One can also relate each X alternative to each Y goal by showing the degree of relationship and also the extent to which nonlinear diminishing returns are involved rather than just whether the relation is relatively positive or negative. In addition, one could indicate the extent to which a relation between an X and a Y is affected by the probabilistic occurrence of an outside event. An example might be that public defenders tend to provide aggressive representation only when they have adequate resources, but the probability of their having adequate resources is roughly .30 in the sense that only about one out of three public defenders' offices have funding above an adequate threshold of budget divided by cases, although more exact statistics are currently being developed by the National Legal Aid and Defenders' Association.

Bibliography on Finding an Optimum Choice
without Contingent Probabilities

These sources discuss or use methods that emphasize determining whether a given policy provides greater benefits than costs and how much greater, rather than what policy would maximize a given set of goals. Evaluation research and the measurement of benefits and costs are the predominant methods here.

Methods

[1] Bennett, Carl, and Lumsdaine, Arthur, eds. *Evaluation and Experiment: Some Critical Issues in Assessing Social Programs.* Academic Press, 1975.

[2] Black, Guy. *The Applications of Systems Analysis to Government Operations.* Praeger, 1968.

[3] Caro, Francis, ed. *Readings in Evaluation Research.* Russell Sage Foundation, 1971.

[4] Layard, Richard, ed. *Cost-Benefit Analysis.* Penguin, 1972.

[5] Mishan, Ezra J. *Cost-Benefit Analysis.* Praeger, 1976.

[6] Quade, Edward S. *Analysis for Public Decisions.* Elsevier, 1975.

[7] Struening, Elmer, and Guttentag, Marcia, eds. *Handbook of Evaluation Research.* Sage, 1975.

[8] Suchman, Edward. *Evaluative Research: Principles and Practice in Public Service and Social Action Programs.* Russell Sage Foundation, 1967.

[9] Weiss, Carol. *Evaluation Research: Methods for Assessing Program Effectiveness.* Prentice-Hall, 1972.

Applications

[10] Abt, Clark, ed. *The Evaluation of Social Problems.* Sage, 1976.

[11] Guttentag, Marcia, and Saar, Shalom, eds. *Evaluation Studies Review Annual.* Vol. 2. Sage, 1977. (Also see vol. 1, edited by Gene Glass.)

[12] Hinrichs, Harley, and Taylor, Graeme. *Systematic Analysis: A Primer on Benefit-Cost Analysis and Program Evaluation.* Goodyear, 1972.

[13] McKean, Roland. *Efficiency in Government through Systems Analysis: With Emphasis on Water Resources Development.* Wiley, 1958.

[14] Rossi, Peter, and Williams, Walter, eds. *Evaluating Social Programs: Theory, Practice, and Politics.* Seminar Press, 1972.

[15] Wholey, Joseph; Scanlon, John; Duffy, Hugh; Fukumoto, James; and Vogt, Leona. *Federal Evaluation Policy: Analyzing the Effects of Public Programs.* Urban Institute, 1976.

Finding an Optimum Choice
with Contingent Probabilities

Procedure

The legal process, at least in its judicial aspects, involves a series of choices that are made by the participants on the basis of the probability of the occurrence of some contingent event. For example, the would-be criminal chooses to commit or not commit a crime partly on the basis of the probability of getting caught and convicted. Likewise, the personal-injury lawyer accepts a client partly on the basis of the probability of winning the case, especially if the lawyer gets paid only if the case is won. Similar probabilistic decisions are faced by arraignment judges, sentencing judges, parole boards, prosecuting attorneys, and insurance-company lawyers, although each of these decision-makers may be concerned with a different contingent event, different data, and different specific goals to be maximized.

Substantively, we could divide the above situations into criminal-case decisional problems or civil-case decisional problems. From a methodological perspective, however, it would be more meaningful to divide those situations into ones that involve a single decisionmaker trying to make a choice irrespective of anyone else's present choices or interaction, as contrasted to situations involving more than one decisionmaker whose decisions are influenced by the interactive behavior or decisions of another decisionmaker.

The one-person decision situation can be illustrated by the bond-setting decision. It involves the contingent event of the defendant appearing in court as well as the contingent event of the defendant committing a crime while released. It involves the dichotomous decision of release or hold and the numerical decision of what dollar bond to set. The goals, or Y scores (associated with each decision and contingent event), can be expressed in nonmonetary satisfaction units or in dollar units. The bond-setting problem can be thought of as an individual, case-by-case judicial problem or as a more generalized problem of legislating for types of cases. In addition, the bond-setting problem illustrates distinctions between models designed to describe how the legal process operates and models designed to prescribe how the legal process should operate in order to maximize given goals.[11]

The two-person interacting situation can be illustrated by the process of plea bargaining and out-of-court civil settlements. In plea bargaining, the offers of the prosecutor and the defendant or his or her defense counsel are partly determined by their perceptions of the probability of conviction if the case were to go to trial. Likewise, in civil-case negotiations, the offers of the plaintiff and the defendant or their attorneys are partly determined by perceptions of the probability of the defendant being found liable if the case were to go to trial. Both the criminal and the civil negotiators will choose between settlement and trial partly on the basis of what the other side offers, unlike in the bond-setting situation where the defendant does not bargain or make moves with the judge.[12]

The plea-bargaining situation is useful for illustrating not only what is involved in making an optimum choice under probabilistic conditions, but also in a generalized way the sequential steps that are likely to occur from the initial positions of the parties to the final settlement or to a determination that a settlement is impossible. That kind of a sequential analysis may be especially valuable in explaining the occurrence of certain decisions. That kind of sequential analysis, plus the basic decision theory and bargaining models, may also be valuable in analyzing the effect of legal and other system changes on the decisional behavior of the participants. By knowing how system changes are likely to affect decisional behavior, system planners can allow for those effects when instituting various system changes, such as increased pretrial release, reduced delay, or increased allocation of resources to the participants.

In discussing general optimizing, we emphasized that finding an optimum or alternative legal policy involves choosing the alternative that maximizes net benefits, where net benefits are total benefits minus total costs. In situations that involve making an optimum choice under probabilistic conditions, that general rule needs to be slightly modified. The modification involves saying this: Choose the alternative that maximizes expected net benefits, where expected net benefits are expected total benefits minus total expected costs. In that context, expected total benefits equal the benefits to be received if a contingent event happens times the probability of its happening. Likewise, expected total costs equal the costs to be incurred if a contingent event happens times the probability of its happening. Where there is more than one benefit, each benefit to be received is multiplied by the probability on which it is contingent. Therefore, expected total benefits (ETB) equals $P_1B_1 + P_2B_2 + \ldots P_nN_n$, and likewise with expected total costs.

Bibliography on Finding an Optimum Choice with Contingent Probabilities

Methods

[1] Behn, Robert, and Vaupel, James. *Analytical Thinking for Busy Decision Makers.* Basic Books, 1978.

[2] Brown, Rex; Kahr, Andrew; and Peterson, Cameron. *Decision Analysis for the Manager.* Holt, Rinehart, and Winston, 1974.

[3] Matheson, James, and Howard, Ronald, eds. *Readings in Decision Analysis.* Stanford Research Institute, 1977.

[4] Jeffrey, R.C. *The Logic of Decision.* McGraw-Hill, 1965.

[5] Lee, Wayne. *Decision Theory and Human Behavior.* Wiley, 1971.

[6] Mack, Ruth. Planning on Uncertainty: Decision Making in Business and Government Administration. Wiley-Interscience, 1971.

[7] Raiffa, Howard. *Decision Analysis: Introductory Lectures on Choices under Uncertainty.* Addison-Wesley, 1968.

[8] Slovic, Paul; Fischoff, Baruch; and Lichtenstein, Sara. "Behavioral Decision Theory." *Annual Review of Psychology* 28 (1977):1–39.

Applications

[9] Clark, Elizabeth, and van Horn, Andrew. *Risk-Benefit Analysis and Public Policy: A Bibliography.* Harvard Energy and Environmental Policy Center, 1976.

[10] Easton, Allan. *Complex Managerial Decisions Involving Multiple Objectives.* Wiley, 1973.

[11] Halter, Albert, and Dean, Gerald. *Decisions under Uncertainty with Research Applications.* South-Western, 1971.

[12] Keeney, Ralph, and Raiffa, Howard. "Illustrative Applications," in *Decisions with Multiple Objectives: Preferences and Value Tradeoffs,* pp. 354–435. Wiley, 1976.

[13] Nagel, S., and Neef, M. *Decision Theory and the Legal Process.* LexingtonBooks, D.C. Heath, 1978.

Finding an Optimum Level on a Continuum of Alternatives

Procedures

The legal process tends to be epitomized by U-shaped or valley-shaped cost curves and by hill-shaped benefit curves. This is so with regard to both judicial procedure and the more general problem of how strict or lenient legal rules should be made or applied. The due-process or fair-procedure aspects of the legal process involve a constant struggle between going too far and not going far enough in providing due process. On one hand, if too much due process is provided, then many guilty persons will go free in criminal cases and liable persons in civil cases, which will mean high total costs to the system at that end of the due-process scale. On the other hand, if too little due process is provided, then many innocent persons will be found guilty of wrongdoing in criminal cases and nonliable persons in civil cases, which will mean high total costs to the system at the low end of the due-process scale. Somewhere in the middle of that valley-shaped total-cost curve, the costs to the system reach a minimum. At that point we have an optimum balance or optimum level of due process.

Likewise, any legal rule can be worded or applied in an overly strict or an overly lenient way. If environmental-protection standards become too strict, we suffer unduly high cleanup costs; but if the standards become too lenient, we suffer unduly high pollution-damage costs. Likewise, contract-law standards can become too strict, thereby interfering with freedom of contract and possibly incurring large societal costs in terms of reduction in the free flow of business. If contract-law standards become too lenient, however, then we might encourage large societal costs in terms of exploitation of the side with less knowledge or weaker bargaining power. In tort law, automobile negligence standards could be so strict as to slow traffic almost to a standstill or so lenient as to paralyze potential drivers and pedestrians from venturing into the streets. Similar problems of doing too much or too little can occur in criminal law, divorce law, housing law, or any field of law. Somewhere between those extremes, however, is an optimum point where a minimum is reached on the sum of the total costs, with or without weights to consider different valuations of each cost.

The optimum-level problem can be analyzed with empirical data from the pretrial-release situation. If too high a percentage of defendants is held in jail prior to trial, then high holding costs will be incurred with regard to jail maintenance, lost gross national product, and the bitterness generated from being held in jail in spite of the fact that one's case results in a dismissal or an acquittal. If too low a percentage of defendants is held in jail prior to trial, then high releasing costs will be incurred with regard to the costs of rearresting defendants who fail to appear for their trials and of crimes committed by defendants prior to trial that would not have been committed if they had been held in jail. The object is to find an optimum percentage of defendants to hold or release prior to trial in order to minimize the sum of the holding and the releasing costs.[13]

Another optimum-level problem is the optimum-jury-size problem. If juries are too large, too many guilty defendants may fail to be convicted; if juries are too small, too many innocent defendants may be convicted. Unlike the percentage-to-release problem, however, virtually no empirical data can be obtained which meaningfully show for various jury sizes the quantity of defendants convicted, let alone the quantity of guilty or innocent defendants. This is so because when the jury size changes in a given state, the type of cases decided by jury trials rather than bench trials also tends to change. There is no empirical way of separating the effect of jury size and case types on changes in the conviction percentages. Therefore, to arrive at an optimum jury size requires a substantial amount of deductive modeling from premises that are acceptable, flexible, empirical, and normative. That kind of model involves probabilistic conditions, but it is basically an optimum-level model.[14]

In discussing general optimizing, we emphasized that finding an optimum alternative legal policy involves choosing the alternative that maximizes net benefits, where net benefits are total benefits minus total costs. In the optimum-level situation, generally we convert all the relevant effects to costs and then seek to minimize the unweighted or weighted sum of the costs. One reason for making that conversion is that generally it is easier to obtain cost data than benefit data in dealing with social problems, although an important type of benefit is the dollars saved (or the negation of the costs) by not having to rearrest a defendant who fails to appear, by not having to lose the gross national product lost by holding a defendant in jail, or by not incurring some other cost. Another reason for expressing effects as costs, especially in the optimum-level situation, is that doing so emphasizes that the optimum-level problem is basically one of minimizing the sum of type I errors or costs (where a true hypothesis is rejected, such as convicting an innocent defendant contrary to the presumption of innocence) plus type II errors or costs (where a false hypothesis is accepted, such as acquitting a guilty defendant in accordance with the presumption of innocence).

In spite of the tendency to express optimum-level problems in terms of minimizing total costs, often they can be expressed in terms of maximizing total benefits or maximizing certain benefits minus certain costs. For example, we could express the percentage-to-release problem as the problem of finding the percentage to release at which the sum of the releasing benefits (holding costs avoided) plus the holding benefits (releasing costs avoided) will be maximized. We could also express it in terms of finding the percentage to release at which the releasing benefits minus the releasing costs are maximized, or the holding benefits minus the holding costs are maximized, and still arrive at the same solution. The problem of the optimum school-integration enforcement level seems to be best stated as finding the level at which we avoid the lowered integration benefits both associated with tokenism and associated with white flight and resegregation, and thus we obtain a maximum point on a hill-shaped total-benefits curve. The important thing is that we recognize that both overenforcement and underenforcement of any law can cause us to lose benefits or suffer costs, including opportunity costs, thereby necessitating a search for the optimum balance or optimum level with empirical data, deductive models, or a combination of both.

Bibliography on Finding an Optimum Level
on a Continuum of Alternatives

These sources discuss or use methods that emphasize finding the point on a continuum policy which minimizes a valley-shaped total-cost curve, maximizes a hill-shaped total-benefits curve, or maximizes net benefits minus costs where doing too much or too little is socially undesirable. Calculus maximization is the predominant method here.

Methods

[1] Brennan, Michael. *Preface to Econometrics: An Introduction to Quantitative Methods in Economics.* South-Western, 1973.
[2] Fisher, Gene. *Cost Considerations in Systems Analysis.* Elsevier, 1971.
[3] Henry, S. *Elementary Mathematical Economics.* Sage, 1969.
[4] Shockley, James. *The Brief Calculus: With Applications in the Social Science.* Holt, Rinehart and Winston, 1971.
[5] Starr, M.K., and Miller, D.W. *Inventory Control: Theory and Practice.* Prentice-Hall, 1962.

Applications

[6] Buchanan, James, and Tullock, Gordon. *The Calculus of Consent: Logical Foundations of Constitutional Democracy.* University of Michigan Press, 1962.
[7] Hite, James; Macaulay, Hugh; Stepp, James; and Yandle, Bruce. *The Economics of Environmental Quality.* American Enterprise Institute for Public Policy Research, 1972.
[8] Nagel, S.; Neef, M.; and Wice, Paul. *Too Much or Too Little Policy: The Example of Pretrial Release.* Sage Administrative and Policy Studies Series, 1977.
[9] Phillips, Llad, and Votey, Harold. "An Economic Basis for the Definition and Control of Crime." In *Modeling the Criminal Justice System,* pp. 89–109. Edited by Stuart Nagel. Sage, 1977.
[10] Stigler, George. *The Theory of Price.* Macmillan, 1966.

Finding an Optimum Mix in Allocating Scarce Resources

The legal process can be expressed as a series of probabilistic decisions or as an attempt to find an optimum balance of type I and type II errors. It can also be expressed as an attempt to allocate scarce social resources. This is especially the case with legislative and administrative programs that involve the allocation of funds for various societal purposes. Since money is a scarce resource, the object of those aspects of the legal process is to allocate those funds among activities and/or places in such a way as to maximize total benefits obtained, where all effects are expressed as benefits (or desirable social indicators such as increased longevity) or to minimize the total costs where all effects are expressed as costs (or undesirable social indicators, such as disease or crime occurrence). The allocation or optimum-mix model also applies to the legal process where nonmonetary values are being allocated, such as some measure of effort on the part of civil-rights organizations or agencies.

The basic rule for handling the optimum-mix problem for allocating scarce resources is to allocate to activities or places in accordance with the budget available and the slopes or marginal rates of return for each activity or place. A *slope*, or *marginal rate of return*, is simply the ratio between a change in output produced for an activity or place and the corresponding change in input or resources expended to that activity or place. If the relation between inputs and outputs is constant or linear, then one would allocate to the activities or places with the largest slopes after satisfying whatever minimum constraints are required. If the relation between inputs and outputs involves diminishing returns or nonlinear relations, then one would allocate to the activities or places until their changing nonlinear slopes are equalized such that nothing could be gained by shifting from one activity or place to another. Under either type of relation, all the budget should be expended if one wants to maximize benefits without exceeding the budget, but less than all the budget should be expended if one wants to minimize costs while providing a minimum benefit or satisfaction level.

These general principles can be illustrated with regard to allocating effort among civil-rights activities relating to voting, schools, criminal justice, employment, housing, and public accommodations. The problem is one of trying to determine how to allocate the total civil-rights effort to those six input activities in order to maximize the total equality improvement as the collective output activity which represents the sum of the improvements obtained in each of the six civil-rights fields. The model deals with linear relations for the sake of simplicity and because the range of the data fits a linear model about as well as a nonlinear one. To further simplify the presentation, the optimum-mix model can be presented first in the context of finding an optimum mix between just two civil-rights activities, namely those that relate to efforts against government discrimination and efforts against private discrimination. In effect, the model represents a combination of linear regression analysis and linear-programming optimization. The regression analysis is especially useful for obtaining slopes between each input activity and each output criterion for use in developing an input-output matrix that enables one to see how the outputs would change given various changes in the inputs, or how the inputs would have to change in order to satisfy changes in the output goals.[15]

The general principles can also be illustrated with regard to allocating dollars among geographical places in order to minimize the national crime occurrence. Here the emphasis is on places rather than activities, which changes the methodology from a single equation (relating the overall output goal to various input activities) into multiple equations (in which the crime occurrence in each place is related to anticrime dollars spent in that place). The emphasis here is also on diminishing-returns nonlinear relations rather than linear regression and linear programming.[16] In both examples, concern is expressed for obtaining change data or data at more than one point in time, but dollars and anticrime data lend themselves to more precise measurement than effort and antidiscrimination data. Both examples involve an attempt to deal with the crucial problem of controlling for demographic, socioeconomic, and other variables which affect crime and discrimination besides antidiscrimination effort or anticrime dollars. Likewise, both examples in differing ways involve an attempt to deal with minimum and maximum political, legal, and economic constraints on the allocation of scarce resources to either activities or places.

In discussing general optimizing, we emphasized that finding an optimum alternative legal policy involves choosing the alternative that maximizes net benefits, where net benefits are total benefits minus total costs. In the optimum-mix situation, in effect we seek that goal by looking to the dynamic benefit-cost ratio of each activity or place to which we are considering allocating our scarce resources. By *dynamic benefit/cost ratio,* we mean the ratio between a change in benefits and a change in costs in moving from any one point with regard to resources allocated (for that activity or place) to any other point. By observing that benefit/cost ratio, slope, or marginal rate of return and allocating accordingly, at least in theory we can maximize the total benefits we can obtain from our total expenditures. In practice, we may run into considerable difficulty obtaining meaningful data for measuring those ratios, especially in view of our inability to hold constant or statistically control for other variables that may influence the benefits or outputs while changes are occurring in our costs or inputs.

Bibliography on Funding an Optimum Mix
in Allocating Scarce Resources

These sources discuss or use methods that stress allocating scarce resources to maximize satisfaction within a budget constraint or to minimize expenditures while providing a minimum satisfaction level. Mathematical programming (linear, nonlinear, and so on) is the predominant method here, or program budgeting on a less sophisticated level.

Methods

[1] Kotler, Philip. *Marketing Decision Making: A Model Building Approach.* (Holt, 1971).
[2] Lee, Sang. *Goal Programming for Decision Analysis.* Auerbach, 1972.
[3] Llewellyn, Robert. *Linear Programming.* Holt, 1963.
[4] Lyden Frement, and Miller, Ernest, eds. *Planning-Programming-Budgeting: A Systems Approach to Management.* Rand McNally, 1972.
[5] McMillen, Claude, Jr. *Mathematical Programming: An Introduction to the Design and Applications of Optimal Decision Machines.* Wiley, 1970.

Applications

[6] Beltrami, Edward. *Models for Public Systems Analysis.* Academic, 1977.
[7] Goldman, Thomas, ed. *Cost-Effectiveness Analysis: New Approaches in Decision-Making.* Praeger, 1967.
[8] Haveman, Robert, and Margolis, Julius, eds. *Public Expenditures and Policy Analysis.* Markham, 1970.
[9] Laidlaw, C. *Linear Programming for Urban Development Plan Evaluation.* Praeger, 1972.
[10] Nagel, S. *Minimizing Costs and Maximizing Benefits in Providing Legal Services to the Poor.* Sage Administrative and Policy Studies Series, 1973.
[11] Shoup, Donald, and Mehay, Stephen. *Program Budgeting for Urban Police Services.* Praeger, 1971.

Miscellaneous Methods

In this section we have conceptualized the legal process as a choice model, a probabilistic model, an optimum-level model, and an optimum-mix model. It is useful to think of each of those models separately since they involve different concepts, methods, and, to some extent, causal and prescriptive theories. Nevertheless, there is considerable overlap among the models in that both the same problem often can be viewed from more than one perspective and each model often can be translated into each other model. We previously mentioned that the optimum-jury-size problem can be viewed as both a probabilistic and an optimum-level model. The pretrial-release problem can be viewed from three perspectives. It is a probabilistic problem in the sense that the individual judge is trying to decide whether releasing or holding the defendant produces the highest expected value, in light of the probability that the defendant will appear for trial and the costs of making a type I error (holding a defendant who would have appeared) versus a type II error (releasing a defendant who would not appear). It is an optimum-level problem in the sense that the system is trying to arrive at an optimum percentage of defendants to hold in order to minimize the sum of the holding costs and the releasing costs. It is an optimum-mix problem in the sense that the system can also be said to be trying to arrive at an optimum mix between defendants who are held and defendants who are released.

The last point illustrates how one model sometimes can be translated into another. Any optimum-level problem involving the question of what is the optimum level of due process or enforcement severity can be expressed as a problem of finding the optimum mix between type I and type II errors or between severity and leniency, although that conceptualization may be more awkward than the optimum-level conceptualization. Likewise, any optimum-mix problem can be reduced to an optimum-level problem. This is more clearly seen when there are just two activities or two places to which to allocate. Instead of asking what the optimum mix is of $10 between place 1 and place 2, we could ask what the optimum level is to allocate our $10 to place 1 given the fact that the more we allocate to place 1, the less we have to allocate to place 2. If there are three places, then the latter statement becomes "given the fact that the more we allocate to place 1, the less we will have to allocate collectively to places 2 and 3." That conceptualization, though, may be more awkward than the optimum-mix approach.

To illustrate how the optimum-mix and optimum-level models can be virtually interchangeable, one can use the problem of what is the optimum mix between free press and fair trial in the context of allowing newspapers to report on pending criminal trials where their reporting may tend to prejudice the defendant's case. To express it in other terms, one is dealing with the problem of what is the optimum level of free press in that context, or what is the optimum level of fair trial in that context. The optimum-mix perspective tends to appeal to political scientists because of its emphasis on policy tradeoffs in arriving at a solution. The optimum-level perspective tends to appeal to econometricians because of its mathematical simplicity, given its emphasis on only one variable.[17]

An interesting methodology that combines the optimum-mix perspective and the probabilistic perspective is portfolio analysis.[18] It originated in the context of trying to decide the optimum mix of stocks to purchase in order to maximize total dividends, profits from resale, or both in light of the probabilistic nature of various dividends being paid or various increases in the value of the stock. One researcher has proposed the use of portfolio analysis to determine the optimum mix of prisoners in a prison between, say, armed robbers and burglars, given their differing probabilities of recommitting their crimes and the different costs to society or certain segments within society.[19]

One other set of models that crosses our typologies is that set in which the minimization of time consumption is the primary consideration. This would include queuing models which inform us how much waiting and processing time could be saved for court cases by adding judges, reducing the time needed for processing an average case, or reducing the number of cases entering into the waiting lines. Time-oriented models would also include dynamic programming, which could inform us of the optimum order in which to process cases so as to minimize the average waiting time plus processing time per case. A third kind of time-oriented model is PERT analysis, which can tell us the optimum path of alternative processing steps to follow in order to minimize time consumed by the average court case. Those three models are prescriptive time-oriented models in the sense that they tell us about means to use to minimize the antigoal of delay. Related time-oriented models that are descriptive or causal in nature include time-series analysis which relates variables to each other over time, and Markov chain analysis, which indicates how a change in one variable will affect a series of other variables that are indirectly influenced by the first variable in a kind of domino effect.[20]

Bibliography on Miscellaneous Methods

These sources discuss or use methods that emphasize either saving time as the key benefit-cost consideration or the need to think in terms of chain reactions or future values in making present choices. Queuing, dynamic programming, PERT, Markov chains, and difference-differential equations are the predominant methods here.

Methods

[1] Archibald, Russell, and Villoria, Richard. *Network-Based Management Systems: PERT/CPM.* Wiley, 1967.
[2] Baker, Kenneth. *Introduction to Sequencing and Scheduling.* Wiley, 1974.
[3] Cortes, Fernando; Przeworski, Adam; and Sprague, John. *Systems Analysis for Social Scientists.* Wiley, 1974.
[4] Gross, Donald, and Harris, Carl. *Fundamentals of Queuing Theory.* Wiley, 1974.
[5] Wheelwright, Steven, and Makridakis, Spyros. *Forecasting Methods for Management.* Wiley, 1973.

Applications

[6] Bohigian, Haig. *The Foundations and Mathematical Models of Operations Research with Extensions to the Criminal Justice System.* Gazette, 1971.

[7] Byrd, Jack, Jr. *Operations Research Models for Public Administration.* LexingtonBooks, D.C. Heath, 1975.

[8] Chaiken, J.; Crabill, T.; Holliday, L.; Jaquette, D.; Lawless, M.; and Quade, E. *Criminal Justice Models: An Overview.* Rand, 1975.

[9] Nagel, S., and Neef, M. "Time-Oriented Models and the Legal Process: Reducing Delay and Forecasting the Future." Paper presented at the annual meeting of the American Society for Public Administration, 1978.

[10] Reed, John. *The Applications of Operations Research to Court Delay.* Praeger, 1973.

Value Decisions and Policy Analysis

One particularly interesting set of issues worth raising when discussing the problems of optimizing in public-policy analysis is the issues that relate to the role of values in policy analysis. A number of points might be mentioned concerning those matters. On the most basic level is the issue of being value-free in doing research. By definition, policy analysis at least partly involves seeking to achieve or maximize given values or social goals rather than ignoring them. Policy analysts, like other researchers, should, however, be value-free in the sense of not allowing their values to influence how they record or present information. In fact, the concern for objectivity and replicability in policy analysis research should probably manifest itself in taking extra precautions to keep the bias of researchers from influencing their results, given the stronger feelings that generally exist about policy problems as contrasted to research problems that lack policy implications. These precautions can include drawing upon multiple sources and individuals for cross-checking information, making available raw data sets for secondary analysis, and making assumptions more explicit.

Many policy-analysis problems involve taking goals as givens and determining what policies will maximize those goals. The goals, however, may be only intermediate values directed toward achieving other more general values. For example, a policy-analysis problem might involve determining how to reduce pretrial jail populations (Y). The proposals might relate to methods for increasing pretrial release (X_1) and reducing delay from arrest to disposition (X_2). There might, however, be some policymakers who think the pretrial jail population should be increased (rather than reduced) as a means for punishing arrested defendants who might otherwise escape punishment through plea bargaining or lack of admissible evidence. A second-stage policy analysis could deal with the effect of the pretrial jail experience on reducing crime rates (Z), which can be taken as a higher-level goal. To make policy analysis more manageable between X and Y, one may merely refer to the possibility of doing further research on the relation between Y and Z without actually undertaking it.

Like any research tool (including a calculator or a typewriter), policy analysis can be used for good or evil purposes. A computerized analysis of the effects of alternative legislative-redistricting patterns, for example, can be used to facilitate a kind of proportional representation whereby the percentage of districts dominated by Democrats roughly approximates the percentage of Democrats in the state. On the other hand, the same redistricting programs can be used to minimize black representation in a state legislature. Quantitative policy analysis, however, is less likely to be used for purposes that are unconstitutional or on which there is a negative consensus, because policy analysis tends to make more explicit the values, assumptions, input data, and other parameters used in arriving at the decisions than more traditional decision-making does. In the computer redistricting example, one can check the programs and the input data to see what the basis was for the redistricting outputs.

Sometimes people involved in policy analysis may be asked to maximize what they consider to be socially undesirable goals. This brings out the need for policy analysts to choose carefully whom they work for, to try to improve the caliber of those people if they can, to call illegal matters to the attention of appropriate authorities, and to look elsewhere if they are dissatisfied with the goals of their government agency or employer. Normally, in a democratic society, elected officials and their political appointees do try to achieve goals that will make them popular and that will be in conformity with the law. Therefore, a policy analyst's desire to do things in the public interest and be legal is not so likely to conflict with the people he or she works for.

Value decisions are particularly relevant to policy analysis in the sense that optimizing solutions are very much influenced by the values that are plugged into the analysis. In the redistricting example, the optimum plan is likely to depend on whether the goal is merely to provide equality of population across the districts or also to provide such things as proportionality of party representation and competitiveness within districts. Likewise, what constitutes an optimum jury size depends partly on how many guilty people we are willing to acquit in order to save one innocent person from conviction. A tradeoff higher than ten to one may, however, be irrelevant if the maximum reasonable jury size is twelve persons. As another example, the optimum mix of funds in the Legal Services Corporation between law reform and routine case handling may depend on who is evaluating the legal services agencies that constitute the data on which the analysis is based. Lawyer evaluators may tend to give higher ratings to agencies involved in more difficult appellate court precedent-setting cases, but representatives of the poor may give higher ratings to agencies involved in easier but more immediate family, housing, and consumer negotiations. Policy analysts should be particularly concerned with presenting sensitivity analyses in their projects, whereby they show how the optimum would vary when changes are made in the values being maximized.[21]

The main thing that all these models have in common is that they are capable of provoking useful insights that might otherwise be missed by viewing legal-process problems from other research perspectives only. Optimizing models provide insights for comparing various forms of optimum behavior with empirical behavior so that one can make legal policy recommendations to bring the empirical closer to the optimum, or so that one can revise the values attributed to the policymakers in order to bring the alleged optimum closer to the empirical. They also provide insights for understanding the effects on other variables of changing legal policies and decisions, and the effects on legal policies and decisions of changing other variables. They help to clarify assumptions, goals, alternative means, payoffs from alternative means, contingent probabilities, and other elements essential to understanding more fully the basic simplicities and subtle complexities of the legal process.

Summary of the Main Formulas in Optimizing Analysis

This section pulls together on a more abstract, symbolic level the major optimizing principles which are presented verbally and illustrated with legal-policy examples in this chapter. By seeing the principles on a more abstract level, their interrelations and generalizability are further clarified. Here we also briefly refer to some important general matters which did not seem appropriate to discuss elsewhere, given the emphasis on verbal and legal-policy presentation.

Basic Symbols

$$X = \text{policy, means, or input}$$

This policy can be dichotomous or continuous. It can be a single policy or a combination of policies.

$$Y = \text{goal, end, or output}$$

This goal can be dichotomous or continuous. It can be a single goal or a combination of goals. It can be something to maximize or minimize.

B = desirable output or a benefit

C = undesirable output or a cost

b_{YX} = slope of Y to X (the change in Y with a 1-unit change in X)

Z = occurrence or variable that affects the relation between an X policy and a Y goal

$X*$ = policy that optimizes one's goals, that is, that maximizes a desirable Y or minimizes an undesirable Y

$Y*$ = value of Y when $X = X*$

$f(X_1)$ = function of X_1

Thus if $X_2 = 5X_1^3$, then $X_2 = f(X_1)$.

The General Formula for Optimizing

$$X* = X \rightarrow \max(B - C)$$

That is, the optimum policy is the policy that causes total benefits minus total costs to be a maximum, or that simply maximizes net benefits subject to economic, legal, political, or other constraints.

Optimum Choice without Probabilities

$$X* = X \rightarrow \max[\Sigma(VQ)_B - \Sigma(VQ)_C]$$

V = value per unit or normative weight; also symbolized W_{Y_i} for the weight of output i

Q = quantity of units or empirical weight; also symbolized $b_{Y_iX_j}$ for the slope of the relation between goal i and policy j

Optimum Choice with Probabilities

$$X* = X \rightarrow \max(EB - EC), \quad \text{or} \quad \max[\Sigma(BP) - \Sigma(CP)]$$

E = expected Y in view of the probability of the B's and C's occurring

P = probability of B, C, or Z occurring

$P*$ = threshold probability such that $+ X = X*$ if $P > P*$ and $- X = X*$ if $P < P*$

Solve for P in $(1 - P)(a) + Pb = (1 - P)(c) + Pd$. Now,

$$P* = B/A+B \quad \text{or} \quad P* = A/A+B$$

depending on how the choice problem is worded, where $A =$ the costs of making an error of rejecting a true hypothesis and $B =$ the costs of making an error of accepting a false hypothesis. And,

$$P* = a-c/a-b-c+d \quad \text{when } +Z \text{ has a probability of } P \text{ and } -Z \text{ has a probability of } 1 - P$$

where $\quad a = Y$ if one chooses $+X$ when Z is negative

$\qquad b = Y$ if one chooses $+X$ when Z is positive

$\qquad c = Y$ if one chooses $-X$ when Z is negative

$\qquad d = Y$ if one chooses $-X$ when Z is positive

Also $\quad P* = 1/R+1 \quad$ or $\quad P* = R/R+1 \quad$ where $R = A/B$

Optimum-Level Problems

With relations that go in only one direction (*monotonic* relations), where Y is desirable and b_{YX} is positive, $X* =$ highest X within the constraints on X. This also applies where Y is undesirable and b_{YX} is negative. And where Y is desirable and b_{YX} is negative or zero, $X* =$ lowest X within the constraints on X. This also applies where Y is undesirable and b_{YX} is positive.

With relations that involve valley-shaped or hill-shaped curves (parabolic relations),

$$X* = X \quad \text{where } b_{YX} = 0$$

If

$$Y = aX^b + AX^B$$

then

$$b_{YX} = ba(X)^{b-1} + BA(X)^{B-1}$$

and so if

$$b_{YX} = 0$$

then

$$X^* = [-ab/(AB)]^{1/(B-b)}$$

Optimum-Mix Problems

With linear relations, the following hold:

1. Where Y is desirable and b_{YX_j} is greater in a positive direction than the slope of the other X's, then $X_j^* = $ highest X_j, within the constraints. If there is any budget left over after maximizing X_j, give it to the next highest X, and so on.
2. Before allocating to the X with the greatest slope, provide each X with whatever minimum allocations are required. With the exception of these minimum allocations, nothing should be allocated to X's with zero slopes or negative slopes where Y is desirable.
3. Where Y is undesirable, give to the X with the greatest negative slope, and so on.
4. These rules assume one wants to maximize or minimize Y within a budget. If one wants to merely reach a satisfactory level on Y and minimize budget expenditures, then allocate to the best X, and then the next best X, and so on, until that satisfactory level is reached.

With nonlinear relations, the following hold:

1. If one wants to maximize or minimize Y within a budget, then spend the total budget while equalizing the slopes of the X's. For allocating to places, simultaneously solve the following types of equations:

$$X_1 + X_2 = G \qquad \text{where } G \text{ is the grand total available}$$
$$ba(X_1)^{b-1} = BA(X_2)^{B-1} \qquad \text{since } Y_1 = aX^b \text{ and } Y_2 = AX^B$$

Thus $X_1^* = $ solving for X_1 in $X_1 + f(X_1) = G$, which requires reiterative guessing, and $X_2^* = G - X_1^*$. For allocating to activities, simultaneously solve the following types of equations:

$$X_1 + X_2 = G$$
$$b(aX_2^B)X_1^{b-1} = B(aX_1^b)X_2^{B-1}, \qquad \text{since } Y = aX_1^bX_2^B$$

Thus

$$X_1^* = Gb/(b + B) \qquad \text{and} \qquad X_2^* = GB/(b + B)$$

2. If one wants to merely reach a satisfactory level on Y and minimize budget expenditures, then set Y at a minimum while equalizing the slopes of the X's. For allocating to places, simultaneously solve

$$\min Y = aX_1^b + AX_2^{B^-} \quad \text{and} \quad ba(X_1)^{b-1} = BA(X_2)^{B-1}$$

Thus

$$X_1^* = \text{solving for } X_1 \text{ in } aX_1^b + A[f(X_1)]^B = \min Y \text{ and } X_2^* = f$$
$$[\min (Y, X_1^*)]. \text{ For allocating to activities, simultaneously solve}$$

$$\min Y = aX_1^b X_2^B \quad \text{and} \quad b(aX_2^B)X_1^{b-1} = B(aX_1^b)X_2^{B-1}$$

Thus

$$X_1^* = \text{solving for } X_1 \text{ in } aX_1^b[f(X_1)]^B = \min Y \text{ and } X_2^* = f[\min (Y, X_1^*)].$$

3. If each X place or X activity is supposed to receive a minimum amount, then change the above formulas so that wherever X_1 appears, you substitute $X_1 + M_1$, and wherever X_2 appears, you substitute $X_2 + M_2$.

4. If there are N X's, there will be N terms in the first of the above pairs of equations and N slopes to be equalized in the second pair. Solving for each X^* may then require a computer program for solving nonlinear simultaneous equations, just as a regression-analysis computer program may be needed to find the numerical values for a, b, A, B, and the other parameters.

5. If one wants to reach a different satisfactory level on each component of a composite Y and minimize budget expenditures, then simultaneously solve the following types of nonlinear equations (where the exponents are other than 1) or linear equations (where the exponents are all 1):

$$\min Y_1 = aX_1^b + AX_2^B$$
$$\min Y_2 = aX_1^b + AX_2^B$$

Thus

$$X_1^* = \text{solving for } X_1 \text{ in } Y_1 = aX_1^b + A[f(X_1)]^B \text{ and } X_2^* = f[\min (Y_1, X_1^*)].$$

Bibliography on the Pros and Cons
of Systems Analysis in Policy Studies

Over the years, a body of literature has developed dealing with advocacy of or attacks on systems analysis in policy studies. In this context by *systems analysis* we mean planning, benefit-cost analysis, operations research, management science, deductive modeling, optimizing, or other related approaches to systematically determine the effect of alternative policies and to make recommendations to increase the effects that are considered desirable and to decrease the undesirable effects.

The sources cited here take a relatively pro or con position on some of the basic issues or discuss the pro and con positions, rather than simply explaining what systems analysis is. Explanatory sources include E.S. Quade, *Analysis for Public Decisions* (Elsevier, 1975); Roland McKean, *Efficiency in Government through Systems Analysis* (Wiley, 1958); Guy Black, *The Application of Systems Analysis to Government Operations* (Praeger, 1969); and S. Nagel with Marian Neef, *Operations, Research Methods: Applied to Political Science and the Legal Process* (Sage, 1976). All the sources listed are scholarly rather than polemic. They all recognize other points of view, but tend to emphasize a relatively pro or con position, although the pro sources do not agree on all aspects of systems analysis, as with the con sources.

Sources that advocate greater use of social science in policy making do not necessarily advocate a systems-analysis perspective since social science includes a variety of other methodologies. Sources dealing with evaluation research generally are not included because they stress evaluation of adopted policies rather than the use of preadoption analytic techniques to forecast the effects of alternative policies. This controversy is not the same as the quantitative versus nonquantitative controversy in social science, since many quantitative social scientists are not doing policy analysis and some nonquantitative social scientists may be highly involved with policy problems. Neither is this a liberal-conservative, left-right controversy since systems analysis can be used for a variety of ideological goals.

Some of the Relatively Pro Literature

[1] Bennis, Warren; Benne, Kenneth; and Chin, Robert. *The Planning of Change: Readings in the Applied Behavioral Sciences.* Holt, 1964.
[2] Beutel, Frederick. *Experimental Jurisprudence and the Scienstate.* Rothman, 1975.
[3] Blumstein, Alfred; Kamrass, Murray; and Weiss, Armand. *Systems Analysis for Social Problems.* Washington Operations Research Council, 1970.

[4] Cherns, Albert, ed. *Sociotechnics.* Malaby Press, 1976.
[5] Churchman, C. West. *The Systems Approach.* Delcorte Press, 1968.
[6] Dror, Yehezkel. *Public Policymaking Reexamined.* Chandler, 1968.
[7] Hovey, Harold. *The Planning Programming Approach to Government Decision Making.* Praeger, 1968.
[8] Lerner, Daniel, and Lasswell, Harold, eds. *The Policy Sciences.* Stanford University Press, 1951.
[9] Lynd, Robert. *Knowledge for What?* Princeton University Press, 1939.
[10] Olson, Mancur. *Toward a Social Report.* Department of Health, Education, and Welfare, 1969.
[11] Suchman, Edward. *Evaluative Research: Principles and Practice in Public Service and Social Action Programs.* Russell Sage, 1977.

Some of the Relatively Con Literature

[12] Berlinski, David. *On Systems Analysis: An Essay Concerning the Limitations of Some Mathematical Methods in Social, Political, and Biological Science.* M.I.T. Press, 1976.
[13] Braybrooke, David, and Lindblom, Charles. *A Strategy for Decision.* Free Press, 1963.
[14] Guttman, Daniel, and Willner, Barry. *The Shadow Government: The Government's Multi-Billion-Dollar Giveaway of Its Decision-Making Powers to Private Management Consultants, "Experts," and Think Tanks.* Pantheon, 1976.
[15] Hayek, Frederick. *The Road to Serfdom.* Routledge, 1944.
[16] Hoos, Ida. *Systems Analysis in Public Policy: A Critique.* University of California Press, 1972.
[17] Jewkes, John. *The New Ordeal by Planning.* St. Martin's Press, 1968.
[18] Levine, Robert. *Public Planning: Failure and Redirection.* Basic Books, 1972.
[19] Tribe, Laurence. "Policy Science: Analysis or Ideology?" *Philosophy and Public Affairs* 2 (1973).
[20] Wildavsky, Aaron. "The Political Economy of Efficiency: Cost-Benefit Analysis, Systems Analysis, and Program Budgeting." *Public Administration Review* 26 (1966):292–310.

Some of the Literature Presenting Both Perspectives

[21] Archibald, Kathleen. "Three Views of the Experts' Role in Policymaking: Systems Analysis, Incrementalism, and the Clinical Approach." *Policy Sciences* 1 (1970):73–86.

[22] Brock, Bernard; Chesebro, James; Cragan, John; and Klumpp, James. *Public Policy Decision-Making: Systems Analysis and Comparative Advantages Debate.* Harper & Row, 1973.

[23] Charlesworth, James, ed. *Integration of the Social Sciences through Policy Analysis.* American Academy of Political and Social Science, 1972.

[24] Etzioni, Amitai. "Mixed Scanning: A 'Third' Approach to Decision-Making." *Public Administration Review* 27 (1967):385–402.

[25] Gates, Bruce. "Management Science and the Administration of Public Policy." In *Public Administration and Public Policy.* Edited by George Frederickson and Charles Wise. LexingtonBooks, D.C. Heath, 1977.

[26] Gregg, Phillip, ed. *Problems of Theory in Policy Analysis.* Lexington-Books, D.C. Heath, 1976.

[27] Horowitz, Irving. *The Use and Abuse of Social Science.* Transaction Books, 1971.

[28] Williams, Alan. "Cost-Benefit Analysis: Bastard Science and/or Insidious Poison in the Body Politik?" *Journal of Public Economics* 2 (1972):199–226.

Notes

1. Roland McKean, *Efficiency in Government through Systems Analysis* (Wiley, 1958), pp. 25–102. For general works on optimizing methods in public-policy analysis, although presenting different perspectives from this article, see Edward Quade, *Analysis for Public Decisions* (Elsevier, 1975); Guy Black, *The Application of Systems Analysis to Government Operations* (Praeger, 1969); Alvin Drake, Ralph Keeney, and Philip Morris, eds., *Analysis of Public Systems* (M.I.T. Press, 1972); and S. Nagel and M. Neef, *Operations Research Methods: As Applied to Political Science and the Legal Process* (Sage, 1976).

2. S. Nagel, "Choosing among Alternative Public Policies," in *Public Policy Evaluation,* edited by Kenneth Dolbeare (Sage, 1975), pp. 153–174.

3. S. Nagel and M. Neef, "Bail, Not Jail, for More Defendants," *Judicature* 60 (1976):172–178.

4. S. Nagel, "How to Provide Legal Counsel for the Poor: Decision Theory," in *Analyzing Poverty Policy,* edited by Dorothy James (Lexington-Books, D.C. Heath, 1975), pp. 215–222.

5. "Computers and the Law and Politics of Redistricting," in *Improving the Legal Process: Effects of Alternatives,* edited by S. Nagel (Lexington-Books, D.C. Heath, 1975), pp. 173–190.

6. S. Nagel and M. Neef, "Deductive Modeling to Determine an Optimum Jury Size and Fraction Required to Convict," *Washington University Law Quarterly* 1975 (1976):933–978.

7. S. Nagel and M. Neef, "The Policy Problem of Doing Too Much or Too Little: Pretrial Release as a Case in Point" (Sage Professional Papers in Administrative and Policy Studies, March 1977).

8. S. Nagel, "Minimizing Costs and Maximizing Benefits in Providing Legal Services to the Poor" (Sage Professional Papers in Administrative and Policy Studies, 1973).

9. S. Nagel and M. Neef, "Allocating Resources Geographically for Optimum Results," *Political Methodology,* 1976, pp. 383–404.

10. An alternative conceptualization would involve saying that in some situations, we have semantically reduced all effects to positive or negative costs. In those situations, the total benefits are zero, and the net benefits equal the total costs. Likewise, in some situations, we semantically reduce all effects to positive or negative benefits, and the net benefits then equal the total benefits.

11. S. Nagel, M. Neef, and S. Schramm, "Decision Theory and the Pretrial Release Decision in Criminal Cases," *University of Miami Law Review* 31 (1977):1433–1491.

12. S. Nagel and M. Neef, "Plea Bargaining, Decision Theory, and Equilibrium Models," *Indiana Law Journal* 51 and 52 (1976):987–1024, 1–61; and "The Impact of Plea Bargaining on the Judicial Process," *American Bar Association Journal* 62 (1976):1020–1022.

13. See S. Nagel and M. Neef, "The Policy Problem of Doing Too Much or Too Little," Sage Professional Papers in Administrative and Policy Studies, March 1977. That study involves benefit/cost data obtained from police chiefs, prosecutors, judges, defense attorneys, and bail officials in twenty-three cities.

14. See S. Nagel and M. Neef, "Deductive Modeling to Determine an Optimum Jury Size," *Washington University Law Quarterly* 1975 (1976):933–978.

15. S. Nagel and M. Neef, "The Application of Mixed Strategies: Civil Rights and Other Multiple-Activity Policies" (Sage Professional Papers in American Politics, 1976). That study involves civil-rights input-output data obtained from NAACP chapter presidents in thirty-one cities.

16. See S. Nagel and M. Neef, "Allocating Resources Geographically for Optimum Results," *Political Methodology,* 1976, pp. 383–404.

17. S. Nagel, K. Reinbolt, and T. Eimermann, "A Linear Programming Approach to Problems of Conflicting Legal Values like Free Press versus Fair Trial," *Rutgers Journal of Computers and the Law* 4 (1975): 420–461. This study involves attitudinal questionnaire data obtained from about 250 police chiefs, prosecutors, defense attorneys, and newspaper editors.

18. William Baumol, *Portfolio Theory: The Selection of Asset Combinations* (McCaleb-Seiler, 1970).

19. Peter Aranson, "Post Conviction Decisions in Criminal Justice," Research proposal to the Law Enforcement Assistance Administration, 1975.

20. Jack Byrd, Jr., *Operations Research Models for Public Administration* (LexingtonBooks, D.C. Heath, 1975), pp. 115–220; and Haig Bohigian, *The Foundations and Mathematical Models of Operations Research with Extensions to the Criminal Justice System* (Gazette, 1971), pp. 171–247.

21. For other discussions of value decisions in policy analysis, see Phillip Gregg, ed., *Problems of Theory in Policy Analysis* (LexingtonBooks, D.C. Heath, 1976); Duncan MacRae, Jr., *The Social Function of Social Science* (Yale University Press, 1976); Gideon Sjoberg, "Politics, Ethics and Evaluation Research," in Guttentag, ed., *Handbook of Evaluation Research* (Sage, 1975), pp. 29–51; Laurence Tribe, "Policy Sciences: Analysis or Ideology?" *Philosophy and Public Affairs* 2 (1973): 66–110; Peter Brown, "Ethics and Policy Research," *Policy Analysis* 2 (1976): 325–340; and S. Nagel, ed., *Policy Studies and the Social Sciences* (LexingtonBooks, D.C. Heath, 1975) (part VI deals with social philosophy and includes relevant chapters by John Ladd, Eugene Meehan, and Martin Golding).

10 Disciplinary Contributions to Policy Studies

Policy Studies Across the Social Sciences

Policy studies or policy analysis can be broadly defined as the study of the nature, causes, and effects of alternative public policies. All fields of scientific knowledge, but especially the social sciences, are relevant to such a study. The main purpose of this book is to discuss some aspects of the dovetailing potential contributions to policy studies of each of the social sciences, along with appropriate bibliographic references. For discussions of the interdisciplinary nature of policy studies in general, see Duncan MacRae, Jr., *The Social Function of Social Sciences* (Yale University Press, 1976); James Charlesworth, *Integration of Social Sciences through Policy Analysis* (American Academy of Political and Social Science, 1972); Stuart Nagel, ed., *Policy Studies and the Social Sciences* (LexingtonBooks, D.C. Heath, 1975); and George Webber and George McCall, *Social Scientists as Advocates: Views from the Applied Disciplines* (Sage, 1978).

Although there are differences of opinion on the relevance of various social sciences for policy-studies research and teaching, there seems to be agreement on some of the basic aspects of what each social science may have to contribute to policy causal analysis and policy-evaluation analysis. Sociology, for example, has developed a substantial amount of factual knowledge and theory in broad fields such as social control, socialization, and social change which can be helpful in understanding the effects of alternative policies and the behavior of policymakers and policy appliers. Sociology is also especially concerned with why certain societal practices are considered social problems and how society seeks to cope with them. Sociology has also attempted to cover (more so than other social sciences) the special policy problems of race relations, family problems, and criminology. On sociology and policy studies, see Paul Lazarsfeld and Jeffrey Reitz, *An Introduction to Applied Sociology* (Elsevier, 1975); N.J. Demerath, Otto Larsen, and Karl Schuessler, *Social Policy and Sociology* (Academic Press, 1975); Alvin Gouldner and S.M. Miller, eds., *Applied Sociology: Opportunities and Problems* (Free Press, 1965); and Paul Lazarsfeld, William Sewell, and Harold Wilensky, eds., *The Uses of Sociology* (Basic Books, 1967).

Of all the social sciences, clearly the field of economics has developed the most sophisticated mathematical models for synthesizing normative and empirical premises in order to deduce means-ends policy recommendation. These mathematical models relate to the optimum allocation of scarce resources, the optimum level at which to pursue a given policy which has a curvilinear relation with net benefits achieved, and the optimum strategy to follow when the net benefits achievable are dependent on the occurrence of a contingent event. Economic reasoning, which assumes people attempt to maximize their perceived benefits minus costs, can often lead to deductive models which enable one to predict the effects of some policies before they are adopted. Institutional economists have been especially relevant in discussing the role of economic class structures, ownership systems, and technology in determining policy choices. Economics has also concerned itself, more so than other social sciences, with the specific policy problems of union-management relations, consumer problems, unemployment, and inflation. On economics and policy studies, see Ryan Amacher, Robert Tollison, and Thomas Willett, eds., *The Economic Approach to Public Policy* (Cornell University Press, 1976); Llad Phillips and Harold Votey, Jr., eds., *Economic Analysis of Pressing Social Problems* (Rand McNally, 1977); and Robert Haveman and Robert Hamrin, eds., *The Political Economy of Federal Policy* (Harper & Row, 1973).

Anthropology, geography, and history provide a broader perspective than the other social sciences. That kind of cross-cultural and historical perspective can help to make policy analysis less culture-bound and less time-bound. The theoretical and practical findings of policy studies thereby become more broadly meaningful when the causes and effects of alternative public policies are dealt with. Anthropology also has a special relevance to policy problems that affect present or former preliterate peoples. Geographers are becoming increasingly concerned with the optimum location of various facilities or districts. By extrapolating trends or analogizing to the past historians can add a futuristic element of policy studies. On anthropology, geography, and history in a policy-studies context, see H. Barnett, *Anthropology in Administration* (Row Peterson, 1956); R. Bastide, *Applied Anthropology* (Harper & Row, 1973); G. Foster, *Applied Anthropology* (Little, Brown, 1969); David Harvey, *Social Justice and the City* (Johns Hopkins University Press, 1973); Gilbert White, "Geography and Public Policy" [*Professional Geographer* 24 (1972):103]; David Landes and Charles Tilly, *History as Social Science* (Prentice-Hall, 1971).

Without philosophy, especially normative social philosophy, policy studies might tend to lack direction with regard to what it seeks to achieve. Indeed, one of the major criticisms of quantitative policy analysis is that it is too capable of being used to maximize socially undesirable goals as well as socially desirable ones. Philosophy, in spite of its contemporary emphasis on positivism, is still the leading discipline for discussing what is socially desirable on a high level of abstraction. Philosophy also provides a high level of abstraction with regard to discussing ultimate-type causes as to why societies make certain basic policy choices. In addition to its normative and causal components, philosophy provides the most developed principles of logical and semantic analysis on which the more narrow social sciences can build. On philosophy and social studies, see Phillip Gregg, ed., *Problems of Theory in Policy Analysis* (LexingtonBooks, D.C. Heath, 1976); Duncan MacRae, Jr., *The Social Function of Social Science* (Yale University Press, 1976); and Peter Brown, "Ethics and Policy Research" [*Policy Analysis* 2 (1976):325–340].

Without the quantitative and computer-science tools that are ultimately associated with *mathematics,* policy studies might tend to overemphasize evaluative gut reactions, armchair speculation, and isolated historical anecdotes. Mathematics provides the basis for both an empirical, statistical approach to policy studies and a deductive, syllogistic approach. Through the mathematics of algebraic equations and the calculus of change, the syllogistic premises can take on a much greater precision than is provided by the kind of dichotomous reasoning normally associated with symbolic logic. Physical and biological sciences to some extent provide models to emulate in the development of mathematically scientific laws, provided one always considers the differences in the behavioral instability of people as compared to physical or biological objects. Natural science is also quite relevant substantively to certain specific policy problems, such as environmental protection, energy development, and population control. On mathematics and policy studies, see William Fairley and Frederick Mosteller, eds., *Statistics and Public Policy* (Addison-Wesley, 1977); Martin Greenberger, Matthew Crenson, and Brian Crissey, *Models in the Policy Process* (Russell Sage, 1976); and Edward Tufte, ed., *The Quantitative Analysis of Social Problems* (Addison-Wesley, 1970).

The field of law has important social-science elements when it involves studying why the law is what it is or the effects of alternative laws, as contrasted to what the law is and how to use it as a lawyer. As a social science, the legal field is close to the heart of policy studies because virtually all policy problems are capable of at least attempted solution by legislatures, courts, or lawmaking administrative agencies. Legal literature can be helpful in generating policy hypotheses, providing large quantities of data, especially with regard to policy decisions, and providing a better understanding of the societal rules which relate to the problems of such institutions as the family, the economy, and the criminal-justice system. On law and policy studies, see Jay Sigler and Benjamin Beede, *The Legal Sources of Public Policy* (LexingtonBooks, D.C. Heath, 1977); Richard Posner, *Economic Analysis of Law* (Little, Brown, 1977); Stuart Nagel and Marian Neef, *Legal Policy Analysis: Finding an*

Optimum Level or Mix (LexingtonBooks, D.C. Heath, 1977); and F.R. Marks, *The Lawyer, the Public, and Professional Responsibility* (American Bar Foundation, 1972).

Since policy studies particularly refers to the study of the causes and effects of government policy, one would expect political science to be especially relevant, even though political scientists may be very dependent on other social sciences for a variety of methodological tools and substantive knowledge. Traditionally political scientists have devoted much of their intellectual resources to analyzing how government policy is made and administered, with special emphasis on the role of interest groups and, more recently, of individual decisionmakers. Political scientists are now turning more toward the analysis of specific policy-problem areas (such as welfare and taxation) rather than more abstract studies of the policy-making process. Along with this concern for specific policy problems, political scientists have shown increasing interest in studying the impact of various policies, such as those in the civil-liberties field. Along with civil liberties, the subject matter of political science has made the discipline especially relevant to policy problems related to the reform of elections, legislatures, courts, administrative agencies, and reform of other government institutions, as well as relevant to problems of international relations and foreign policy. On political science and policy studies, see Austin Ranney, ed., *Political Science and Public Policy* (Markham, 1968); Robert Spadaro, Thomas Dye, Robert Goliembiewski, Murray Stedman, and L. Harmon Zeigler, *The Policy Vacuum: Toward a More Professional Political Science* (LexingtonBooks, D.C. Heath, 1975); and Ira Sharkansky, *Policy Analysis in Political Science* (Markham, 1970).

From this material one can probably conclude that the study of government policy problems is indeed an *interdisciplinary* activity, at least in the sense that many disciplines have something to contribute. For any social scientist, it would be too much to acquire expertise in all the relevant perspectives. Indeed, it is too much to become an expert in all the subfields within one's own social science. Nevertheless, if one is interested in developing competence in policy-studies work, she or he would probably be familiar in a general way with the potential contributions and drawbacks of the various social sciences. Such familiarity will at least enable one to know when to call on another social scientist or a treatise in another social science, just as a layperson has a general idea of the meaning of what the doctor or lawyer says.

Policy Studies by Political-Science Fields

Policy studies can be defined as the study of the nature, causes, and effects of public policies, with a special emphasis on the systematic evaluation of alternative policies for achieving given goals. *Public policies,* in turn, can be defined as the ways in which a society seeks to deal with problems relating to its effective operation. Thus political science is especially relevant to policy studies because political science, by definition, is concerned with societal decision making.

More specifically, political scientists have developed a body of knowledge concerning how government policy is adopted and administered, with special emphasis on the role of government institutions and interest groups and more recently on the role of individual decisionmakers. Now political scientists are showing increasing concern for studying policy formation or determinants, and implementation or impact with regard to all major policy problems, literally from A to Z as reflected in studies of air pollution by Charles Jones and studies of zoning and housing by Harold Wolman.

The purpose of this section is not to indicate how political science as a whole is relevant to policy studies as compared to other disciplines. That has been done elsewhere. Rather the purpose is to indicate how each field within political science is relevant to policy studies and how a policy-studies perspective is becoming increasingly important within each field of political science. Political-science fields can be organized in terms of government institutions, levels of government, and general matters. Fields emphasizing certain government institutions include public law (courts), public administration (executive agencies), the legislative process (legislatures), and political dynamics (voters, interest groups, and parties). Fields emphasizing levels of government include state and local government, U.S. government, comparative government, and international relations. The more general fields include political theory and political-science methodology.

On the relation between political science in general and policy studies, see Austin Ranney, ed., *Political Science and Public Policy* (Markham, 1968); Robert Spadaro, Thomas Dye, Robert Golembiewski, Murray Stedman, and L. Harmon Zeigler, *The Policy Vacuum: Toward a More Professional Political Science* (LexingtonBooks, Heath, D.C. 1975); Ira Sharkansky, ed., *Policy Analysis in Political Science* (Markham, 1970); and S. Nagel, ed., *Policy Studies in America and Elsewhere* (LexingtonBooks, D.C. Heath, 1975).

Governmental and Political Institutions

Public Law and the Courts. The field of public law traditionally has been concerned with policy analysis in the sense that public-law teachers and researchers have always been analyzing the nature of Supreme Court policies and often speculating on their causes and evaluating their effects. Public-law people have developed a special competence with regard to such policy problems as those relating to freedom of speech, fair procedure in criminal and civil proceedings, equality of opportunity for minorities, and judicial reform to enable the courts to operate more efficiently. That competence has extended to being cited in Supreme Court cases and by other government policymakers in these fields. Political scientists from the public-law field recently have been cited before the Supreme Court in cases dealing with acceptable jury sizes, search and seizure, and voting rights.

On a more general level, the public-law field is especially relevant to evaluating alternative public policies by clarifying the constitutional and legal-system constraints that should be taken into consideration. For example, a paper on a 1975 APSA panel discussed the possibility of providing shorter sentences for higher-salaried defendants in order to avoid the lost GNP that would be incurred by imprisoning such people. The same paper discussed the possibility of providing longer sentences for black defendants in order to avoid what was thought to be higher recidivism (crime-repeating) costs among black defendants. The paper, however, did not discuss the constitutional constraints by way of the equal-protection clause with regard to having explicitly differential sentences along class or racial lines.

The public-law field also may clarify the drawbacks of policies that rely on court enforcement rather than administrative enforcement in implementing policy goals. The dissertation research of Charles Hamilton showed, for example, the folly of relying on a case-by-case approach to get blacks registered in the South, as contrasted to the system of federal registrars which was established by the 1965 Voting Rights Act. Some of that dissertation research may have played a part in the enactment of that important statute. Likewise, the research of Jack Peltason showed the folly of relying on a case-by-case approach to get Southern schools desegregated, as contrasted to the administrative enforcement of HEW, especially after the passage of the federal aid-to-education legislation of 1964.

Bibliography on Public Law and Policy Studies

[1] Becker, Theodore, and Feeley, Malcolm, eds. *The Impact of Supreme Court Decisions.* Oxford, 1973.
[2] Casper, Jonathan. *The Politics of Civil Liberties.* Harper & Row, 1972.
[3] Gardiner, John, ed. *Public Law and Public Policy.* Praeger, 1977.
[4] Jacob, Herbert, ed. *The Potential for Reform of Criminal Justice.* Sage, 1974.
[5] Nagel, Stuart. *Improving the Legal Process: Effects of Alternatives.* LexingtonBooks, D.C. Heath, 1975.
[6] Sigler, Jay. *American Rights Policies.* Dorsey, 1975.
[7] Wasby, Stephen, ed. *Civil Liberties: Policy and Policy Making.* LexingtonBooks, D.C. Heath, 1976.

Public Administration and the Executive Agencies. The field of public administration has long been concerned with how to administer policies more effectively in order to achieve given goals. Also relevant is the interest of public administrators in developing government structures that can produce a greater degree of goal achievement. The budgeting field within public administration has become particularly important as an area focusing on how to explain and evaluate alternative allocation decisions. Contemporary public administration discusses the improvement of public administration, not in terms of intuitive clichés about the need for hiring more competent people and spending money more efficiently. It has also moved beyond the institutional description of hiring rules and budgeting procedures. Instead, there is now more emphasis on the psychology of organizational behavior and allocating in accordance with a combination of incrementalism, functionalism, and management science.

On a more general level, public administration may be especially relevant to clarifying alternative administrative arrangements for implementing government policies. For example, in the field of housing policy, economists in the late 1960s often recommended government programs designed to convert poor people from tenants to homeowners. In theory, the idea sounds find. By becoming homeowners, poor people would have a greater stake in their dwelling units and thus take better care of them. They would be especially unlikely to burn them down, as they were sometimes doing during the 1960s. By becoming homeowners, poor people might acquire a more positive self-image and a more favorable attitude toward society, thereby becoming better citizens in ways other than just taking better care of their homes. Partly in reliance on that kind of economic analysis, the Nixon administration pushed a homeownership program for the poor that would involve government-guaranteed mortgages with low payments per month comparable to what the Federal Housing Authority for years had been providing for middle-class people. The program turned out to be a rather dismal failure. Homes were sold to poor people at inflated assessments often as a result of sellers bribing government assessors to exaggerate the value of the homes in order to increase the government guarantee. Homes were also sold to poor people without their being adequately informed of the expensive maintenance costs and defects in the plumbing, heating, or electrical systems. As a result, maintenance and repair costs often were too high for poor people to handle, and they used the mortgage payments for repairs, thereby incurring foreclosures. Some of those foreclosed houses exchanged hands more times than a repossessed used car, since houses are normally more durable than cars. The program was wracked with the same kind of supplier fraud as the Medicaid and Medicare programs with doctors, dentists, pharmacists, optometrists, nursing-home owners, and others overcharging for services rendered and not rendered.

What may have been needed in designing the program is more concern for the effects of alternative administrative systems. Perhaps a big mistake of the

Nixon homeownership program was that it involved government funding through the private-sector real-estate system. An alternative way of administering or delivering the program would be for salaried government employees to sell homes to the poor that the government would have previously obtained by tax foreclosures, government purchases, or government construction. Salaried government employees selling government-owned housing to poor people would have no incentive to inflate the assessed valuation of the property or to withhold information on likely maintenance or repair costs. An analogous government program is the Legal Services Corporation, which consists of salaried government attorneys providing legal services to the poor. No attorney from the Legal Services Corporation or its predecessor, the OEO Legal Services Agency, has been involved in any scandal related to overcharging the poor for actual or fictitious services. Such a system would be administratively feasible for selling houses or supplying medical services to the poor. However, the system might not be politically feasible for medical services, given the fear of the American Medical Association that such a system would lead to socialized government medicine for the total population. There is no likelihood that the government is going to go into the real-estate business for the total population, and thus having salaried government homefinders for the poor might be politically feasible.

The negative income-tax experiments represent another related example where economic modeling may have missed some important insights by not adequately considering alternative administrative systems. More specifically, over $10 million was spent in New Jersey to test such relations as the effects on getting a job or being given alternative amounts of money. Families were randomly assigned to various income-receiving groups. One group may have received enough money to satisfy only about 33 percent of minimum needs, as is done under the Mississippi welfare system; a second group may have received income at the 66 percent level, which corresponds roughly to the Texas welfare system; and a third group may have received income at the 100 percent level, which is what most Northeastern states provide. Conservatives hypothesize that as welfare payments go up, ambition to get a job goes down because the welfare recipient has less need for a job. Liberals hypothesize that as low welfare payments go up, ambition to get a job may also go up, because the welfare recipient may have his or her appetite whetted and expectations raised. The true relation might involve job getting going up to a point and then going down. The expensive experiment, however, shows a rather flat relation between job getting and welfare payments within the monetary range of the experiment.

Perhaps, however, a much steeper relation might have been observed if the families had been randomly assigned to alternative delivery systems as well as, or instead of, alternative welfare amounts. The basic alternative delivery system consists of the compulsory caseworker, as exists under the present aid-to-dependent-children system, or the check in the mail, which is associated with the negative-income-tax system that seeks to minimize administrative interference in the lives of the poor. On one hand, maybe the compulsory caseworker stimulates job getting by informing the welfare recipient about available jobs or by harrassing the welfare recipient into taking a job. On the other hand, maybe the compulsory caseworker lowers the self-esteem of the welfare recipient and makes him or her more dependent than would be the case in the absence of a caseworker. Unfortunately, that kind of alternative administrative hypothesis was never tested, possibly because of a lack of participation by public-administration people in the negative-income-tax experiments.

Bibliography on Public Administration and Policy Studies

[1] Frederickson, George, and Wise, Charles, eds. *Public Administration and Public Policy.* LexingtonBooks, D.C. Heath, 1977.
[2] Golembiewski, Robert. *Public Administration as a Developing Discipline.* Marcel Dekker, 1977.
[3] Henry, Nicholas. *Public Administration and Public Affairs.* Prentice-Hall, 1975.
[4] Marini, Frank, ed. *A New Public Administration: The Minnowbrook Perspective.* Chandler, 1971.
[5] Mosher, Frederick. *Democracy and the Public Service.* Oxford University Press, 1968.
[6] Ostrom, Vincent. *The Intellectual Crisis in American Public Administration.* University of Albama, 1974.
[7] Pressman, Jeffrey, and Wildavsky, Aaron. *Implementation.* University of California, 1973.
[8] Reagan, Michael. *The Administration of Public Policy.* Scott, Foresman, 1969.
[9] Rourke, Francis. *Bureaucracy, Politics, and Public Policy.* Little, Brown, 1972.

The Legislative Process. The legislative-process field within political science is partly concerned with reforming or improving legislative procedures, so as to increase the legislative outputs and their impact (as a measure of effectiveness), decrease unnecessary time consumption and expense (as a measure of efficiency), and increase the representativeness of legislative bodies (as a measure of equity). The legislative-reform literature deals with such specific issues as the seniority system for choosing committee chairpersons, the power of committees in approving or blocking votes on bills, rules governing filibustering and speaking arrangements, the number of committees and how legislators are assigned to them, ethics within legislatures, supportive staffs and policy information, devices to stimulate party responsibility, and relations with executive agencies.

On a more general level, the legislative-process field may be especially relevant to clarifying legislative constraints that prevent government policies from being adopted and that also clarify how those constraints can sometimes be overcome in order to facilitate policy adoption. For example, for years liberals in the Senate sought to pass legislation to regulate the oil industry, but were unable to do so given the power of the industry. That power was partly based on making large campaign contributions. The power may have rested more, however, on historical accidents that could not be readily overcome by merely passing laws regulating the financing of congressional campaigns. The historical accidents included the interrelations of (1) the dominance of the Democratic Party in Congress since 1932, partly because of the severe Republican defeat resulting from the Depression and the advent of the New Deal; (2) the division within the Democratic Party between the North and the South stemming from the Civil War; (3) the logical tendency of the Democrats to pick their leaders from border states such as Texas and Oklahoma (for example, Lyndon Johnson and Sam Rayburn) in order to attempt to draw together the regional factions; and (4) the coincidence of those two states being the major oil states in the United States. The power of the oil industry to defeat attempts to repeal the depletion allowance or import quotas could be broken only when the worldwide oil shortage of the 1970s began, and the oil industry could then prosper greatly without the indirect government subsidies of the depletion allowance and import quotas.

Another example of where an understanding of the legislative process can help provide insights into matters of legislative feasibility is in farm price supports. A favorite solution of some economists to the problem of inadequate farm income is the Brannan plan, whereby farm families who have less than a minimum level of income are subsidized by the government enough to bring them up to a minimum level. Such a solution has the advantages of (1) making clear the costs of boosting farm income and thereby facilitating a benefit/cost analysis, (2) excluding farmers who do not need government support in order to achieve a minimum income level, and (3) allowing the prices of farm products to fall to a natural unsupported level to the benefit of consumers and the free market. All those economic advantages represent political disadvantages. The farmers receiving such direct support resent that type of program because it sounds like a welfare program. The well-off and politically powerful farmers not receiving support under that type of program might resent having their present support withdrawn. In the past, in general farmers have preferred and obtained indirect supports that increase demand, decrease supply, and thus increase prices. What may ultimately enable the economic optimum and the politically feasible to come together is the reduction in the power of farm interests as a result of the decreased quantity of farmers. An understanding of the farm-bloc senators and their ability to control farm legislation is necessary to evaluate the legislative feasibility of alternative farm-support proposals.

Bibliography on the Legislative Process
and Policy Studies

[1] Clausen, Aage R. *How Congressmen Decide: A Policy Focus.* St. Martins Press, 1975.

[2] Davidson, Roger, Kovenock, David; and O'Leary, Michael. *Congress in Crisis: Politics and Congressional Reform.* Wadsworth, 1966.

[3] Herzberg, Donald, and Rosenthal, Alan, eds. *Strengthening the States: Essays on Legislative Reform.* Doubleday, 1972.

[4] Ornstein, Norman, ed. *Congress in Change: Evolution and Reform.* Praeger, 1975.

[5] Rieselbach, Leroy. *Legislative Reform.* LexingtonBooks, D.C. Heath, 1977.

[6] Rieselbach, Leroy. *People vs. Government: The Responsiveness of American Institutions.* Indiana University Press, 1975.

[7] Ripley, Randall. *Congress: Process and Policy.* Norton, 1974.

[8] Welch, Susan, and Peters, John, eds. *The Impact of Legislative Reform.* Praeger, 1977.

Political Dynamics concerning the Public, Pressure Groups, and Parties. The political-dynamics field is concerned with voting behavior, public opinion, the role of interest or pressure groups, and political parties. Political scientists in that field contribute directly to policy evaluation when they attempt to improve the electoral process by analyzing the effects of alternative redistricting criteria, registration methods, voting procedures, changes in the electoral college, government funding of elections, campaign allocation strategies, nomination systems, and eligibility rules.

A good example of the influence of political-science voting-behavior experts might include the role of Steven Brams in attempting to convince the New Hampshire legislature that it should adopt approval voting for the Presidential primary, whereby voters indicate approval or disapproval for each candidate. Such a system would attract centrist Presidential aspirants without fear of splitting the vote among themselves since centrist voters can vote for all of them. Such a system would also attract noncentrist aspirants since noncentrist voters need not worry about wasting their one vote under such a system.

Another example might be the role of political scientists in developing the Voting Rights Act of 1965. The work of Donald Matthews and James Prothro showed that literacy tests were the key factor which correlated with low black voter registration across Southern counties rather than lynchings or other violent activities. This pointed up the need to avoid emotional antilynching laws and to stress having objective registration requirements. They also showed the need for abolishing the poll tax in view of the correlation between its presence and relatively low black voter registration among the Southern counties. That kind of political-science analysis aided the campaign for the Twenty-fourth Amendment abolishing poll taxes.

On a more general level, a study of the role of interest groups may be especially important to evaluating the political feasibility of alternative public policies. For example, in the field of environmental policy, often economists recommend some form of pollution tax, discharge fee, or effluent charge in order to minimize pollution. Such a tax in the water-pollution field might involve requiring all firms on a given river segment to be taxed in accordance with the amount of pollution generated by each firm. Before the tax was levied, engineers could determine the total cost of keeping the river segment at a given quality level by building a downstream filtration plant. If that total cost were $10 million a year and a firm contributes 5 percent of the pollution in the river segment, then it should pay 5 percent of the $10 million. Under such a system, each firm would have an incentive to reduce its pollution in order to reduce its assessment. If reducing its pollution is more expensive than the assessment, the firm can pay the assessment, which can then be used to clean up the river segment before the pollutants damage downstream communities. The main advantage of such a system is that it internalizes the cost of the external damage that business firms are doing by polluting rivers or other water systems. In the absence of such a system, the costs are absorbed by the general public in the form of waterborne diseases and general taxes; thus the potential deterrent effect of a pollution tax is lost.

That economic advantage, however, is the main political disadvantage of such a system. By making the business firms so explicitly bear the costs of their expensive pollution, they would be aroused to exert great efforts to prevent such legislation from being adopted. If the sky over Washington was supposedly dark with Lear jets when the Carter administration sought to deregulate natural gas, one can imagine how black the sky would be if the Carter administration were to propose a pollution tax which would affect virtually all industries, not just the natural-gas industry. The political infeasibility of such a solution to the pollution problem under present circumstances is illustrated by the fact that when Congress established the National Water Quality Commission, the Commission was prohibited from even investigating the pollution tax as an alternative to the regulatory antipollution system which is part of the 1972 water-pollution legislation and the 1970 air-pollution legislation. Therefore, what may be needed as a politically feasible antipollution policy is more indirect and selective approaches. These include federal government subsidies to municipalities and tax rewards to business firms. In other words, legislation that subsidizes is generally more politically feasible than legislation that taxes, especially legislation that taxes business firms. Politically feasible antipollution policies also include ones that emphasize case-by-case litigation through the courts, rather than an expensive blanket requirement for a given industry. Thus business interests do not seem to be as opposed to allowing rare or occasional damage suits, injunctions, or even fines as contrasted to prohibiting automobiles or cigarettes that exceed strict pollution thresholds. Therefore an optimum antipollution policy could be defined as one that minimizes pollution within the political constraints of present adoptability.

Tariff reduction is another example of a policy almost universally endorsed by economists. The endorsement, however, is generally made without adequately considering whose ox is going to be gored and how to minimize that perceived damage. In 1930, thousands of economists signed petitions calling on the Hoover administration to reduce tariffs in order to facilitate international trade. The Hoover administration, however, raised tariffs in order to satisfy the political demands of the numerous business firms that felt they needed such protection from foreign competition. Instead of simply cutting tariffs, it would have been more politically feasible to provide substitutes along with the tariff reductions, as was learned subsequent to World War II. Those tariff-offsetting sweeteners have included negotiating reciprocal tariff reductions, offering government credit and aid to facilitate foreign purchases of U.S. goods, and providing government subsidies or tax benefits to industries and firms hurt by tariff reductions.

Bibliography on Political Dynamics and Policy Studies

[1] Carlson, Richard, ed. *Issues on Electoral Reform*. National Municipal League, 1974.

[2] Crotty, William. *Political Reform and the American Experiment.* Thomas Crowell, 1977.

[3] Lehnen, Robert. *American Institutions, Public Opinion, and Public Policy.* Dryden Press, 1976.

[4] Luttbeg, Norman, ed. *Public Opinion and Public Policy.* Dorsey, 1974.

[5] Rae, Douglas. *The Political Consequences of Electoral Laws.* Yale University Press, 1966.

[6] Ranney, Austin. *The Doctrine of Responsible Party Government.* University of Illinois Press, 1962.

[7] Tufte, Edward, ed. *Electoral Reform.* Symposium issue of the *Policy Studies Journal,* 1974.

[8] Weisberg, Robert. *Public Opinion and Popular Government.* Prentice-Hall, 1976.

[9] Zisk, Betty. *Local Interest Politics.* Bobbs-Merrill, 1973.

Levels of Government

State and Local Governments. The field of state and local governments now tends to emphasize urban affairs, because urban areas tend to increasingly dominate state governments and consume an increasingly larger percentage of the population. Analyzing the urban political-affairs literature, one observes that six policy problems tend to be emphasized: housing, transportation, poverty, crime, education, and pollution. Within each a number of issues have been addressed by political scientists interested in urban-policy problems.

One set of housing issues relates to providing adequate housing for low-income people. Those issues include (1) eligibility criteria and processing procedures for government-aided housing; (2) the use of clustered public housing versus scattered-site public housing; (3) a balance between government-owned housing and government rent or building subsidies in private landlord-tenant relations; (4) government programs to facilitate home ownership for the poor; (5) urban renewal and rehabilitation procedures; (6) government policy toward reducing racially segregated public and private housing; and (7) issues dealing with allowable defenses in landlord-tenant disputes over rent or housing conditions. Many of these issues also affect middle-class housing problems.

Urban-transportation issues include (1) developing a rapid-transit rail and subway system, including how to finance it and what neighborhoods or communities it should service; (2) the location of urban airports, railroad stations, and bus terminals; (3) the development of urban freeways and the accompanying problems of condemning land to create the freeways; (4) regulating, subsidizing, and municipal ownership of urban bus systems; (5) providing for special segments of the population, such as senior citizens, school children, and low-income people; (6) regulation of taxis, trucking companies, delivery services, the transportation of dangerous products, and other specialized transportation matters; and (7) nontransportation problems that also affect the urban transportation industry, such as pollution, crime, labor relations, consumer safety, and energy consumption.

The main poverty issues deal with matters of income maintenance and welfare, or how to provide funds to bring poor people closer to a minimum annual family income. Subissues of that general controversy relate to (1) whether welfare programs should be decentralized with different standards and procedures in each state or a more uniform approach taken throughout the country; (2) how welfare payments should be related to employment incentives, especially where one or two parents are capable of working; (3) what the eligibility criteria, benefit levels, and obligations to repay should be; and (4) what procedures should be provided for investigations, caseworkers, and hearings. Other important poverty issues deal with the problems of poor people in various roles which they have in common with other people, but in which poverty increases the likelihood of being taken advantage of. These roles include (1) being an employee with little bargaining power for better wages, hours, working conditions, and nondiscriminatory treatment; (2) being a tenant who may be more subject to housing-code violations in private housing and lack of due process in public housing; (3) being a consumer more subject to credit-collection abuses, broken warranties, and defective merchandise; (4) being a family member where charges of delinquency, neglect, and abuse may be more prevalent; (5) being a person more lacking in good health and in the funds and facilities to obtain it; and (6) being a child who is provided with relatively poor school facilities and possibly other government services.

The crime field basically involves two sets of somewhat conflicting issues. On the one hand are the issues that relate to how to reduce street crime, white-collar crime, and criminal behavior by public officials. On the other hand are issues that relate to how to safeguard the innocent from conviction and harassment by criminal-justice decisionmakers. Methods for reducing crime tend to relate to three kinds of activities. One kind of activity involves increasing the probabilities of wrongdoing being detected, adjudicated, and negatively sanctioned. Increasing those three probabilities may require greater professionalism on the part of criminal-justice decisionmakers, although some advocate increasing those probabilities by relaxing the constraints on police surveillance, evidence needed for convictions, and the imposition of severe penalties such as capital punishment. A second kind of activity involves decreasing the benefits that come from illegal behavior. Doing that may require changing the nature of peer-group recognition and hardening the targets of criminal wrongdoers. A third kind of activity involves increasing the costs that come from illegal behavior. For many people that means longer prison sentences under harsher conditions, but for other people that might mean increasing the realistic opportunities lost as a result of illegal behavior, which may be the main reason middle-class people do not take the risks involved in committing street crimes.

Urban educational issues especially deal with (1) desegreation of students and faculty; (2) allocating government funds and personnel to schools in low-income areas; (3) how to find the tax money to support a school system when antitax voters often control bond issues and changes in tax-assessment rates; (4) government regulation and mediation relevant to the unionization of educational personnel, collective bargaining, and strikes; (5) the involvement of the courts in suspensions, dismissals, and disciplinary proceedings of students and faculty; (6) the role of the government with regard to parochial schools and religious education; (7) the need for special education programs for the handicapped, non-English-speaking, culturally deprived, and other groups; (8) providing balance in the curriculum among classical, vocational, life-adjustment, college preparation, and other educational goals; and (9) providing both citizen involvement and independent professionalism in the administration of the schools.

Urban environmental protection involves a number of major issues. The main issue concerns the extent to which the effects of various types of pollution are detrimental enough to warrant large-scale regulatory and grant programs. Water pollution, for example, is damaging to public health, recreation, aesthetics, commerical fishing, agriculture, and industrial water supplies. Air pollution is damaging even more so to public health because of the inability to clean the air, as well as damaging to plant life, materials, visibility, and climate. However, massive environmental programs use resources and human effort that could be better devoted to problems of domestic and worldwide poverty. Such programs may also interfere with industrial production and the raising of living standards. Sometimes there may also be too much emphasis in environmental programs on middle-class aesthetics and recreation, as contrasted to the public-health problems of pollution, especially in inner-city areas. The concern for developing new energy sources may also sometimes conflict with environmental standards, although energy conservation and environmental protection tend to go together. Other important environmental-protection issues deal with such matters as (1) devising government structures to reduce pollution, which is a public-administration matter; (2) devising government procedures to reduce pollution, which is largely an administrative-law matter; (3) devising pollution-reducing incentives, which is where environmental economics can be especially helpful; and (4) partly philosophical issues such as whether and how to compensate victims of pollution, provide for displaced workers, and protect consumers from bearing anti-pollution costs. Pollution problems in the inner city are worse than in the suburbs or in rural areas with regard to polluted air, water, noise, solid waste, and land use. Radiation pollution is the only major form of pollution that may be more of a problem in rural areas than in cities, given the more frequent location of nuclear reactors in rural areas.

Bibliography on State and Local Governments and Policy Studies

[1] Bish, Robert, and Ostrom, Vincent. *Understanding Urban Government: Metropolitan Reform Reconsidered.* American Enterprise Institute for Public Policy Research, 1973.

[2] Dye, Thomas R. *Politics, Economics, and the Public: Policy Outcomes in the American States.* Rand McNally, 1966.

[3] Levy, Frank; Meltsner, Arnold; and Wildavsky, Aaron. *Urban Outcomes: Schools, Streets and Libraries.* University of California Press, 1974.

[4] Lineberry, Robert, and Masotti, Louis, eds. *Urban Problems and Public Policy.* LexingtonBooks, D.C. Heath, 1975.

[5] Lineberry, Robert, and Sharkansky, Ira. *Urban Politics and Public Policy.* Harper & Row, 1978.

[6] Ostrom, Elinor, ed. *The Delivery of Urban Services: Outcomes of Change.* Sage, 1976.

[7] Palley, Marian, and Palley, Howard. *Urban America and Public Policies.* D.C. Heath, 1977.

[8] Sharkansky, Ira. *The Maligned States: Policy Accomplishments, Problems and Opportunities.* McGraw-Hill, 1972.

[9] Wilson, James, (ed.) *City Politics and Public Policies* (Wiley, 1968).

Federal Government. The importance of the federal government in understanding U.S. policy outputs, and vice versa, can be seen by analyzing the relations shown in figure 10–1. The figure lists five basic characteristics of the federal government: federalism, separation of powers, judicial review, a two-party system with weak ideologies, and democracy manifesting itself through universal adult voting rights while allowing freedom for minority viewpoints to try to convert the majority. The figure relates those five characteristics to the key domestic policy of having a regulatory and welfare-oriented government and the key foreign policy which emphasizes competition with the Soviet Union for international influence. Each of the government structures influences, and is in turn influenced by, each of those two public policies, thereby generating twenty relations, ten for each of the two policies, five in each reciprocal direction.

Beginning with relation 1, we see that federalism has had some important effects on government regulation. It has made government regulation more decentralized than would otherwise be so (for example, telephone company regulation). It has provided testing grounds for new forms of government regulation in particular states (for example, workmen's compensation in Wisconsin). It has also provided a less uniform regulatory program than a unitary government system would, with accompanying possibilities of intergovernmental conflict (for example, trucking regulation) and of intergovernmental vacuums (for example, union-management regulation). Government regulation also has a feedback effect on federalism. Increased responsibility has tended to increase the power of both the federal and the state governments; but, relatively speaking, the increase has been substantially greater at the federal level because to be effective, so many regulatory programs require

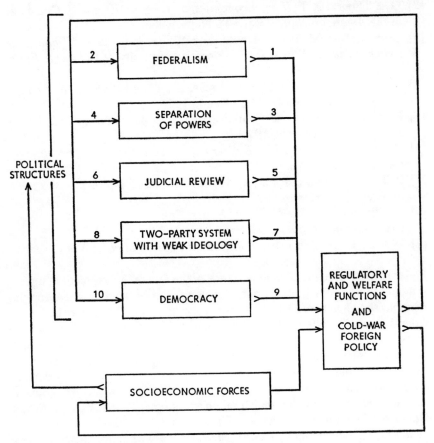

Figure 10–1. Mutual Relations Between U.S. Government Structures and Functions

interstate regulation (for example, programs designed to prevent depression and inflation).

Just as federalism has produced relatively uncoordinated regulatory programs in terms of intergovernmental relations, separation of powers has likewise produced relatively uncoordinated regulatory programs in terms in interbranch relations. Separation of powers makes possible the control of Congress and the administration by opposed political parties or opposed ideologies, which leads to at least temporary inaction (for example, the lack of a vigorous relief and recovery program between 1930 and 1932). On the other hand, increased government regulation has tended to weaken separation of powers by concentrating more quasi-legislative and quasi-judicial power in the hands of administrative agencies, where quicker and more expert action can generally be taken than in Congress or the courts (for example, transportation-rate making or the adjudication of stock-brokerage violations).

Judicial review has had the effect of slowing the increase in governmental regulation (for example, the child-labor cases), but not preventing it. On the other side of the picture, the increase in government regulation has grown so large that this phenomenon, along with personnel and social changes, has probably been a major cause of the withdrawal of the federal courts from nullifying economic regulatory legislation since 1937.

The check and balance provided by the two-party system has probably tended to make regulatory programs operate more efficiently. The "out" party is constantly trying to find and reveal to the public examples of waste, corruption, and unresponsiveness on the part of the "in" party. However, the two-party system has meant that the planning of regulatory programs must be more short run than would be so with a one-party system. Federal economic programs, for instance, generally cannot be planned for more than one Presidential administration ahead because of the possibility of a change in the party occupying the White House. The relatively weak ideological split in the U.S. party system, however, has meant that when the out party comes in, it will not drastically change all the economic programs of the former in party. It has also meant that campaign disputes over regulatory issues generally tend to be fought along pragmatic lines rather than along ideological lines of socialism versus capitalism. Viewed from the other side of the conceptual scheme, increased government regulation and regulatory issues probably have sharpened the differences between Democrats and Republicans. In the 1964 Congress, for instance, the sharpest interparty disputes were over Keynesian fiscal policy, Medicare for the aged, and President Johnson's incipient antipoverty program. Upsurges in economic regulation during the Wilson and Roosevelt administrations clearly sharpened interparty differences.

That the United States has a meaningful universal adult suffrage combined with relative freedom for unpopular viewpoints has enabled substantial economic reforms to be introduced without violent revolution. In both England and the United States, socialistic-reformist philosophies were able to win acceptance without generating reactionary repression. Probably the most controversial relation shown in figure 6-1 is the impact of economic regulation on democracy. If, on the one hand, one defines democracy so as to include the right to operate a business for profit as the owner sees fit, without being subject to government regulation, then government regulation, by definition, has decreased democracy. If, on the other hand, one defines democracy in terms of universal adult suffrage combined with freedom for unpopular viewpoints, then most regulatory programs of the twentieth century have directly or indirectly helped to increase U.S. democracy. Surely, universal adult suffrage can be exercised more effectively by workers who have the time to familiarize themselves with politics instead of merely working long hours at a bare subsistence wage starting in early childhood. Maximum-hour laws, minimum-wage laws, and child-labor laws have helped to free the worker so that she or he can gain increased political familiarity, and business regulation legislation has probably helped (along with the mass media and increased education) to decrease the undue power that business concerns exercised over state and federal legislatures in the past.

Bibliography on the Federal Government and Policy Studies

[1] Dolbeare, Kenneth, and Edelman, Murray. *American Politics: Policies, Power, and Change.* D.C. Heath, 1971.

[2] Hendel, Samuel, and Bishop, Hillman. *Basic Issues in American Democracy.* Prentice-Hall, 1976.

[3] Lockard, Duane. *The Perverted Priorities of American Politics.* Macmillan, 1971.

[4] Mitchell, William. *Public Choice in America: An Introduction to American Government.* Markham, 1971.

[5] Ripley, Randall. *American National Government and Public Policy.* Free Press, 1974.

[6] Salisbury, Robert. *Governing America: Public Choice and Political Action.* Appleton, 1973.

[7] Sharkansky, Ira, and Van Meter, Donald. *Policy and Politics in American Governments.* McGraw-Hill, 1975.

[8] Wade, Lawrence, and Meek, Roy. *Democracy in America: A Public Choice Approach.* Duxbury, 1976.

Comparative Government. Having a cross-national perspective on policy problems can be justified in terms of developing broader theories of the causes and effects of alternative public policies than can be developed by merely working with states or cities within the United States or another single country at one point or even many points in time. Having such a perspective also has practical significance in terms of providing insights into what policies ought to be adopted in light of given goals, constraints, and environmental cir-cumstances. For example, an analysis of the effects of abortion policies in the United States made during the 1960s might lead one to conclude that making abortions easier to obtain has virtually no effect on decreasing deaths from illegal abortions, unwanted births, or other social indicators. In reality, however, the slope, or marginal rate of return, of relevant social indicators to the leniency of abortion policy might be quite substantial if the units of analysis had been countries where there is a wider range of scores on the leniency variable than among U.S. states. Like many policies, abortion policy may have an S-shaped relation to its goals such that the slope is relatively flat at low and high levels on the policy, but relatively steep in the middle. Determining the role of possible fundamental policy causes like industrialization, capitalism-socialism, and democracy-dictatorship cannot be meaningfully done within the limited variation of U.S. states rather than U.N. members.

The main problem in cross-national policy comparisons is the difficulty of holding constant other variables (besides the policy variable) that may affect the goal indicators. The traditional approach has been to use a cross-sectional analysis of many countries at one point in time and divide the countries into similar subsamples or use a form of predictive regression analysis that attempts to statistically control for differences among the countries. Those approaches, however, are limited by the number of countries available and by the difficulty of determining what variables to control for. An improvement on that methodology is the increased concern for time-series analysis. By comparing a set of ten or N countries before and after they adopt a policy, one generally controls for extraneous variables better than comparing ten countries that have adopted the policy with ten countries that have not. For example, it would probably be more meaningful to do an interrupted time series on a set of countries to determine the effects on sex crimes of legalizing pornography than to compare countries that legally allow pornography with those that prohibit it, although with either approach one would want to consider other causal variables. Both approaches can be combined by trying to compare countries over time that have adopted a policy with related countries over the same periods that have not adopted the policy. Likewise, over-time analysis may be especially helpful in determining the effects of policy causes like population change, the business cycle, or per capita income.

Related to the control problem and the use of time-series analysis is the problem of determining the degree of reciprocal causation between policies and other variables. For example, does crime occurrence increase anticrime efforts on a cross-national basis, or do anticrime efforts decrease crime, or both, or neither? If one uses countries at one point in time to determine the relationship, the slope tends to be positive regardless of which variable is used as a dependent variable and what other variables are held constant. If, however, one uses countries at two points in time and relates crime occurrence as an effect at time t to anticrime expenditures as a cause at time $t - 1$, holding constant crime occurrence at time $t - 1$, then the relation tends to be negative and substantial. Likewise, if one relates anticrime expenditures as an effect at time t to crime occurrence as a cause at time $t - 1$, holding constant anticrime expenditures at time $t - 1$, then that relation tends to be positive and substantial. Thus, with two points in time data, we are able to show that there is a positive relation in one direction and a negative relation in the other, as well as in which direction the relation is stronger. This also illustrates the relevance of the concepts and methods of cross-national comparisons to cross-state and cross-city comparisons.

The above conceptual and methodological problems emphasize the use of empirical data, which may be more difficult to obtain at the cross-national level than the subnational level. As a result, there may be even greater need in cross-national theory building and practice for the use of deductive modeling to analyze the causes and effects of alternative public policies. The most useful models for deducing the effects of policy changes on society or social changes on policy may be models which assume that political decisionmakers and people in general try to maximize their perceived expected benefits minus costs. Models like that are helpful not only in the absence of hard evaluation data, but also for determining the effects of changes before the changes occur, even if data might be available afterward. For example, one can predict many effects of the adoption of a pollution tax on business or managerial polluters from such a model without having to adopt the tax. Likewise, one can probably better explain why some countries have adopted national health insurance and others have not by using such a model to understand the choices made by legislators in the adopting countries and the opposite choices made by legislators in the other countries.

Bibliography on Comparative Government and Policy Studies

[1] Groth, Alexander. *Comparative Politics: A Distributive Approach.* Macmillan, 1971.

[2] Hayward, Jack, and Watson, Michael, eds. *Planning, Politics and Public Policy: The British, French and Italian Experience.* Cambridge University Press, 1975.

[3] Heidenheimer, Arnold; Heclo, Hugh; and Adams, Carolyn. *Comparative Public Policy: The Politics of Social Change in Europe and America.* St. Martin's Press, 1975.

[4] Liske, Craig; Loehr, William; and McCamant, John; eds. *Comparative Public Policy: Issues, Theories, and Methods.* Wiley, 1975.

[5] Rose, Richard, ed. *The Dynamics of Public Policy: A Comparative Analysis.* Sage, 1975.

[6] Siegel, Richard, and Weinberg, Leonard. *Comparing Public Policy: United States, Soviet Union and Europe.* Dorsey, 1977.

[7] Wilensky, Harold. *The Welfare State and Equality: Structural and Ideological Roots of Public Expenditures.* University of California Press, 1975.

International Relations. Foreign-policy problems have been especially important in political science, although such problems have historical, economic, demographic, psychological, technological, and ethical aspects, as well as relevance to other disciplines. Perhaps the most meaningful division of the issues is into those that deal with international conflict versus issues of international cooperation. The conflict issues relate to conflict prevention, mainly through alliances and international organization, and conflict resolution, mainly through negotiation and sometimes war. The cooperation issues relate to cooperation in trade, environmental protection, energy, communications, transportation, postal service, food, labor, health, education, and banking.

An alternative way of organizing foreign-policy issues would be in terms of the country or region whose foreign policy is being studied, which is a kind of cross-national perspective that can be applied to any policy problem. A related organization of the issues would be to think of foreign policy just from a U.S. perspective but to divide the issues in terms of the countries and regions with which the United States interacts. That kind of geographical perspective, however, tends to miss issues that cut across U.S. relations with other countries and tends to focus unduly on current events rather than on matters of a more lasting nature.

Another meaningful way of organizing foreign-policy issues involves stressing the goals and means of state departments or foreign ministries in dealing with other countries. These goals include winning allies, consumers for U.S. products, sources of raw materials, and human rights for foreign nationals. The means include trade, economic aid, military aid, propaganda, subversion, institutions of diplomacy, and international organization. Closely related to this division of goals and means are issues that relate to the structures, personnel practices, and administrative procedures used within the State Department and the government in general, to make the means more efficient in furthering the goals and to make both means and goals more responsive to elected officials and the public.

Defense policy emphasizes developing a capability for deterring foreign aggression, and arms-control policy stresses mutual reduction or restraint in armament development. Defense policy issues include (1) balancing air, naval, and land power; (2) balancing massive strategic power versus the ability to fight limited wars or engagements; (3) balancing the ability to engage in conventional warfare versus guerrilla and counterinsurgency activities; (4) civil defense with regard to shelter programs, antiballistic missiles, industrial relocation, and aftermath planning; (5) civilian control over the military; (6) intelligence-gathering activities; (7) problems involved in recruiting, training, and retaining military personnel; (8) coordinating military capabilities with one's allies; (9) development and implementation of new weapons technologies; (10) policy toward the use of atomic, chemical, and bacteriological weapons systems which are oriented toward civilian destruction; (11) administrative structures to facilitate rational responses to defense problems; and (12) internal-security matters, especially in time of war.

Arms-control issues include (1) provisions for monitoring compliance with agreements, which formerly meant debating the degree of on-site inspection, but which now can be handled partly through satellite surveillance; (2) the extent to which there should be a mutual reduction in armaments or merely restraint in the development of new armaments; (3) the extent to which there has to be a settlement of political issues before or after arms-control agreements; (4) the administrative structures for negotiating arms-control agreements; (5) bilateral versus multilateral arms-control agreements; (6) balancing conventional arms control and nuclear arms control; (7) disengagement or arms-free zones; (8) agreements to limit arms sales and military aid to other countries; (9) agreements concerning the banning of certain types of nuclear weapons testing; and (10) the role of the United Nations in achieving arms control.

An increasingly important perspective in international relations involves studying the international implications of domestic policy problems such as human rights, crime, economic regulation, education, pollution, health, race relations, poverty, food, science policy, population, transportation, labor, and energy, as contrasted to the more traditional fields of diplomacy and defense. Various specialized agencies of the United Nations are relevant to these domestic policy problems, such as the Food and Agriculture Organization, International Labor Organization, UNESCO, World Health Organization, and numerous others. Of increasing importance are regional international organizations designed to deal with economic and social problems, such as the Common Market, OPEC, and the Eastern European version of the Common Market. Of related importance is the role of multinational business corporations which have necessitated some international cooperation to deal with them and their effects on domestic economic matters.

Bibliography on International Relations and Policy Studies

[1] Bliss, Howard, and Johnson, M. Glen. *Beyond the Water's Edge: America's Foreign Policies.* Lippincott, 1975.
[2] Coplin, William. *Introduction to International Politics.* Rand McNally, 1974.
[3] East, Maurice; Salmore, Stephen; and Hermann, Charles. *Why Nations Act: Theoretical Perspectives for Comparative Foreign Policy Studies.* Sage, 1977.
[4] Merritt, Richard L., ed. *Foreign Policy Analysis.* LexingtonBooks, D.C. Heath, 1975.

[5] Nye, Joseph, and Koehane, Robert. *International Relations.* Harvard University Press, 1971.
[6] Rosenau, James, ed. *International Politics and Foreign Policy: A Reader in Research and Theory.* Free Press, 1969.

General Fields of Political Science

Political Philosophy. A key part of the relation between political theory or political philosophy, on the one hand, and policy studies or policy analysis, on the other, is the question of the role of values in arriving at policy decisions. A number of points might be mentioned. On the most basic level is the issue of being value-free in doing research. By definition, policy analysis at least partly involves seeking to achieve or maximize given values or social goals rather than ignoring them. However, policy analysts, like other researchers, should be value-free in the sense of not allowing their values to influence how they record or present information. In fact, the concern for objectivity and replicability in policy-analysis research should probably manifest itself in taking extra precautions to keep the bias of researchers from influencing their results, given the stronger feelings which generally exist about policy problems, as contrasted to research problems that lack policy implications. These precautions can include drawing on multiple sources and individuals for cross-checking information, making available raw-data sets for secondary analysis, and making assumptions more explicit.

Many policy-analysis problems involve taking goals as givens and determining what policies will maximize those goals. The goals, however, may be only intermediate values directed toward achieving other more general values. For example, a policy-analysis problem might involve determining how to reduce pretrial jail populations (Y). The proposals might relate to methods for increasing pretrial release (X_1) and reducing delay from arrest to disposition (X_2). However, there might be some policymakers who think the pretrial jail population should be increased (rather than reduced) as a means for punishing arrested defendants who might otherwise escape punishment through plea bargaining or lack of admissible evidence. A second-stage policy analysis could deal with the effect of the pretrial jail experience on reducing crime rates (Z), which can be taken as a higher-level goal. To make policy analysis more manageable between X and Y, one may merely refer to the possibility of doing further research on the relation between Y and Z without actually undertaking it.

Like any research tool (including a calculator or a typewriter), policy analysis can be used for good or evil purposes. A computerized analysis of the effects of alternative legislative redistricting patterns, for example, can be used to facilitate a kind of proportional representation whereby the percentage of districts dominated by Democrats roughly approximates the percentage of Democrats in the state. But the same redistricting programs can be used to minimize black representation in a state legislature. Quantitative policy analysis, however, is less likely to be used for purposes that are unconstitutional or on which there is a negative consensus because policy analysis does tend to make more explicit the values, assumptions, input data, and other parameters used in arriving at the decisions than more traditional decision making does. In the computer redistricting example, one can check the programs and the input data to see what was the basis for the redistricting outputs.

Sometimes people involved in policy analysis may be asked to maximize what they consider to be socially undesirable goals. This brings out the need for policy analysts to choose carefully those for whom they work, to try to improve the caliber of those people if they can, to call illegal matters to the attention of appropriate authorities, and to look elsewhere if they are dissatisfied with the goals of their government agency or employer. Normally in a democratic society, elected officials and their political appointees do try to achieve goals that will make them popular and that will be in conformity with the law. Therefore, a policy analyst's desire to do things in the public interest and be legal is not so likely to conflict with the people for whom he or she works.

Value decisions are particularly relevant to policy analysis in the sense that optimizing solutions are very much influenced by the values plugged into the analysis. In the redistricting example, the optimum plan is likely to depend on whether the goal is merely to provide equality of population across the districts or to also provide such things as proportionality of party representation and competitiveness within districts. Likewise, what constitutes an optimum jury size depends partly on how many guilty people we are willing to acquit in order to save one innocent person from conviction. A tradeoff higher than 10 to 1 may, however, be irrelevant if the maximum reasonable jury size is twelve persons. As another example, the optimum mix of funds in the Legal Services Corporation between law reform and routine case handling may depend on who is evaluating the legal-services agencies that constitute the data on which the analysis is based. Lawyer evaluators may tend to give higher ratings to agencies involved in more difficult appellate-court precedent-setting cases, but representatives of the poor may give higher ratings to agencies involved in easier but more immediate family, housing, and consumer negotiations. Policy analysts should be particularly concerned with presenting sensitivity analyses in their projects in which they show how the optimum would vary when one makes changes in the values being maximized.

On a higher level of generality, political philosophy can contribute a greater awareness of alternative values that one might ultimately seek to maximize. Those values are generally not explicitly part of the criteria involved in evaluating alternative public policies, but they may underlie those criteria. Such value systems are associated with the great thinkers of political philosophy such as Plato, Aristotle, Aquinas, Hobbs, Locke, Rousseau, and Marx. The sensitivity of policy analysts to value problems probably would be substantially heightened by including in their training readings from such political theorists.

Bibliography on Political Theory and Policy Studies

[1] Buchanan, James, and Tullock, Gordon. *The Calculus of Consent: Logical Foundations of Constitutional Democracy.* University of Michigan Press, 1962.

[2] Easton, David. *Systems Analysis of Political Life.* Wiley, 1965.

[3] Gregg, Phillip, ed. *Problem of Theory in Policy Analysis.* Lexington-Books, D.C. Heath, 1976.

[4] Lowi, Theodore. *The End of Liberalism: Ideology, Policy, and the Crisis of Public Authority.* W.W. Norton, 1969.

[5] Meehan, Eugene. *Value Judgment and Social Science: Structures and Processes.* Dorsey, 1969.

[6] Riker, William, and Ordeshook, Peter. An Introduction to Positive Political Theory. Prentice-Hall, 1973.

Political-Science Methodology. Political-science methodology has tended to incorporate methodologies developed in other social sciences rather than create its own methodologies. In the context of policy analysis, six kinds of methodologies may be especially important. They relate to inference, prediction, causation, goal measurement, optimizing, and deduction. They can be considered in a hierarchy such that each methodology builds on the previous one.

The basic level in social-science research involves summarizing data to indicate univariate measures of both central tendency and spread for a number of data points on a given variable. For example, what is the average age of a set of state-supreme-court judges, and what is the range in their ages? At the same basic level, one is likely to make comparisons between averages or other measures for two or more groups. For example, how does the average age of elected judges compare with that of appointed judges? If one asks that kind of question, one is logically led into asking to what extent the difference found may be readily attributable to chance. One intuitively recognizes that chance could be more easily the reason for the difference if the difference is small or if the size of the samples is small. Standard statistics textbooks provide formulas for calculating the probability of a given statistic really being zero (or some other number) with given sample sizes. An interesting controversy at that level of analysis involves how low that chance probability has to be before one will conclude that the difference or the statistic is not due to chance, but rather is based on a real difference, relation, or nonchance occurrence.

On the next level of analysis, one is not just concerned with summarizing data and indicating to what extent one can generalize from a sample: instead, one is interested in bivariate and multivariate relations for the purpose of predicting how a unit of analysis will be positioned on one variable, given its position on one or more other variables, or given the distribution of the units of analysis on the main variable. For example, to what extent can we predict the decisional propensities of judges in criminal cases from knowing their ages, or from knowing that the average judge tends to favor the prosecution? That question raises two kinds of controversies. One asks what the best method of prediction is, with the choices including predicting from another variable, predicting from the distribution on a given variable, and many variations on those two. The second asks what the best criterion is for deciding among those alternative prediction methods, with the choices mainly relating to either squaring or not squaring the deviations from each predicted score to each actual score.

Moving up in the hierarchy, one might logically ask, "Just because I know there is a nonchance predictive relation between the age of judges and their propensity to decide for the prosecution in criminal cases, how do I know that it is a causal relation, and especially how do I know what kind of causal relation?" In other words, will being an older judge consistently correlate well with deciding for the prosecution, or does the correlation substantially change when some other variable is manipulated, such as off-the-bench liberal attitudes. For example, if only old liberal judges are compared with young liberal judges, and only conservative old judges are compared with young conservative judges, then the relation between age and deciding for the prosecution might tend to disappear, possibly indicating that liberalism is an intervening variable between age and decisional propensity. However, there may be a low propensity to decide for the prosecution among young liberal, old liberal, and young conservative judges, but a high propensity to decide in favor of the prosecution by old conservative judges, possibly indicating a joint causal relation by conservatism and age on decisional propensities. But maybe being conservative causes one to decide for the prosecution, but deciding for the prosecution tends to reinforce one's conservatism, thereby possibly indicating some reciprocal causation in the model.

After tentatively resolving some of the methodological controversies concerning hypothesis testing, prediction, and causation, one might then logically ask, "So what?" In other words, how does one make use of that kind of knowledge in order to arrive at a decision concerning what alternative public policies ought to be adopted that relate to one's subject matter? Not all social science has policy implications. Before arriving at a decision as to what ought to be adopted, one has to clarify what goals we are seeking to maximize, minimize, or optimize, as well as determine how those goals relate to the policy alternatives being considered. Clarifying goals may especially involve determining how one is going to combine multiple and sometimes conflicting goals. For example, in deciding between an elected or an appointed judicial system, we might have as our goals securing judges who are either economic liberals or economic conservatives, when economic issues arise that cannot be resolved by clear precedents, and securing judges who are civil-libertarian liberals or conservatives, when legal or factual civil-liberties issues arise. If elected judges were to score favorably or unfavorably on both goals, there would be no problem. However, when relating those goals to the alternative policies, we might find that elected judges tend to be somewhat more liberal on economic matters given their more working-class backgrounds, but less liberal on civil-liberties matters given their fear of being voted out of office by majority pressures.

Merely determining our goals and relating them to the policy alternatives do not necessarily resolve the question of what is the optimum policy alternative. Answering that question may require working with a model involving formulas for (1) choosing among discrete alternatives without or with contingent probabilities, (2) finding an optimum level on a hill-shaped total-benefits curve or a valley-shaped total-cost curve, or (3) finding an optimum mix among a variety of places or activities. For example, the optimum solution to the policy problem of having an elected or appointed judiciary may involve a mix between the two, in which one's goals are maximized by initially electing judges, but providing for the long tenure that is associated with appointing judges. That mix might provide judges with liberal backgrounds for economic decision making, but freedom from majority pressures for civil-libertarian decision making. Determining what constitutes the optimum length of tenure may also be an optimum-level problem because tenure that is either too short or too long may be undesirable, since short tenure brings a lack of independence, but unduly long tenure may bring staleness and unresponsiveness.

On the highest methodological level, one might ask the question, "How can I use all this knowledge about inference, prediction, causation, goals, and optimizing in order to deduce a prediction about the effect of X on Y, or to deduce a prescription as to what X should be adopted, without having to gather difficult empirical data to test those conclusions?" For example, if one knows how twelve-person juries decide criminal cases under a unanimity rule, how can one deduce how six-person juries (or twelve-person juries under a nonunanimity rule) would decide criminal cases? Having to experiment with real criminal cases might be practically impossible as well as unfair to the defendants and might produce meaningless results because of our inability to statistically control for other variables (besides jury size) that influence case outcomes. For another example, if one knows or deduces the empirical relation between jury size and propensity to convict and one tentatively accepts the Blackstonian norm that it is worse to convict one innocent person than to free ten guilty people, then how does one use those kinds of premises to deduce a prescriptive conclusion as to the optimum jury size? As social science does more analysis of hypotheses, predictions, causation, and optimizing, there develops a body of potential premises that can be used in deducing conclusions, just as chemistry was able to deduce the existence of new elements before they were empirically discovered.

Bibliography on Political-Science Methodology

[1] Coplin, William, and O'Leary, Michael. *Everyman's Prince: A Guide to Understanding Your Political Problems*. Duxbury, 1972.
[2] Dolbeare, Kenneth, ed. *Public Policy Evaluation*. Sage, 1975.
[3] Nagel, Stuart, Neef, Marian. *Operations Research Methods: As Applied to Political Science and the Legal Process*. Sage, 1976.
[4] Scioli, Frank, Jr., and Cook, Thomas, eds. *Methodologies for Analyzing Public Policies*. LexingtonBooks, D.C. Heath, 1975.
[5] Sharkansky, Ira, ed. *Policy Analysis in Political Science*. Markham, 1970.
[6] Tufte, Edward. *Data Analysis for Politics and Policy*. Prentice-Hall, 1974.

Some Conclusions

From this analysis, one can readily conclude that all fields of political science are relevant to understanding the effects of alternative public policies. There is a need for more awareness of options and constraints with regard to law, administration, legislative feasibility, and the politics of adoption and implementation. There is an increasing concern for public-policy issues among people who study state-local government, the federal government, comparative government, international relations, and the use of those political arenas for testing the effects of alternative public policies. Both political philosophy and methodology are becoming more relevant to discussing policy goals and statistical or mathematical models for determining the effects of policies on those goals.

The increasing concern of all fields of political science for the study of the nature, causes, and effects of public policies is shown in the contents of textbooks, convention panels, articles, journals, and job descriptions in each of those fields. The future looks particularly good for the fields of political science that are especially involved in policy studies, such as public administration, and state-local government. All fields, however, seem to be benefiting by their association with policy studies. The benefits are not just increased publishing and job opportunities. The association of political science with policy studies also enables one to combine the scholarly orientation of developing general theories of cause-and-effect relations among policies, determinants, and impacts, while simultaneously developing practical findings and principles relevant to enabling public policies to be more effective in achieving societal goals.

Epilogue: Policy Analysis as a Career Activity

This memo was prepared mainly for distribution to undergraduate political-science majors attending the Illinois Pi Sigma Alpha Political Science Honorary initiation ceremonies in October 1978, as part of a panel on "Alternatives to Law School for Political Science Majors." Perhaps others will find the references and ideas helpful in themselves or for preparing related materials for other undergraduate or graduate students.

Policy analysts are involved mainly in determining the effects of alternative public policies in working for government agencies, nonuniversity research centers, university research centers, teaching units, or interest groups. The work is generally not full-time policy-analysis work; rather, policy analysis tends to be part of a full-time position in public administration, research, or teaching. The government agencies could be executive agencies such as HEW or HUD, legislative agencies such as the Congressional Reference Service and General Accounting Office, or judicial agencies such as the Federal Judicial Center and the National Center for State Courts. The government agencies could also be at the federal, state, or local level. For further information on what policy analysts do, see Arnold Meltsner, *Policy Analysts in the Bureaucracy* (University of California Press, 1976); Michael White, Michael Radnor, and David Tansik, *Management and Policy Science in American Government* (D.C. Heath, 1975); and Yehezkel Dror, *Design for Policy Sciences* (Elsevier, 1971). On the more general subject of the utilization of social science in government decision making, see Carol Weiss, ed., *Using Social Research in Public Policy Making* (D.C. Heath, 1977); Irving Horowitz and James Katz; *Social Science and Public Policy in the United States* (Praeger, 1975); and S. Nagel and M. Neef, eds., *Political Science Utilization Directory* (PSO, 1975).

In order to acquire the training needed for policy-analysis work, it is normally necessary to acquire a graduate degree in one of the social sciences, preferably economics, political science, social psychology, planning, or one of the newer interdisciplinary policy-studies programs. The best of the interdisciplinary programs, in random order, are probably those at the Harvard Kennedy School, Princeton Woodrow Wilson School, Michigan Institute of Public Policy Studies, Berkeley Graduate School of Public Policy, Duke Institute of Policy Sciences and Public Affairs, Minnesota Hubert Humphrey Institute of Public Affairs, Rand Graduate Institute, Texas L.B.J. School,

Syracuse Maxwell School, Southern California School of Public Administration, SUNY Stony Brook Harriman School, Wisconsin Center for the Study of Public Policy and Administration, Washington Graduate School of Public Affairs, and SUNY Binghamton Program in Public Policy Analysis and Administration. For further information on those programs, see NASPAA, *Graduate Programs in Public Affairs and Public Administration* (National Association of Schools of Public Affairs and Administration, 1976); S. Nagel and M. Neef, eds., *Policy Studies Directory* (PSO, 1976); and Harry Weiner, ed., "Education for Public Services" (symposium issue of the *Journal of Urban Analysis,* October 1976).

The methodological training of policy analysts should include courses in social-science research methods, especially methods that relate to questionnaires, interviewing, sampling, goal measurement, prediction, causal analysis, data processing, systematic observation, and report writing. The methodological training should also include courses in optimum decision making, such as those offered in business administration, industrial engineering, and economics under titles such as *operations research* or *management science.* For further information on the relevant skills, see Edith Stokey and Richard Zeckhauser, *A Primer for Policy Analysis* (Norton, 1978); Edward Quade, *Analysis for Public Decisions* (Elsevier, 1975); S. Nagel and M. Neef, *Policy Analysis: In Social Science Research* (Sage, 1978); Elmer Struening and Marcia Guttentag, eds., *Handbook of Evaluation Research* (Sage, 1975); and Ruth Mack, *Planning on Uncertainty: Decision Making in Business and Government Administration* (Wiley, 1971).

The substantive training of policy analysts should include courses that deal with how and why alternative policies get adopted and implemented, as well as courses that cover the basic issues and references in at least a few specific policy fields. For further information on policy adoption and implementation, see James Anderson, *Public Policy-Making* (Praeger, 1975), and Charles Jones, *An Introduction to the Study of Public Policy* (Duxbury, 1977). For surveys of a number of specific policy problems, see Theodore Lowi and Alan Stone, *Nationalizing Government: Public Policies in America* (Sage, 1978), and James Anderson, David Brady, and Charles Bullock, *Public Policy and Politics in America* (Duxbury, 1978).

Policy problems are inherently interdisciplinary, but political science has an important role to play. A political-science or political perspective is essential to considering adequately the likelihood of a proposed policy being adopted, such as pollution taxes to promote environmental protection. That kind of taxing scheme may, if adopted, be quite effective, but its chances of being adopted seem quite slight given the strong opposition of virtually all business groups in view of how explicitly they would bear the antipollution costs. Likewise, a political-science perspective is essential to considering adequately the problems of administering various policies. For example, the negative-income-tax experiments in New Jersey found little relation between money awarded and incentives to work. However, they might have found some relation to work incentives by comparing the alternative delivery systems of the compulsory caseworker versus the receipt in the mail without a caseworker. Caseworkers may stimulate job finding by providing information or by harassing welfare recipients, or they may decrease job finding by lowering self-esteem and increasing the dependency of welfare recipients. Regardless of the effects, this is an interesting hypothesis that political scientists and public-administration people would be more likely, than economists or social psychologists, to be concerned with. For books emphasizing the role of political science in policy analysis, see Austin Ranney, ed., *Political Science and Public Policy* (Markham, 1968); Robert Spadaro, Thomas Dye, Robert Golembiewski, Murray Stedman, and L. Harmon Zeigler, *The Policy Vacuum: Toward a More Professional Political Science* (LexingtonBooks, D.C. Heath, 1975); and S. Nagel, ed., *Policy Studies in America and Elsewhere* (LexingtonBooks, D.C. Heath, 1975).

For developing a general background in policy analysis, see the back issues of such journals as the *Policy Studies Journal, Policy Analysis, Policy Sciences,* and *Public Policy*. Also see the annual volumes of the *Policy Studies Review Annual*. Although this book was prepared as part of a panel on "Alternatives to Law School for Political Science Majors," policy analysis and law can go together since lawyers interested in influencing the legal system would probably be aided by a supplementary background in policy analysis. Likewise, policy analysts who are also lawyers would be more effective in some government positions, such as working with legislative committees or judicial agencies. Policy analysis, however, can be considered an even more exciting field than traditional law practice for those who are interested in the intellectual challenge of trying to determine the effects of alternative public policies and who are interested in being relevant to important policy problems.

Index of Names

Aaron, Henry, 43
Abt, Clark C., 89, 125, 150
Adams, Carolyn T., 7, 33, 196
Adler, Richard, 44
Alford, Robert, 51
Allen, Herb, 103
Allensworth, Don, 43
Allison, David, 88
Allison, Graham, 38, 132
Altshuler, Alan, 44
Amacher, Ryan, 176
Anderson, James E., 7, 31, 42, 208
Andrews, F. Emerson, 103
Applebaum, Judith, 125
Aranson, Peter, 173
Archibald, Kathleen, 170
Archibald, Russell, 161
Aroesta, Jean L., 103
Ashford, Douglas, 33

Bachrach, Peter, 49
Baker, Kenneth, 161
Banfield, Edward, 132
Bardach, Eugene, 32
Barnett, H., 176
Barzun, Jacques, 125
Bastide, R., 176
Bauer, Michael, 129
Bauer, Raymond, 31
Baumol, William, 147, 172
Becker, Theodore, 180
Beede, Benjamin, 177
Behn, Robert, 152
Beltrami, Edward, 159
Benne, Kenneth, 169
Bennett, Carl, 150
Bennis, Warren, 169
Bergman, Elihu, 49
Berlinski, David, 170
Bernstein, Ilene, 88
Bernstein, Marver, 42
Beutel, Frederick, 169
Beuthel, William E., 77, 90
Beyer, Janice, 120
Biderman, Albert, 88, 89
Bish, Robert, 190
Bishop, Hillman, 194
Black, Guy, 7, 150, 169
Blau, Peter, 132
Bliss, Howard, 198
Blumstein, Alfred, 147, 169
Bohigian, Haig, 162, 173
Bonjean, Charles, 120

Book, John, 147
Bouxsein, Peter, 72
Boyum, Keith, 32
Brady, David, 208
Braybrooke, David, 170
Brennan, Michael, 156
Brock, Bernard, 171
Brown, Peter, 173, 177
Brown, Rex, 152
Browne, William, 54
Buchanan, James, 147, 156, 201
Buckdruker, Elliot, 103
Bullock, Charles, 208
Bunker, Douglas, 72
Burkholder, Kathy, xii
Burns, James M., 7
Byrd, Jack Jr., 162, 173

Caldwell, L.K., 50
Cannon, Mark, 129
Caplan, Nathan, 89
Carey, George, 140
Carlson, Richard, 39, 187
Caro, Francis, 150
Carroll, James D., 103
Casper, Jonathan, 41, 180
Cater, Douglass, 44
Chaiken, J., 162
Charlesworth, James, 35, 139, 171, 175
Chase, Janet, 120
Cherns, Albert, 170
Chesebro, James, 171
Chin, Robert, 169
Christensen, Daphne, 44
Church, David M., 103
Churchman, C. West, 170
Clark, Elizabeth, 153
Clausen, Aaga R., 185
Clayton, Ross, 147
Clinton, Richard, 49
Cochran, Wendell, 125
Colvard, Richard, 113
Cook, Thomas J., 7, 29, 68, 204
Coplin, William, 29, 72, 198, 204
Cortes, Fernando, 161
Coser, Lewis, 125
Crabill, T., 162
Cragan, John, 171
Crecine, John P., 72, 89
Crenson, Matthew, 148, 177
Crissey, Brian, 148, 177

Davidson, Roger, 185
Davis, Dan, 123
Davis, David, 53
Dean, Gerald, 153
Dekker, Marcel, xiii
de Neufville, Richard, 147
Dermer, Joseph, 103
Dexter, Lewis, 129
Deutsch, Karl, 132
Dickson, Evelyn, 88
Dolbeare, Kenneth M., 7, 29, 68, 171, 194, 204
Downs, Anthony, 132
Drake, Alvin, 148, 171
Dresang, Dennis L., 6
Dror, Yehezkel, 6, 7, 28, 73, 132, 139, 170, 207
Duffy, Hugh, 150
Dye, Thomas, 6, 7, 28, 31, 46, 132, 139, 178, 179, 191, 209

East, Maurice, 198
Easton, Allan, 153
Easton, David, 139, 201
Edelman, Murray, 194
Eimermann, T., 172
Eldredge, H. Westworth, 73
Ericson, Richard, 73
Etzioni, Amitai, 171
Eulau, Heinz, 139, 140
Evans, Nancy, 125

Fairley, William, 177
Feeley, Malcolm, 32, 180
Fischoff, Baruch, 153
Fisher, Gene, 156
Foster, G., 176
Fraenkel, Richard, 54
Frederickson, George, 32, 171, 183
Freeman, David, 53
Freeman, Howard, 88
Freeman, Jo, 46
Friedman, Renee, 88, 89
Fromm, Gary, 148
Fukumoto, James, 150
Fuller, David, 103

Gardiner, John, 41, 47, 180
Gass, Saul, 148
Gates, Bruce, 171
George, Alexander, 38
Gergen, Kenneth, 31
Glaser, E.M., 140
Glatt, Evelyn, 88
Glazer, Nathan, 6
Goldberg, Peter, 89
Golden, Hal, 103

Golden, Joseph, 103
Golding, Martin, 173
Golembiewski, Robert, 7, 178, 179, 183, 209
Goldman, Thomas, 159
Gorham, William, 6, 89
Gouldner, Alvin, 175
Gove, Samuel, 48, 73
Grad, Frank, 52
Graff, Henry, 125
Graham, George, 140
Grannis, Chandler, 125
Greenberg, Daniel, 50, 104
Greenberger, Martin, 148, 177
Greenstein, Fred, 140
Gregg, Phillip, 6, 171, 173, 177, 201
Gross, Donald, 161
Grosse, Richard, 147
Groth, Alexander, 33, 196
Guttentag, Marcia, 150, 173, 208
Guttman, Daniel, 88, 170

Haas, Michael, 139
Haberer, Joseph, 50, 104
Hadwiger, Don, 54
Hagstrom, Warren, 113
Hall, Mary, 104, 125
Halter, Albert, 153
Hamilton, Charles, 180
Hamilton, Diane, 148
Hamilton, William, 148
Hamrin, Robert, 176
Handy, Rollo, 113
Harberger, Arnold, 148
Hargrove, Edwin, 32
Haro, Robert, 77, 90
Harris, Carl, 161
Harris, Fred, 140
Harvey, David, 176
Hathaway, Dale, 54
Havelock, Ronald, 30, 140, 141
Haveman, Robert, 148, 159, 176
Hayek, Frederick, 170
Hayward, Jack, 196
Healy, Robert, 43
Heclo, Hugh, 7, 33, 196
Heidenheimer, Arnold, 7, 33, 196
Heimann, Fritz, 104
Helly, Walter, 148
Hendel, Samuel, 194
Henry, Nicholas, 183
Henry, S., 156
Hermann, Charles, 198
Herzberg, Donald, 40, 185
Hill, Mary, 125
Hill, William, 104
Hinrichs, Harley, 150
Hite, James, 156

Hofferbert, Richard, 7
Holliday, L., 162
Holtzman, Abraham, 129
Hoos, Ida, 170
Hopkins, Anne, 121
Horowitz, Irving Louis, xiii, 30, 35, 88, 141, 171, 207
Hoselitz, Bert, 114
Houck, James, 54
Hovey, Harold, 170
Howard, Ronald, 152
Huenefeld, John, 125
Hullum, Jan, 120
Hyneman, Charles, 140

Ikenberry, Stanley, 88

Jacob, Herbert, 47, 180
James, Dorothy, 46, 171
Jaquette, D., 162
Jeffrey, R.C., 153
Jewkes, John, 170
Johnson, M. Glen, 198
Jones, Charles O., 7, 31, 73, 140, 179, 208

Kahr, Andrew, 152
Kallgren, Joyce, 121
Kamrass, Murray, 147, 169
Kariel, Henry, 139
Karlesky, Joseph, 88, 89
Kassouf, Sheen, 7, 147
Katz, Arnold, 6, 35, 88, 207
Keeney, Ralph, 148, 153, 171
Kirst, Michael, 8
Kloek, Teun, 147
Klumpp, James, 171
Knezo, Genevieve, 141
Koehane, Robert, 199
Koeppen, Sheillah, 73
Kotler, Philip, 150
Kraft, Michael, 49
Krathwohl, David R., 104
Krislov, Samuel, 32, 73
Kurtz, Paul, 113

Ladd, John, 173
Laidlaw, C., 159
Landes, David, 176
Larsen, Otto, 175
Lasswell, Harold, 6, 28, 35, 73, 140, 141, 170
Lawless, M., 163
Lawrence, Robert, 53
Lawson, Anne, 121
Layard, Richard, 150
Lazarsfeld, Paul, 88, 141, 175
Lear, Julia, 6
Lee, Sang, 159

Lee, Wayne, 153
Lehman, Edward, 89
Lehnen, Robert, 187
Lepawsky, Albert, 73
Lerner, Daniel, 35, 141, 170
Levine, Robert, 38, 170
Levy, Frank, 191
Lichenstein, Sara, 153
Limsdaine, Arthur, 150
Lindblom, Charles, 7, 28, 31, 170
Lineberry, Robert, 28, 191
Linowes, Robert, 43
Liske, Craig, 196
Llewellyn, Robert, 159
Loavenbruck, Grant, 141
Lockard, Duane, 194
Loehr, William, 196
Lowi, Theodore, 132, 201, 208
Luttbeg, Norman, 187
Lyden, Fremont, 159
Lynd, Robert, 141, 170
Lynn, Lawrence, 148
Lyons, Gene, 141

Macaulay, Hugh, 156
McCall, George, 175
McCamant, John, 196
McCune, Srar Miller, xiii
McDougal, Myres, 73
Mack, Ruth, 153, 208
McKean, Roland N., 7, 150, 169, 171
McMillen, Claude Jr., 159
MacRae, Duncan, 35, 73, 147, 173, 175, 177
Mahoney, Margaret E., 104
Mahood, H.R., 129
Makridakis, Spyros, 161
Mancke, Richard, 53
Mann, Lawrence, 73
Mann, Thomas, 140
March, James G., 104, 132, 139
Margolis, Julius, 148, 159
Marien, Michael, 121, 123
Marini, Frank, 183
Marks, David, 147
Marks, F.R., 178
Marmor, Theodore, 46, 51
Marshall, Dale Robert, 121
Masotti, Louis, 191
Masteller, Frederick, 177
Matheson, James, 152
Mechanic, David, 51
Meehan, Eugene, 173, 201
Meek, Roy, 194
Mehay, Stephen, 159
Meltsner, Arnold, 7, 191, 207
Mercer, Jane R., 104
Merritt, Richard, 38, 89, 121, 198

Michalos, Alex, 121
Milbrath, Lester, 129
Miller, Arthur S., 73
Miller, D.W., 156
Miller, Ernest, 159
Miller, S.M., 175
Mishan, Ezra J., 7, 150
Mitchell, John, 121
Mitchell, Joyce, 140
Mitchell, William, 140, 194
Monsen, Joseph, 129
Morris, Philip, 171
Morse, Philip, 148
Mosher, Frederick, 183
Mosteller, Frederick, 177
Mulkey, Michael, 47
Mullins, Carolyn, 121
Munshaw, Nancy, xii
Murray, Michael, 90
Myrtle, Robert, 147

Nadel, Mark, 42
Nagel, Stuart S., xii, 6, 7, 28, 29, 35, 47, 52,
    67, 68, 73, 76, 82, 90, 140, 141, 147, 148,
    153, 156, 159, 162, 169, 171, 172, 173,
    175, 177, 179, 180, 204, 207, 208, 209
Nash, Keir, 49
Neef, Marian, xii, 6, 7, 29, 73, 76, 82, 90, 147,
    148, 153, 156, 162, 169, 171, 172, 177,
    204, 207, 208
Neustadt, Richard, 132
Niskanen, William, 148
Nutt, Thomas, 74
Nye, Joseph, 199

O'Leary, Michael, 185, 204
Olson, Mancur, 170

Ordeshook, Peter, 201
Orlans, Harold, 88
Ornstein, Norman, 185
Orstrom, Elinor, 191
Ostrom, Vincent, 183, 190
Owen, Harry, 7

Palley, Howard, 191
Palley, Marion, 46, 191
Palmer, Archie, 77, 90
Pechman, Joseph, 45
Peltason, J.W., 7, 180
Peters, John, 40, 185
Peterson, Cameron, 152
Phillips, Llad, 156, 176
Pierce, Lawrence, 45
Pilarsky, Milton, 44
Polsby, Nelson, 140
Posner, Richard, 177

Powell, Walter, 125
Pressman, Jeffrey, 32, 183
Preston, Michael, 46
Price, Don, 132
Przeworski, Adam, 161
Putnam, John, 125
Pyszka, Gloria, 121

Quade, Edward S., 7, 29, 147, 150, 162, 169,
    171, 208

Radner, Michael, 30, 141, 207
Rae, Douglas, 187
Raiffa, Howard, 153
Ranney, Austin, 6, 28, 140, 178, 179, 187,
    209
Rathjens, George, 52
Reagan, Michael, 183
Reed, John, 162
Reinbolt, K., 172
Reitz, Jeffrey, 175
Richmond, Samuel, 147
Rieselbach, Leroy, 40, 185
Riker, William, 201
Ripley, Randall, 185, 194
Rivlin, Alice, 132
Robinson, D.Z., 104
Robinson, James, 74
Rodgers, Harrell, 47
Rokkan, S., 89
Rose, Aaron, 147
Rose, Richard, 33, 196
Rosenau, James, 38, 199
Rosenbaum, Walter, 52
Rosenthal, Alan, 40, 185
Rosenthal, Albert, 52, 105
Ross, H.L., 140
Ross, Lawrence, 121
Ross, Ruth, 121
Rossi, Peter, 88, 150
Rourke, Francis, 183
Ruttan, Vernon, 54

Saar, Shalom, 150
Salisbury, Robert, 129, 194
Salmore, Stephen, 198
Scanlon, John, 150
Schmandt, Jurgen, 104, 105
Schneider, Mark, 49
Schultze, Charles, 7
Schwartz, P., 105
Scioli, Frank Jr., 7, 29, 68, 204
Sclar, Deanna, 103
Seidman, Larry, 74
Sewell, William, 175
Shapiro, Gilbert, 90
Sharkansky, Ira, 45, 140, 178, 179, 191, 194,
    204

Sharp, Laura, 88
Shelley, Maynard, 88
Shockley, James, 156
Shoup, Donald, 159
Siegel, Richard, 147, 196
Sigler, Jay, 41, 177, 180
Silk, Tom, 103
Silberstein, JoAnn, 103
Simon, Herbert, 132
Sinclair, John, 129
Sisson, Roger, 148
Sjoberg, Gileon, 173
Slovic, Paul, 153
Smerk, George, 44
Smigel, Erwin O., 7
Smith, Bruce, L.R., 88, 89, 90
Smith, David, 67, 74
Smoke, Richard, 38
Somers, Ann, 51
Somers, Herman, 51
Somit, Albert, 114, 140
Spadaro, Robert N., 7, 178, 179, 209
Speckhard, Roy, 90
Sprague, John, 161
Starr, M.K., 156
Stedman, Murray, 7, 178, 179, 209
Steiner, Gilbert, 46
Stepp, James, 156
Stigler, George, 156
Stokey, Edith, 29, 147, 208
Stone, Alan, 208
Strickland, Ida, 103
Struening, Elmer, 150, 208
Suchman, Edward, 150, 170
Sunderland, John, 74
Susskind, Lawrence, 74

Talbot, Ross, 54
Tanenhaus, Joseph, 114, 140
Tansik, David, 30, 141, 207
Tarpey, J., 105
Taylor, Graeme, 150
Theil, Henri, 147
Theriauf, Robert, 147
Tilly, Charles, 176
Tollison, Robert, 176
Tribe, Lawrence, 170, 173
Truman, David B., 129
Tufte, Edward, 39, 177, 187, 204
Tullock, Gordon, 29, 147, 156, 201

Useem, Michael, 104

Van Dyke, Vernon, 140
van Horn, Andrew, 153

Van Leunen, Mary-Claire, 121
Van Meter, Donald, 194
Vaupel, James, 152
Villoria, Richard, 161
Vogt, Leona, 150
Votey, Harold, 156, 176

Wade, Lawrence, 6, 194
Wagner, Richard, 29
Waldo, Arley, 54
Walton, Ann D., 103
Wasby, Stephen, 8, 32, 41, 180
Waters, Anita, 89
Watson, Michael, 196
Webber, George, 175
Weinberg, Leonard, 196
Weiner, Harry, 7, 74, 208
Weisberg, Robert, 188
Weiss, Armand, 147, 169
Weiss, Carol, 8, 30, 105, 141, 150, 207
Welch, Susan, 40, 185
Wheelwright, Steven, 161
White, Gilbert, 176
White, Michael, 30, 141, 147, 207
White, Susan, 32
White, Virginia P., 104
Whitson, William, 38
Wholey, Joseph, 150
Wice, Paul, 156
Wilcox, Clair, 46
Wildavsky, Aaron, 32, 45, 132, 170, 183, 191
Wilde, James, 147
Wilensky, Harold, 33, 175, 196
Willett, Thomas, 176
Williams, Alan, 148, 171
Williams, C.W., 105
Williams, Walter, 88, 89, 150
Willner, Barry, 88, 170
Wilson, Everett K., 116
Wilson, James, 191
Wilson, John Q., 132
Winston, Eric, 91
Wirt, Frederick, 48
Wise, Charles, 32, 171, 183
Wolf, Charles Jr., 90
Wolman, Harold, 43, 179
Woottan, Graham, 129

Yandle, Bruce, 156
Yates, Douglas Jr., 74
York, Carl M., 105

Zeckhauser, Richard, 29, 147, 148, 208
Zeigler, L. Harmon, 7, 129, 178, 179, 209
Zisk, Betty, 129, 188
Zurcher, Arnold J., 105

Index of Subjects

Academic disciplines,
  policy analysis and, 34–35
Academic programs,
  policy studies, 74–76
Agriculture,
  natural science policy problem, 53–54
Allocating scarce resources:
  finding optimum mix, 156–159;
    applications, 159; bibliography, 159;
    methods, 159
Alternative policy, finding optimum, 145–148;
  bibliography, 147–148;
    basic methods, 147; policy applica-
    tions, 147–148
Alternatives, continuum:
  finding optimum level, 153–156
    bibliography, 156; applications, 156;
    methods, 156
    procedures, 153–156
Applicants, policy studies funding, 97–100
  bibliography, 103–104
  suggestions for, 97–102
Applied research,
  funding for, 101
Arms control:
  political science policy problem, 38–39
Associations:
  policy-relevant, 109–144
  scholarly, 109–113
    bibliography, 113–114
Audience, disciplinary orientation and, 119–
  120

Background characteristics:
  policy studies people, 19–22
Basic concepts:
  policy studies, 27–35
Basic methods:
  optimum alternative policy, 147
Basic symbols:
  optimizing analysis formulas, 164–165
Bibliographies:
  alternative policy, 147–148
  alternatives, optimum level continuum,
    155–156
  applicants, 103–104
  applications for funding, 103–104
  book publishing, 125
  comparative government, 196
  federal government, 191–194
  Finding optimum policy, alternative,
    147–148

Choice, with contingent probabilities, 152,
  without contingent probabilities, 150
level on continuum probabilities, 156
mix in allocating scarce resources, 158–159
funding sources, 102–105
interest groups, 129
international relations, 198–199
legislative process, 185
methods,
  optimum, alternative policy, 147, choice,
    with contingent probabilities, 150,
    without contingent probabilities, 152–
    153
level on continuum of alternatives, 153–
  156
mix allocating scarce resources, 159
Policy analysis, 6–8; 28–29
Policy research,
  centers, 88–91
  utilization, political science, 139–140;
    social science, 140–141
Policy studies, 5–8
  comparative government, 196
  federal government, 194
  international relations, 198–199
  legislative process, 185
  policy analysis, 6–8
  political dynamics, 187–188; science
    methodology, 204; theory, 201
  public administration, 183, public law,
    180
  state and local government, 190–191
  systems analysis, 169–171
  teaching policy studies, 72–74
  utilization of policy research, 139–141
pros and cons of systems analysis, 169–171
scholarly associations, 113–114
scholarly journals, 120–121
social-science, utilization, 141–141
Blacks,
  sociology-psychology policy problem, 46–
    47
Book publishers,
  policy-relevant, 121–125

Career activity:
  policy analysis as, 207–208
Civil liberties:
  political science policy problem, 40–41
Communication:
  economic policy problem, 43–44

Communications:
  policy studies improvements, 65
Comparative, government:
  bibliography, 196
  policy studies and, 194–196
Courts:
  public law and, 179–180
Criminal justice:
  sociology-psychology policy problem, 47
Cultures:
  policy analysis and, 32–33

Defense:
  political science policy problem, 38–39
Directories:
  policy research centers, 90–91
Disciplinary orientation:
  audience and, 119–120
Dynamics, political:
  policy studies and, 185–188

Economic, policy problems, 41–46
  communications, 43–44
  housing, 42–43
  land use, 42–43
  poverty, 45–46
  regulation, 41–42
  spending, 44–45
  taxing, 44–45
  transportation, 43–44
  welfare, 45–46
Education:
  sociology-psychology policy problem, 48
Electoral policy:
  political science policy problem, 39
Employment positions:
  policy studies people, 17–19
Energy:
  political science policy problem, 52–53
Engineering policy:
  policy studies problem, 49–54
Environmental policy:
  political science policy problem, 51–52
Executive agencies:
  public administration and, 181–182

Foreign policy:
  political science policy problem, 37–38
Formulas, optimizing analysis, 164–168
  basic symbols, 164–165
  choice with probabilities, 165–166
  general, 165
  level on continuum of alternatives, prob-
    lems, 166–167
  mix allocating scarce resources problems,
    167–168

Funding sources, bibliography, 102–105
  applications for, 103–104
  data on sources, 102–103
  items for sources, 104–105
  policy studies research, 93–105
  suggestions for, 101–102

Government:
  agencies, 131–141
  political science in, 131–141
    personnel, 135–139
    research, 132–135
  federal,
    policy studies and, 191–194
    political science field, 191–194
  level of, 188–197
    comparative, 194–196
    federal, 191–194
    state and local, 188–191
  state and local,
    policy studies and, 188–191
    political science field, 188–191
Governmental and political institutions:
  policy studies and, 179–188

Health:
  engineering policy problem, 51
Housing:
  economic policy problem, 42–43

Institutions, governmental and political:
  policy studies and, 179–188
Interest groups:
  bibliography, 129
  social science, 125–128
International relations:
  bibliography, 198–199
  policy studies and, 196–199
  political science field, 196–199
Issues:
  balanced policy studies program, 66–72

Journals:
  policy-relevant, 114–120
    meeting selection criteria, 119
    presubmission suggestions, 118–119
  scholarly
    bibliography, 120–121

Land use:
  economic policy problem, 42–43
Law, public:
  policy studies and, 179–180
Legislative process:
  bibliography, 185
Legislative reform:
  political science policy problem, 39–40

Methodology,
  political science, 201–204
Methods,
  bibliographies, 147; 151; 152–153; 156;
    159
  miscellaneous,
    bibliography, 161–162, applications,
      162, methods, 161
  policy analysis, 145–171
    finding optimum alternative, 147–148;
      choice, with contingent probabilities,
      151–153, without contingent probabili-
      ties, 148–150; level on continuum al-
      ternatives, 153–156; mix in allocating
      scarce resources, 158–159
Minorities:
  sociology-psychology policy problems, 46–
    47

Nations:
  policy analysis and, 32–33
Natural science:
  policy problems, 49–54
    agriculture, 53–54
    energy, 52–53
    environmental protection, 51–52
    science and technology, 49–51

Optimizing analysis:
  miscellaneous methods, 159–162
  bibliography, 161–162
Optimum alternative policy:
  bibliography, 147–148
  basic methods, 147
  policy applications, 147–148
Optimum choice:
  policy finding, 148–153
    with contingent probabilities, 151–153,
      bibliography, 152–153, applications,
      153, methods, 152–153; procedures,
      148–149
    without contingent probabilities, 148–
      150, bibliography, 150, applications,
      150, methods, 150; procedures, 148–
      149
    probabilities formula, 165–166
Optimum level,
  policy finding, 153–156
    continuum of alternatives, bibliography,
      155–156, applications, 156, methods,
      156; procedures, 153–155
    problems formula, 166–167
Optimum mix,
  policy finding, 156–159
    allocating scarce resources, 156–159,
      bibliography, 159, applications,
      methods, 159
    problems formula, 167–168

Parties
  policy studies and, 185–187
People:
  policy studies, 3–23
    background characteristics, 19–22
    employment positions, 17–19
    problems, 12–17
    questionnaires, 8–12
    research activities, 22–24
Philosophy, political:
  policy studies, 199–201
Policy analysis:
  academic disciplines and, 34–35
  bibliography, 5–8
  career activity, 207–209
  cultures, 32–33
  finding, 147–161
    optimum choice, with contingent prob-
      abilities, 151–153, without contingent
      probabilities, 148–150
    optimum level, on continuum of alter-
      natives, 153–156
    optimum mix in allocating scarce re-
      sources, 157–159
  methods, 28–29; 145–173
    miscellaneous, 159–162, bibliography,
      161–162, applications, 162, methods,
      161
  nations, 32–33
  optimizing formulas, 163–168
    basic symbols, 163–165
    choice with probabilities, 165–166
    general, 165
    problems, optimum level, 166–167,
      optimum mix, 167–168
    value decisions, 162–164
Policy formation:
  stages in, 30–31
Policy implementation:
  stages in, 31–32
Policy problems, 37–54
  economic, 41–46
    communication, 43–44
    housing, 42–43
    land use, 42–43
    poverty, 45–46
    regulation, 41–42
    spending, 44–45
    taxing, 44–45
    transportation, 43–44
    welfare, 45–46
  engineering, 49–54
    energy, 52–53
    environmental protection, 51–52
    health, 51
    science and technology, 49–50
  natural science, 49–54
    agriculture, 53–54
    health, 51

people, policy studies, 12–17
political science, 37–41
  arms control, 38–39
  civil liberties, 40–41
  defense, 38–39
  electoral, 39
  foreign policy, 37–38
  legislative reform, 39–40
sociology-psychology, 46–49
  blacks, 46–47
  crime, 47
  criminal justice, 47
  minorities, 46–47
  population, 4–49
  women, 46–47
specific, 12–17
Policy research,
  centers, 77–91
  bibliography, 88–91
  stages in, 27–30
  utilization of, 29–30
    bibliography, 139–141
Policy studies,
  academic programs,
    bibliography, 74–76
  activities, 58–62
    changes in, 61–62
    present, 58–60
  basic concepts, 27–35
  bibliographies,
    comparative government, 196
    federal government, 194
    international relations, 198–199
    legislative process, 185
    policy analysis, 6–8
    political dynamics, 187–188
    political methodology, 204
    political theory, 201
    public administration, 183
    public law, 180
    state and government, 190
    teaching, 72–74
  bibliography, 5–8
    causation, 7
    evaluation, 7–8
    general matter, 6
    substance, 6–7
  communications, improvement for, 65
  disciplinary contributions to, 175–206
  improvements for, 63–69
  legislative process and, 183–185
  people, 3–23
    background characteristics, 19–22
    employment positions, 17–19
    problems, 12–17
    approaches to, 16
    questionnaires, 8–12
    research activities, 22–23

political dynamics, 185–188
political philosophy, 199–201
political science field, 178–179
  government, 188–197, comparative,
    194–196, federal, 191–194, state
    and local, 188–191
  international relations, 196–199
  legislative process, 183–185
  political dynamics, 186–188
  public administration, 181–183
  public law, 179–180
political theory, 199–201
pressure groups, 185–187
processes in, 27–35
program, issues of balanced, 66–72
pros and cons of systems analysis, bibli-
    ography, 169–171
public, 185–187
public administration, 181–183
public law, 179–180
publications,
  book selection criteria, 199
  problems in, 120
research,
  centers, 77–91
  funding sources, 93–105
  improvements for, 63–64
  questionnaires, 93–100
social sciences and, 175–178
subject matter, 3–23
systems analysis and, 169–171
teaching,
  bibliography, 72–73
training, 57–76
  improvements, 65–66
  programs, 57–76
Political dynamics:
  bibliography, 187–188
  policy studies, 185–188
  political science field, 186–188
Political institutions:
  governmental and,
    policy studies, 179–188
Political philosophy:
  policy studies, 199–201
Political science:
  bibliography,
    utilization of policy research, 139–141
  fields, 178–205
    executive agencies, 181–183
    general, 199–205, methodology, 201–
      204, political philosophy, 199–201
    government, 188–197, comparative,
      194–196, federal, 191–194, state and
      local, 188–191
    governmental and political institutions,
      179–188
    international relations, 196–199

legislative process, 183–185
    political dynamics, 185–188
    public administration, 181–183
    public law, 179–180
government agencies, use in, 131–141
law school alternative, 207–209
methodology, 201–204
personnel,
    government agencies, 135–139
policy problems in, 37–41
    arms control, 38–39
    civil liberties, 40–41
    defense, 38–39
    electoral policy, 39
    foreign policy, 37–38
    legislative reform, 39
research,
    government agencies and, 132–135
theory,
    bibliography, 201
    policy studies and, 199–201
    utilization, 139–140
Population:
    sociology-psychology policy problem, 48–
        49
Poverty:
    economic policy problem, 45–46
Pressure groups:
    policy studies and, 185–187
Procedures:
    optimum choice, 147–148; 151–152
    optimum level, 153–155
Processes,
    policy studies, 27–35
Program,
    issues for policy studies, 66–72
    issues of balanced, 66–72
Pros and cons of systems analysis,
    bibliography, 169–171
    con, 170
    pro, 169–170
Public,
    policy studies and, 185–187
Public administration, 181–183
    bibliography, 183
    public studies, 181–183
Public law, 179–180
    bibliography, 180
    courts and, 179–180
    policy studies, 179–180
Publications problems,
    policy studies, 120

Questionnaires:
    APSA 131
    funding sources, 93–97
    government agencies, 131

policy studies people, 8–24
policy studies research, 93–96
research centers, 77–83
    responses, 78–83

Regulation:
    economic policy problem, 41–42
Research activities:
    policy studies people, 22–24
Research centers, 77–91
    bibliography, 88–91
        articles and papers, 89–90
        books, 88–89
        directories, 83–89
    generalizations, 83–87
        empirical, 83–85, external relations, 83–
            84, internal relations, 83, substantive
            emphasis, 83
        normative, 85–87, external relations, 86,
            internal relations, 85–87, substantive
            emphasis, 86–87
        improvement of, 85–87
        policy studies and, 77–91
        questionnaires, 77–83, responses, 78–83;
            survey, 77–78
Research, interdisciplinary:
    increase in funding, 101
Research, policy studies funding, 99–105
    applications for, 97–100
    questionnaires, 93–100
        suggestions for sources, 100–102
    policy studies improvements for, 63–64
    political science in government agencies,
        132–135
    science community input as funding source,
        100
Resources:
    allocating scarce, policy analysis and, 156–
        159

Science and technology:
    engineering policy problem, 49–50
Science community:
    funding source for policy studies research,
        100
Social science:
    interest groups in, 125–128
    policy studies and, 175–178
    utilization,
        bibliography, 140–141
Sociology-psychology:
    policy problems, 46–49
        blacks, 46
        crime, 47
        criminal justice, 47
        education, 48
        population, 47–48
        women, 46

Spending policy:
  economic policy problem, 44–45
Stages:
  policy,
    formation, 30–31
    implementation, 31–32
    research, 27–30
State and local government, 188–191
  bibliography, 190–191
  political science field, 188–191
Subject matter:
  policy studies, 3–23
Survey:
  funding sources, 93–94
  research centers, 77–78
Systems analysis:
  bibliography, 169–171
  policy studies and, 169–171

Taxing:
  economic policy problem, 44–45

Teaching policy studies:
  bibliography, 72–74
Training improvements:
  policy studies and, 65–66
Training programs:
  policy studies and, 57–75
Transportation:
  economic policy problem, 43–44

Utilization of policy research, 29–30

Value decisions:
  policy analysis and, 162–164

Welfare:
  economic policy problem, 45–46
Women:
  sociology-psychology policy-problem, 46–47

About the Author

Stuart S. Nagel is a professor of political science at the University of Illinois and a member of the Illinois bar. He is the author with Marian Neef of *Decision Theory and the Legal Process* (1979), *Policy Analysis and Social Science Research* (1978), *Legal Policy Analysis: Finding an Optimum Level or Mix* (1977), and *The Legal Process: Modeling the System* (1977). He is the author or editor of *Improving Policy Analysis* (1980), *Policy Studies Review Annual* (1977), *Modeling the Criminal Justice System* (1977), *Policy Studies and the Social Sciences* (1975), *Policy Studies in America and Elsewhere* (1975), *Improving the Legal Process: Effects of Alternatives* (1975), *Environmental Politics* (1974), *The Rights of the Accused: In Law and Action* (1972), and *The Legal Process from a Behavioral Perspective* (1969). He has been an attorney to the Office of Economic Opportunity, Lawyer's Constitutional Defense Committee in Mississippi, National Labor Relations Board, and the U.S. Senate Judiciary Committee. Dr. Nagel has also been a fellow of the Ford Foundation, Russell Sage, NSP, ACLS, SSRC, East-West Center, Illinois Law Enforcement Commission, and the Center for Advanced Study in the Behavioral Sciences. He has also been a grant recipient through the Policy Studies Organization from the Departments of Justice, Labor, HUD, Energy, Agriculture, Transportation, and HEW, and from the Rockefeller and Guggenheim Foundations.